CAN I GIVE HIM MY EYES?

*A note about the charity, Children in Crossfire to which a portion of the royalties from this book are being donated:*

Children in Crossfire was founded in 1996 by Richard Moore. His own experience has led Richard to dedicate his working life to helping vulnerable children and young people right across the world. Since 1996, Children in Crossfire, through its partners, has supported projects in Africa, Asia and South America to make a significant and lasting contribution to the fight against poverty. Today, Children in Crossfire work in Tanzania and Ethiopia and our main focus is helping vulnerable children under 8 years of age access pre-school education as well as supporting nutrition and water projects.

Children in Crossfire also carries out work across Ireland through the 'Educating the Heart' programme. Educating the Heart incorporates Richard's story as an example of how the true practice of forgiveness can bring lasting peace and reconciliation both on a personal and social level. Through Educating the Heart, Children in Crossfire works to promote active global citizenship for good community development, peace building and reconciliation to build a better world from the local to the global.

# CAN I GIVE HIM MY EYES?

## The Inspiring Story of a Boy Blinded in War Who Found Freedom in Forgiveness

Richard Moore

with Don Mullan

This edition published by Richard Moore in 2016

ISBN 978-1-5272-0234-4

1



A CIP catalogue record for this title is available from the British Library.

ISBN 978-1-5272-0234-4

First published in 2009 by Hachette Books Ireland

Typeset in Sabon
Printed and bound by GPS, Belfast, Northern Ireland.

# Contents

*To my wonderful parents, Liam and Florence Moore, whose world was shattered by the blinding of their ten-year-old son. You faced your hurt with dignity and tremendous courage. I am so proud to be your son. Thank you for your strength, faith and your example of forgiveness. My love for you will endure for ever.*

*And to my wife Rita and our two children, Naoimh and Enya. Thank you for your constant support and encouragement. I know more than anyone the sacrifices that you have made to allow me to follow my dreams and hopes. Thank you for your love and security, which have sustained me through difficult times. You gave so much without expecting anything in return.*
*I love you and always will.*

*Can you say at close of day,*
*Before you meet the night,*
*Of all the troubles in the world*
*You helped to put one right?*

# Foreword

*His Holiness the Dalai Lama*

At the time of writing this foreword, I have met Richard Moore three times. I consider him not only my friend, but also my hero. Why? Because while I talk about forgiveness, Richard Moore lives it.

I was struck by Richard's warm-heartedness and great sense of humour from the first moment I met him. His story is both tragic and inspirational. Aged ten in 1972, he was blinded by a British soldier's rubber bullet as he walked home from school. The darkness of that event could have cast a long shadow of bitterness and resentment across his entire life. Yet through the powerful and compassionate support of his mother and father, Richard learned to find freedom in forgiveness.

Richard has shown immense inner strength and as a result I have told many people around the world about him. I tell them honestly that if I had faced the same tragedy as he has, I cannot say whether I could be forgiving or not. I hope I could, but without having to deal with such an experience myself, I cannot say. However, the great example that Richard has set us is that he has actually implemented one of the great tenets of all world religions – forgiveness.

Forgiveness, let us be clear, is not a sign of weakness. It is a sign of deep inner strength and greatness of heart. I witnessed and experienced this greatness when I visited Richard's home town of Derry, Northern Ireland, on 18 July 2007. That morning, Richard brought me a gift. He said he had thought of many material gifts he might present to me, but the greatest gift he could give me was to introduce me to the man who had blinded him. For me it was wonderful to see that Richard had not only forgiven the soldier who fired the rubber bullet, but he had also befriended him.

That afternoon I brought Richard and the soldier together on the stage at the Millennium Forum where I was addressing the Tenth Anniversary Conference of the charity, Children in Crossfire. It was a risk, but one I thought worth taking in the city of Derry/Londonderry, where there have been decades of pain and enmity between much of the civilian population and the British Army. It was in this city, in 1972, that the infamous tragedy known as Bloody Sunday occurred, just a few months before Richard was blinded.

It was humbling to witness the standing ovation that both Richard and the former British soldier received as they stood beside me. It was also a sign of how powerful and important the Northern Ireland Peace Process has become. During this visit to Northern Ireland, I was conscious of far more smiling faces and found the atmosphere to be much calmer and more peaceful, which I found really encouraging.

Richard Moore shows us that through forgiveness we can enjoy greater peace of mind, warm-heartedness and a happy family life. As one of the bedrocks of the Peace Process, he is an important example to us all in a world where strife and conflict continue to generate pain and anguish. Courageous human beings like Richard are living testimony to the power of kindness and compassion that naturally arise when we acknowledge how interconnected we all are as human beings.

It is a privilege for me to contribute this foreword to Richard's memoir. I encourage people across the world to read what he has to say, for then they will understand why I consider Richard to be both a friend and a hero. Despite his own loss, he has found freedom through forgiveness. This is not only a wonderful blessing for Richard personally, but because of the example he sets for international relations, for the entire world. This is non-violence in action.

26 February 2008

# Preface

*John Hume*

In July 2007, His Holiness the Dalai Lama visited Derry to mark the ten-year anniversary of Children in Crossfire, a remarkable and inspiring organisation founded by Richard Moore. At that conference, he described Richard as one of his heroes. His Holiness explained his accolade in simple terms: 'I preach forgiveness. Richard lives it.'

Richard's life and his work serve as illustrations of the active, living hope that I, with many others, strove to hold on to during many bleak and heartbreaking years of violence and destruction in Ireland. His is a vision that is deeper, wider and infinitely wiser than much of the prevailing culture of the twenty-first century. It is a huge honour to be asked to write a preface to this book.

1972 in Derry was the year of Bloody Sunday, a year that few people here will remember without pain. Among the innocent men killed on that day was Gerry McKinney, a father of six, soon to be seven children, who was Richard's uncle. It was a few months later, in May 1972, while still in a state of grief and shock over the loss of her brother, that Florrie Moore learned of the shooting and blinding of her ten-year-old son. During this prolonged period of pain and distress for her family, Florrie held on to hope and to life through her faith and through the kindness and love of family and neighbours. She and her husband did not seek revenge but remained anchored in their deeply humane and hopeful view of humanity. The depth of their love for their son and family and their ability to shoulder the pain of his injury helped to nurture a depth and strength of vision in Richard which now enlightens all our lives.

Richard's meeting with Charles, the soldier who fired the bullet that blinded him, has been well documented and was the inspiration behind the Dalai Lama's speech in July 2007. The development of a very real respect and friendship between these two men says much about the courage and generosity of both. It offers a living alternative to Gandhi's fear that 'an eye for an eye leaves everyone blind'.

Over recent years, I have been privileged to witness some of the fruits of Richard's vision. Children in Crossfire is an organisation dedicated to helping children and families affected by illness, domestic violence, war and poverty. Currently largely based in Africa, Children in Crossfire's projects aim to build capacity within communities and families to nurture hope, self-belief and strength. Recognising that gross material inequality in today's world represents an extreme form of violence against those who suffer its effects, Children in Crossfire aims to challenge our blindness on this issue and on many issues affecting the poor in today's world. It is an organisation characterised by dynamism and energy.

On a lighter note, I have also been privileged to hear Richard sing and play, alone and with the Long Tower folk group, which he has run for many years with the help of his wife and daughters. His love of music is but one reflection of his infectious passion for life and his belief that life should be lived and enjoyed to the full. He is a man of great humour and humility. Few of those who meet Richard leave without a smile on their face, even when he is speaking about very serious issues. Like many who do not shy away from the pain of life, he appreciates the value of light-heartedness.

Like many people, I am deeply grateful for the journey that Richard Moore has taken, beyond injustice and personal disability to the strong, inspiring and immensely fruitful life he lives today. He provides us with a vision of hope and open-heartedness well beyond the culture of fear that led to his injury. I hope that many will be inspired by this book, as I have been inspired by the depth, width and clarity of Richard Moore's vision.

# Prologue

## 'What's Your Name, Son?'

I was confused. It had been daytime on Thursday, 4 May 1972, as I ran home from primary school, but now it was suddenly dark. I was ten years old. There was urgency and commotion around me. People were speaking, some shouting, with panic and concern in their voices. I could feel my clothing being tugged at – I learned later that people were using scissors to cut open my shirt and the straps of my schoolbag.

There were men and women around me. Some were crying. Amid the confusion I heard one voice I recognised. It was that of my music teacher from Rosemount Primary School, Derry: Mr Giles Doherty. He must have realised I was beginning to come round because he asked me, 'What's your name, son?'

'Richard Moore,' I told him.

I know now that he was shocked. As my music teacher, he knew me reasonably well, but because of the nature and extent of the injuries to my face I was unidentifiable. My nose was totally flattened but my eyes had been torn from their sockets and, apparently, hung close to my cheekbones. I was a bloody mess.

I kept exclaiming: 'I wasn't doing anything! I wasn't doing anything!' Even at that stage, I knew somehow that I had been shot. How I knew it still puzzles me.

I also knew that I was in a big room. Later I learned that Mr Doherty had carried me into the canteen of St Joseph's Secondary School in Derry and laid me on one of the long tables used at lunchtime.

The next thing I remember is waking up again – in the ambulance this time. Shortly after the doors were shut, a voice said, 'There's a woman outside. She's very upset. Will we let her in?'

My daddy glanced through the tinted windows. 'No! Don't. It's his mother.' He didn't want her to see me the way I was. He and my sister Deirdre were beside me, and I remember him repeating over and over to me, 'You'll be all right, son. You'll be okay.'

That's all I remember until about four days later when I woke up in Altnagelvin Hospital, the main hospital in the Derry area. I'd had a couple of operations, been heavily sedated and was in intensive care. Most of my family was at my bedside, but my mammy was trying to come to terms with the death of her younger brother, Gerard McKinney, shot dead just over three months earlier by British paratroopers on Bloody Sunday, 30 January 1972. The controversial circumstances of his murder were hard enough for her to cope with, but now she also had to deal with the shock of my injuries. The family was trying to protect her as much as they could.

They had held a vigil around my bed all the time I was unconscious. It was thought I might die. My eldest sister, Lily, always seemed to be there while I was in intensive care, all day, every day. The others were in and out, but Lily was there all the time. I was very upset if she or anyone else left me on my own. If I woke up and no one was beside me, I'd shout, 'Lily!' or 'Nurse!' because panic gripped me when I was alone.

One day the medical team were preparing me for an operation to insert a metal pin into my nose. I was terrified and held on to Lily, so she was allowed to walk down the corridor holding my hand as they wheeled the trolley towards the operating theatre. So much fear swirled inside this frightened ten-year-old whose world had so utterly and traumatically changed.

It was a huge relief to my family when I was discharged from intensive care. By then my mammy was at my bedside. All she could do was ask, 'Are you okay? Are you okay?' She held my hand all the time and kissed me. She told me later that two hysterical children had arrived at our door within minutes of my being shot and said that both my eyes were hanging out of my head. I still feel upset at the thought of her shock on hearing that.

Physically, I recovered quickly so I was moved from Altnagelvin to the nearby Waterside General Hospital, where I shared a ward with a boy from Strabane, County Tyrone. Throughout the time I was in hospital, I was under the impression that I couldn't see because of the bandages on my eyes. I can remember saying to the other boy, 'I can't wait to get the bandages off my eyes so I can show you how to play football.' I played football for my class in primary school and every day in the street with my friends. I'm not sure if I was any good but I know I loved it, and I still do.

It must have been heartrending for my mother and the rest of the family to hear me talk about playing football when the bandages were off my eyes. I know, too, that there was great anger, especially among my brothers, when they saw the size of my head, which was swollen out of all proportion to the rest of my body. I didn't know this at the time, but two soldiers who had been injured in the Troubles were being treated in a ward close to mine. Two of my brothers were involved in an angry exchange with their guards – that amazed me when I eventually heard about it because my brothers were not violent.

Two weeks after I'd been shot, I left hospital. I can't remember the journey home but I do remember arriving in our street, Malin Gardens, and getting out of the car. My brother Liam drove and I can't remember whether I was sitting in the front or the back, but I could bet that my daddy insisted on me sitting beside Liam to make me feel special. My mammy and the rest of my siblings were in the house waiting to welcome me back to our close-knit family – the warmth and love at number 42 Malin Gardens were one of the greatest gifts of my life.

The short walk from the car to our front door was different from usual but I didn't understand why. Perhaps I sensed that things would never be the same again, even though I still didn't know that I would never see again. My daddy helped me with the five steps that descended from the street towards a short pathway and three ascending steps that led to the front door. It was the first time I was helped to negotiate the surroundings with which I was so familiar, and the beginning of my life as a blind person. Steps that I had run up and down every day, just two weeks earlier, I now required assistance to master.

Nowadays my hearing is very sensitive. I've learned to listen for cues and clues in sounds to help me make sense of a situation and environment, but back then my hearing was less acute. Years afterwards I found out that a large crowd of neighbours and friends had gathered to witness my homecoming. Out of sadness for my family and me, they must have maintained a respectful silence, for I had no idea that they were there. It no longer surprises me that they were there in force: it was a show of support for our family, and in the months and years ahead they were not to let us down. What happened to me was significant and shocking for the entire community, not just my family. That a young boy had been shot and blinded by the British Army was a major event. I was Liam and Florence's wee boy who played up and down the street, and now I was coming home blind.

The unspoken question on everyone's mind must have been: 'What future lies in store for a boy blinded by violence?' If I was to have any chance of getting on with my life, I would need a lot of loving support.

# 1

# Ten Years with Sight

Liam Moore, my daddy, was born on 18 October 1914, into a world at war. His birthplace was Derry, Ireland, then part of the British Empire. He was not yet two when Pádraig Pearse read the Proclamation of Independence outside Dublin's General Post Office – the spark that ignited the Easter Rising and the Irish War of Independence. When Liam was six, in 1920, Ireland was partitioned, and six of the nine counties of the province of Ulster, including Derry, became Northern Ireland, officially part of the United Kingdom of Great Britain and Northern Ireland. The remaining twenty-six counties, including neighbouring Donegal, achieved partial independence and became known as the Irish Free State, or Saorstát Éireann.

The beautiful river Foyle runs through Derry in a north–south direction, and the city developed along its east and west banks. I have never been able to understand why the Foyle isn't the county border. If it had been, Derry's west bank would have been a natural part of the Donegal hinterland and part of the Irish Republic today. It might even have saved the British government a few headaches. Instead, the border between Derry's west bank and the Irish Republic is a complex mesh of trickling streams and country roads. Not far from where I live today, I can straddle a brook and have one foot on either side of an often-turbulent historical divide.

My daddy was born into a poor family. He grew up in High Street, a sloping terrace that rose from Derry's Bogside towards Waterloo Street, close to the commercial centre of the city. He became a shoemaker and worked in a shop called the Corner Boots Store. His parents died before he was seventeen, so his elder sister, Lila, looked after him. I never met my aunt Lila or, indeed, my daddy's brother Jim or sister Charlotte. My uncle Jim was killed in a tragic accident in England during a storm when a violent gust flung him into the path of an oncoming car. My two aunts also died before I was born.

My mammy, Florence McKinney, was born on 20 June 1919, into a middle-class household, and grew up in Governor Road about a mile north of where my daddy lived. Governor Road was a small terraced street in what was considered a better-class area. It connected with Strand Road, Derry's main commercial artery, which runs parallel to the Foyle. At the northern end, Strand Road forks west and also continues north. Both branches lead to the border with the Republic of Ireland, about three miles away in either direction.

My grandfather, William George McKinney, migrated to Derry from a small townland in Donegal called Iskaheen, eight miles from Derry. He fathered fourteen children in all – two to his first wife, Eliza Baird, a convert to Catholicism who came from Omagh, County Tyrone. Their children were Annie and Margaret Mary. Margaret Mary died at eleven months, from whooping cough, and his young wife Eliza at twenty-four, from tuberculosis.

His second wife was Margaret Ellen Hay, a direct descendant of Edward Hay, a leader in the 1798 rebellion and also associated with Daniel O'Connell's Catholic Emancipation Movement. Edward's brother, Philip Harvey Hay, was captured by the British and beheaded for his part in the rebellion. Margaret Ellen Hay's father, my great-grandfather, was from Wexford. He joined the Royal Irish Constabulary (RIC) and was stationed in Derry. They had four children: Florence, my mother, Willie, Lily and Joseph. Joseph died from pneumonia at the age of fifteen months, having been scalded by boiling milk. Six months later, my grandmother died at thirty-eight, also from tuberculosis.

Eventually my grandfather married again and had eight more children with his third wife, Margaret Coyle: Margaret, Denis, Aileen, Gerard, Laurence, Fred, Lewis and Deirdre. Four died in tragic circumstances: my aunt Aileen died from meningitis at the age of thirteen months; my uncle Gerard on Bloody Sunday, with both his hands in the air; my uncle Fred in a car accident in Donegal, aged twenty-three, on his way home from a dance. He had spent a couple of seasons with Southend United, a team that was later managed by the legendary World Cup-winning England captain, Bobby Moore. Deirdre, the youngest, was born with medical problems and survived only two months.

Grandad McKinney drove a large blue Morris Commercial at a time when cars were scarce. He was, my mammy recalls, a slow and cautious driver. For short journeys, he preferred his bicycle. He enjoyed traditional music and was a good fiddle player. He was also a thrifty man. He worked as manager of the Rosemount Shirt Factory, but also, with the help of his third wife, Margaret, ran a small shop from the front room of Governor Road. He owned two or three other houses, too, which he rented out for extra income, and compared to the majority of Catholics in Derry, including my daddy's family, the McKinneys were quite comfortable.

While unemployment was rife among the men of Derry, employment for women was plentiful in the city's famous linen industry. My mammy worked at the Rosemount Shirt Factory too – her father was very stern, treating her no differently from everyone else in the factory.

During the Second World War, Derry was at the heart of the Allies' strategic defence of the North Atlantic, and the city was under constant threat of German bombing missions. Mercifully, Derry was spared the horrors of the Belfast blitz and the infernos of many cities throughout Britain. However, the Luftwaffe dropped two parachute mines over the town on 15 April 1941, killing fifteen people in the Pennyburn district, less than a mile from Governor Road where my mammy's family lived. Following the bombing, my grandfather moved his family across the border to Iskaheen, where they stayed until the war ended in 1945.

I have only one memory of him. I was seven years old and he was dying. Coincidentally, he had lost his eyesight and fumbled with his pyjama jacket as he tried to find a pocket to put away his rosary beads. He died in 1968, aged eighty-nine.

My parents were friends long before their six-month courtship began. They met on the Strand Road. In the early 1940s, Derry was a small town of about forty thousand civilian inhabitants, swelled by several thousand Allied troops. Mammy says she had no romantic interest in Daddy until he plucked up the courage to ask her out. Then she began to see him in a whole different light. What she loved most was his gentleness.

They were married in St Eugene's Cathedral, Derry, in March 1941, and spent a short honeymoon in the Atlantic seaside town of Bundoran, County Donegal. Only my aunt Lily, who was maid of honour, and the best man, my daddy's friend Jim McGinley, were at the wedding. Grandad McKinney said he didn't like weddings, and with the exception of my uncle Denis's, attended none of his children's. Denis, though, issued an ultimatum: he told my grandfather that if he wasn't at the wedding, he'd never darken the family door again. It was bitter medicine but, for Denis, it worked.

My parents' first home was a rented room in Derry's Glen estate and it was there that they started their family. Between 1942 and 1947 they had six children: Lily, John, Margaret, Liam, Charlotte and Jim. John and Charlotte died at just a few months old of gastroenteritis. After John's death, my mother knew that Charlotte was in danger when she developed the symptoms of vomiting and diarrhoea that John had had. She and Daddy carried her to a doctor, but to no avail.

Even though Derry was a predominantly Irish Nationalist city, during the 1940s local government was controlled by an Ulster Unionist minority. Politics in Northern Ireland is largely divided along pro-Irish and pro-British lines, and sadly the divide is exacerbated by religious affiliations. At this time in Northern Ireland, unlike in Great Britain, the right to vote was not automatically granted to all adults. Until the late 1960s, it was restricted primarily to householders and other property owners. Some people had more than one vote, but many had none. It was not until 1947, when my parents took possession of a house in a new development, the Creggan estate on the west bank of Derry, that they were given the franchise. By then my father was thirty-three and my mother twenty-eight.

Gerrymandering put in place the minority government: the Creggan estate was conceived as a means of containing a huge block of Catholic votes within a limited electoral boundary. In the 1940s my parents and many of their generation were political innocents and their political awareness did not develop until the late 1960s, with the birth of the Northern Ireland Civil Rights Association. They and others seized the opportunity to escape overcrowded tenement accommodation. A home in the Creggan estate offered the possibility of a new beginning. That was certainly how it was for Mammy, Daddy and their surviving children, by then ranging in age from a few months to six years.

The Londonderry Corporation gave my parents tenancy of 42 Malin Gardens, a compact two-storey, red-brick house with three bedrooms, a bathroom and separate toilet upstairs. As an end-of-terrace house, it also had a bay window. Downstairs there were two small sitting rooms, a kitchen and a front and back hallway. We also had a small front and larger back garden.

All of the streets in the lower Creggan estate took their names from places on the Inishowen peninsula in neighbouring Donegal. From Westway Gardens, at the top of our street, I could see the eastern shoreline of the peninsula as it curled northwards along Lough Foyle towards the Atlantic Ocean. Our street was named after Malin Head, the most northerly point in Ireland.

Number 42 Malin Gardens was our family home from 1947 until 1981. Even though others live there now, it will always hold a special place in our hearts. It was there that a second batch of children arrived: Pearse, Bosco, Noel, Deirdre, Martin, Gregory, myself and Kevin.

We shared the three bedrooms: my mammy and daddy had the small back bedroom with Kevin and me. Some mornings I woke up with cold legs sticking through the bars of my cot.

Lily, Margaret and Deirdre had the smaller of the two front rooms and the older boys slept in what we called the big bedroom. In that room, there were two double beds and a set of bunks. I was about three when I was moved into the big room with my brothers, a major step for a wee boy, the first rite of passage in my life that I remember. I shared one of the double beds with Gregory and, eventually, Kevin. The youngest always slept with his head beside smelly feet – not mine, Gregory's.

Later, as the older brothers married or emigrated, we were shuffled about, the next eldest taking the bed closest to the door. I remember waking up in the middle of the night on many occasions thinking I was sweating only to discover that one of my sleeping companions had wet the bed. The problem was that when one of us did that, we all got the blame.

My daddy worked very hard to keep the gardens looking their best. We had a push lawnmower and I loved helping him. I was fascinated by the spinning blades and the green wave of cut grass they threw out. I loved the smell as I raked it into neat piles and distributed it under the hedges. Today I know that the back garden of 42 Malin Gardens is small, but to me as a child, it appeared quite big. I loved to play football there with Bosco, Noel, Gregory, Marty and Kevin, the brothers I was closest to in age.

Mammy was always a worrier. Having lost Charlotte and John, she worried about us all. When I was about seven, I became sick. For a while Mammy fretted, then summoned our next-door neighbour, Mrs Bradley, for a second opinion. Mrs Bradley took one look at me and pronounced, 'Ah! He's got the measles.'

My mammy was a wonderful homemaker. So, too, was my daddy, who was at home for long periods when he was unemployed. For us, like many in the Creggan, times were often tough, but we never seemed to want for anything. Most importantly, we never went hungry. I still shiver at the memory of winter, though. We didn't have central heating in those days and we had no carpets on the floor, only linoleum, which we called oilcloth. I remember the perishing cold when we had five or six blankets on each bed – duvets, of course, were unheard of. The tip of my nose would be icy, and I liked the clouds that came out of my mouth and nostrils when I breathed above the blankets for a minute or two before diving back under the covers to bask in the warmth generated by my brothers. That is, until someone gave in to flatulence. The culprit would take perverse pleasure in counting the seconds before we surfaced, gasping.

Getting up for school on cold mornings was hard, especially when my feet touched the cold lino. My daddy had placed small mats between the bedrooms, the toilet and the bathroom and I used to hop from one to another like stepping stones across a river. I'd wait until the last minute, and then, when the moment of reckoning came, I'd jump out, grab my clothes and run downstairs in my pyjamas to get dressed in the living room where there was a solid-fuel Rayburn range. It had four hotplates and an oven, giving out tremendous heat, night and day. It had a cream enamel finish and came with a long steel poker: we used that to lift off a round lid, then shovelled in the anthracite that fuelled it. We always had hot water boiling on top of the Rayburn. As well as heating the living room, it sparked Noel's imagination: whenever the Beatles appeared on *Top of the Pops*, it substituted for Ringo Starr's drum kit – he beat the living daylights out of the hotplates, kettles and saucepans with the poker and a knitting needle.

When I was dressed, the journey to the bathroom to get washed was bearable. There was no such thing as a daily shower. Soap on the hands and a splash of water on the face seemed to suffice, unless Mammy or Daddy thought we needed scrubbing with a facecloth. We had a weekly bath and our hair was washed regularly, then fine-combed, and if Mammy had been alerted by the school authorities, doused generously with rancid TCP to keep head lice at bay.

In winter, when we stepped outside the living room, our breath vaporised. Even going to the toilet was a nightmare. I had to psych myself up to sit on the seat. It was so cold, it took your breath away. I used to wait until one of my brothers had been so they would have warmed it for me.

The living room was at the back of the house, looking across our garden towards the Hugheses' house in Dunmore Gardens. It had a three-seater sofa and two armchairs and was always crowded in the mornings. Breakfast consisted of tea and toast, nothing else. Coffee was the brew of swanks. Daddy would carry in what I thought of as an enormous teapot; it had no lid but was filled with hot tea, already milked and sweetened, which he poured into our cups. Toast arrived in from the kitchen by the plateload and disappeared in an instant. And it always arrived buttered. Jam and marmalade didn't exist until some of the older ones went to work and supplemented our parents' meagre income.

The 'good room' had a fireplace that was never lit because nobody lived in it. It was used only on occasions when special visitors, such as Father Rooney or Father McLaughlin from St Mary's chapel, called. They were brought into it because it was always tidy and undisturbed.

The kitchen was very cold, too. My mammy seemed to spend her whole day there. During periods of unemployment,

Daddy took over cooking duty while she was endlessly engaged in washing and ironing. She kept the house crisp, tidy and spotlessly clean. As children, we had no regular household tasks to do. I never ironed a shirt or washed a cloth. We were spoiled.

One day I came home from school very pleased with myself: I could count from one to a hundred. As usual, Mammy was standing at the kitchen table, ironing. I announced proudly, 'Mammy, I can count to one hundred.'

'Can you?' she asked. She knew I was bursting to demonstrate and obligingly invited me to begin. The iron never stirred until, breathless, I reached my target.

With a house full of children, there were always piles of laundry to be done. We had a washing machine that was wheeled into the kitchen every day from the back hall. I remember listening to its melodic drone on Sunday mornings before we were called for Mass. It was a Servis twin-tub, bought at cost price by my uncle Gerard, who worked for the manufacturers. Until it arrived, my mother had had to wash everything by hand, then put it all through the mangle to squeeze out as much water as she could before hanging it out to dry. The arrival of the twin-tub was like exchanging a battered Volkswagen Beetle for a Rolls-Royce.

It was an ingenious contraption. One tub was for washing; the other, my favourite, had a spinner that used centrifugal force to drain away the water. The spinner had a black hose attached to the back, which hooked over the sink. I was mesmerised by all the water that came out of our clothes, and would sit and watch it flowing into the sink. Sometimes Mammy asked me to fish out the bits of wool, thread and fabric that had turned into a gooey mess in the plughole and throw them into the bin.

Once spun, Mammy carried the damp clothing to the

clothesline in the back garden. She preferred warm windy days, for there was 'good drying' in them. Later, the endless ironing began. As a child, I thought my mammy lived in the kitchen, for that was where she always seemed to be. It was tiny by modern standards. We had a gas cooker with four cooking rings and an oven we lit with BoPeep matches – in later years, we upgraded to a cooker with a pilot light that made matches redundant. Beside the kitchen window there was a built-in larder with a door. It had high shelving that stored our weekly rations and was a favourite place during games of hide-and-seek. The kitchen wall, facing the cooker, had cupboards in which various culinary items were stored. One of my favourite nooks was the small cupboard beside the sink where the gas meter lived. Back then, it was pay-as-you-go and it was a great treat for the younger ones, when the gas ran out, to be given the job of putting a shilling in the meter. It was never fed more than a shilling at a time because we simply couldn't afford it. To young eyes it was an interesting contraption, a bit like having your very own slot machine at home. The prize was always the same: gas. The coin was placed in a big wing-nut, and when it was turned, the shilling disappeared with a clang. I was intrigued by that clang: it got deeper and had less echo as each additional shilling dropped.

At regular intervals the gasman arrived with his master key, a torch and a grimy cloth bag bulging with shillings. There must have been hundreds of coins in that bag, yet I don't recall hearing of a gasman being robbed before the outbreak of the Troubles. He'd read the meter, remove a metal tray and empty the contents onto the table. He would then calculate the amount of gas used and, to my parents' delight, often replace a shilling or two in the meter before continuing to our next-door neighbours' house.

In the early 1970s, we got a small box fridge about two feet square. We all thought it was marvellous and, with Mammy's twin-tub and the new cooker that didn't need matches, it was a source of pride. With all this fancy new gadgetry, the Moores were coming up in the world.

Because ours was an end-of-terrace house, we had a back wall that ran between our house and the Bradleys'. A side gate gave us access to the back of the house. This meant that we could enter the house at the rear, through what we referred to jokingly as the 'workmen's entrance'. This was the preferred route as it meant the front hallway, which led into the 'good room', was also kept pristine. In the front hall there was an old stand where we hung our coats and hats. It had a marble top and a mirror and was always polished. 'Important' visitors always came in through the front door. The back door was for the rough and tumble of life.

Christmas was very special. Our parents put in a big effort to make it so. The bright red and emerald green decorations that hung from the ceilings changed the atmosphere in the house. We were always happy, but even more so than usual at Christmas. The tree always stood in the bay window of the 'good room'. I loved the shiny coloured balls that were tied to its branches, the fairy lights that sparkled as they blinked on and off, and I liked to look at it from outside in the street on dark December evenings – it made me feel warm inside. Deirdre, the youngest girl in the family, was artistic and could transform our bay window into a winter wonderland. She would spray 'Happy Christmas' across it in white foam.

On Christmas morning, we all went to Mass in St Mary's chapel. We'd have bathed the night before, hair washed, shoes polished, and we paraded there in our new outfits that would see us through the next twelve months. After Mass, we would visit the Christmas crib in which the baby Jesus lay in a manger on real straw. Daddy wasn't overtly religious, but he had a quiet faith. So, too, did Mammy and it became her salvation, literally, in years to come.

I loved Christmas dinner when Daddy and Mammy carried in the turkey with the stuffing oozing out onto the roasting tin lined with tinfoil. Two of the last Christmas movies I remember seeing were the 1939 Victor Fleming classic *The Wizard of Oz*, starring Judy Garland, and the 1965 Robert Wise classic, *The Sound of Music*, with Julie Andrews. As the family got older, I looked forward to seeing my married brothers and sisters on Christmas Day. They'd arrive with presents for Kevin and me.

One of my fondest memories is of being in bed one Christmas Eve when I was seven or eight. The big bedroom had a hearth but never a fire. Throughout the year it lay empty and dark. On stormy nights we could hear the wind groaning eerily around the funnel outside on the chimney. On that Christmas Eve, however, my daddy lit the fire. The glow cast a spell across the walls and ceiling and shadows danced as the flames flickered. Then I began to worry. How was Santa Claus going to get down the chimney? I was fearful he'd get burned and I'd end up the most unpopular boy in the entire world. I stopped worrying when Daddy explained we had a second chimney that went from the roof to the 'good room', where the fire was never lit. It never crossed my mind that, even without a fire, the rotund Santa Claus might have difficulty getting down the narrow chimney. After all, he was magic.

Until I lost my sight, I believed in Santa Claus. Naturally, my younger brother Kevin did too. Santa Claus always came on Christmas Eve. One year he left me a Lego set and another time it was Meccano. I used to look at the pictures on the box and wonder how children could make incredible things like battery-operated motorbikes and cars and tall cranes with movable parts, but the sets we received were basic and what we could make was nothing like as elaborate. But I was always happy with what I got.

The best Christmas of all was the one when I was given a bicycle. I couldn't believe it when I went downstairs on Christmas morning and found it in the sitting room. I was desperate to bring it outside to show off. Very quickly, however, I discovered it wasn't the best bike in the street because my friend Paul Moran, who was younger than me, had got a bigger one. It had gears, too, and I was amazed that he could freewheel without his pedals turning. On my bicycle, when you stopped pushing the pedals still insisted on going round, and because it was small, my knees hit the handlebars. All in all, I wasn't overly impressed with my bike when I compared it to Paul's. The thought crossed my mind that maybe Santa Claus had favourites and I wondered how I could get myself onto his A list. I don't think I whinged to my parents about it – and I hope to God I didn't: now I appreciate the sacrifices they must have made to get it for me. If I had that small bicycle today, I'd hang it on a wall as a reminder of the love and sacrifice we all received from two of the greatest parents ever.

I was forbidden to take my bike onto Westway at the top of Malin Gardens, a long, straight hill with a higher volume of traffic than the streets that branched off it, including our own. One day I disobeyed my parents and ventured out with some friends. We took our bicycles to the top of Westway and the large mound, on a roundabout, which everyone called the Crobie. With our backs to the Crobie, we set off freewheeling down Westway, awed by the accelerating speed. When I tried to make the sharp right turn into Malin Gardens, disaster struck: the front wheel hit the pavement and I was flung head over heels across the Dunlops' beautiful hedge. Thankfully I landed on my backside, and the only thing bruised was my pride.

Today children have all manner of games and gadgets, computers and Wiis, but we had to rely on our own inventiveness. Our childhood was much more active than it would have been today because we had far fewer distractions. All year round we played football and rode bicycles. If we didn't have a ball, we kicked an empty can. Sometimes we played street derbies against Leenan, Dunmore or Melmore Gardens. The passion was as intense as when Celtic played Rangers or Liverpool played Everton.

In the summer we'd search the streets for discarded ice-pop sticks, then make aeroplanes by sticking them together with black tar, softened by the sun, which we picked from the road. Catching butterflies and bumblebees in jam jars was another favourite activity, and in the evening we loved playing knick-knock on our neighbours. We'd either knock on doors and run to a hiding place or tie thread to an ice-pop stick, place it under the knocker, hide in a nearby garden and pull to make the knocker fall after the thread broke. If an adult expressed annoyance, we were delighted. It was better still if he or she hurled a profanity at the hidden phantoms peering from behind nearby hedges and fences.

Tag, or 'Tig', was a favourite game. One person was 'on', meaning they had to chase the others until they touched, or 'tigged', someone, when that person took over.

One of our great adventures, undertaken by two or three of us at a time, was to start at the bottom of the street and sneak up through the back gardens to the top. We pretended to be combat troops on a dangerous mission through enemy territory, which included negotiating various obstacles such as high hedging, fences and walls. The biggest challenge lay in not alerting the neighbourhood dogs, for they could easily blow your cover. The trick was to try and reassure them by calling their name in a whisper. We knew that if we were caught we'd be marched by the offended neighbour to our parents, who'd court-martial us. The punishment was a clip on the ear and getting sent to bed, but the excitement and suspense made the risk worth taking.

The garden that simultaneously provided the greatest challenge and the greatest reward was the one at the top of the street, owned by the Loughreys. Their hedging was very high, but once it was breached the reward was access to an apple tree. My friends and I always referred to it as Loughreys' Orchard.

Now that I've confessed to the world that I participated in such 'dangerous' missions in the service of boyhood bravery, I can also boast that I was never caught. No doubt we were, to varying degrees, a nuisance, but it was harmless fun and even though we knew we were doing things our parents would frown upon, we all had great respect for our neighbours.

And since I'm into confessing, I'd better own up to my worst childhood moment of anti-social behaviour. My daddy and mammy had a little savings scheme and sometimes they sent me on a Saturday morning to the post office on Central Drive to buy a savings stamp, which was added to their savings book. One day I was on my way up Greenwalk – a long street that intersects all the streets in Lower Creggan, from Beechwood Avenue to Fanad Drive. St Mary's Community Centre was being built at the time in the space between Melmore Gardens and Fanad Drive. As I passed, I began to wonder what was inside, but sheets of black tarpaulin covered all the window spaces.

I decided to try to remove a tarpaulin by throwing a fairly large brick at it. This, I reasoned, would allow me to see the interior. To my horror, a massive window shattered. I raced like blue blazes up Fanad Drive and on to the post office. I remember taking the long route home so I didn't have to pass the community centre in case the police and builders were out looking for the vandal. I hadn't meant to break a window and I honestly didn't know there was glass behind the tarpaulin.

When I was a child, foreign holidays were unheard of. The furthest we got was the seaside town of Buncrana on the western shore of the Inishowen peninsula. When money was tight, we'd go only as far as the low sand dunes of Fahan or Lisfannon, a few miles short of Buncrana. The logic was simple: in the town, there were shops and amusements that required extra cash Mammy and Daddy didn't have.

Fahan and Lisfannon are linked by a curving two-mile strand of golden sand along the shores of Lough Swilly, which fills and empties with the ebb and flow of the Atlantic Ocean. The water was always refreshing for a dip, but so cold that unless the weather was very hot we seldom spent more than ten or fifteen minutes in it. My impression was that the Atlantic was a cold ocean. It wasn't until I'd grown up and visited Florida that I discovered the vastness of the Atlantic and that parts of it, especially close to the tropics, are actually pleasantly warm.

We spent hours building sandcastles, digging tunnels and burying one another. The dunes provided great cover for hide-and-seek. We'd arrive with our colourful buckets and spades and, of course, a football. I loved it when Daddy joined us for a kick-about on the beach. We soon discovered that damp sand was a better consistency for the sandcastles. We'd pack each bucket with sand, beat it down with our spades, turn the bucket over and carefully remove it to reveal a shape that resembled a Martello tower. Some children had square buckets with turrets. The Moores, however, worked in numbers, and we prided ourselves on building the biggest and most elaborate castles we could. Sometimes three or four of us would build them close to one another, then connect them with tunnels and sand bridges. As evening approached and the tide began to creep up the beach, we dug channels to let the water flow into moats that protected our constructions from enemies, then watched sadly as they crumbled with the sea's onslaught. If we left before the water reached them, I sometimes felt a bit guilty at abandoning them to their fate.

To this day, I love sausage sandwiches. On the morning we went to the beach, Daddy would be up early to buy a few pounds of Doherty's sausages and two fresh loaves from Mr Pollock's shop on Beechwood Avenue. Mr Pollock had a foreign accent that sounded strange to my childish ears. Years later, I learned he was a European Jew who had fled the Nazis with his family during the Second World War and found refuge among the people of Derry's Creggan estate. Like my daddy, Mr Pollock was a kind and gentle man.

Sometimes the wind sprinkled little grains of sand like salt on our sandwiches, but they were soon washed down with cups of Daddy's best brew, poured from the flasks he had prepared before we walked down from Creggan to the Lough Swilly bus depot at the start of our day.

On the odd occasion when we did make it to Buncrana, our excitement knew no bounds. Shops served cones of pink and white ice cream that swirled around each other into a Matterhorn peak. An extra penny turned them into a 99, a cone with a Cadbury's Flake plunged into the ice cream. But in

Buncrana and Derry we never asked for 'cones'. We called them 'pokes'. That was okay while we were in our own orbit but if we ventured further afield, we received strange looks from ice cream servers when we innocently asked: 'Can I have a poke?' The world is a very big place, and while we think we're at the centre of the universe, we're not!

The candyfloss machine mesmerised us. It was nothing short of miraculous that it could whip sugar into pink sticky webs that wrapped round and round a long thin stick into a hanging beehive. Today whenever anyone mentions candyfloss, my mind goes back to those happy days in Buncrana.

In summertime there were amusements along Buncrana's front shore. In my mind's eye I can still see the bumper cars and a small carousel we called the 'hobby horses'. The chair-a-planes was a favourite – it consisted of seats attached with chains to something like a mechanical maypole. When it reached its maximum speed, you flew round at an exhilarating speed and height. My favourite, however, was the swing-boats. They were Viking ships, in my childish imagination, suspended like giant pendulums. Kevin and I would sit in the middle between two of our older brothers and sisters who each had a firm grip on a heavy rope hanging from the beam to which the boat was attached. The ropes were crossed and, as they pulled, one at a time, they soon had us swaying back and forth. If we got too adventurous, the man in charge would slow us down by applying a large plank of wood to the bottom of the boat like a brake.

I liked the slot machines too. We called them 'one-armed bandits', for inevitably they robbed us of our money. The thrill of pulling the big silver handles and watching the reels of cherries, apples, pears, single, double and treble 'bars' and the lucky 7s spin was magical, especially when three the same lined up in front of you and pennies tumbled gloriously into the metal tray below. It's no exaggeration to say that, back then, a day in Buncrana was, for children from the Creggan, as exciting as a holiday in Barbados. In truth, we were poor and knew nothing else.

It would be nine o'clock in the evening by the time we got home, exhausted and ready for bed. As children, we never worried about who had paid for our day out. I have no doubt that our parents must have saved a few extra pounds to bring us to Buncrana, and I know for certain that they made sure we enjoyed every moment of our time at the seaside.

Streets throughout the Creggan, including our own, sometimes organised a summer bus run to Buncrana. Nowadays it might take a trip to Disneyland to get some children as excited as we were by that bus run, and – believe me – sleep came intermittently the night before. My mammy recalls that as the hour approached for the bus's arrival, children gathered at the top of the street, straining their eyes to see round corners. A huge cheer erupted when the double-decker appeared and an honour guard of boys and girls flanked its slow progress up our narrow street. Parents, mainly mothers, settled into the lower deck while a stampede of children raced up the stairs, anxious to secure the front seats. Songs and laughter cascaded down from the top deck once the journey began. Sadly, when the Troubles started, the bus runs stopped.

During the good weather schools, too, might organise a bus run to an area of historic interest or scenic beauty. I still smile at the songs we sang on those trips. 'Oh You Canny Shove Your Granny Off the Bus' was popular, but the song we had most mischief with was sung to the old American Civil War melody 'John Brown's Body':

*We'll hang Richard Moore to the sour apple tree*
*We'll hang Richard Moore to the sour apple tree*
*We'll hang Richard Moore to the sour apple tree*
*As we go marching along...*

The second verse was similar, but it pleaded with an accompanying relative or, worse still, a girl your schoolmates knew you fancied:

*Oh! Linda Barr don't be angry*
*Oh! Linda Barr don't be angry*
*Oh! Linda Barr don't be angry*
*As we go marching along...*

It went on until everyone ran out of steam.

Today I'm so thankful that I was able to see and experience those summers.

I remember one morning before school my mammy was crying as she buttoned my shirt because my sister Margaret, who had just turned twenty, had decided to leave home and emigrate to England, attracted by the bright lights of foreign shores. For Mammy, it was the beginning of her brood flying the nest, and no doubt it was heartbreaking for her.

Margaret married a Royal Navy sailor, Eddie Edwards, and my first journey out of Ireland was with Mammy, Daddy and Kevin to visit them. It was 1970, a few weeks before my ninth birthday, when we left Derry for Belfast port. I don't remember the journey over the Glenshane Pass that crossed the Sperrin Mountains, but I know I was impressed by the motorway that took us into Belfast. It was my first time in that city and I was spellbound by the noise and dimensions of the docks, in particular the size of the shipyard cranes. It was here that RMS

*Titanic* had been built, and I was excited that we would sail down the river Lagan and across Belfast Lough on what was, in shipping terms, the first highway the great ship travelled shortly before its ill-fated Atlantic crossing in 1912.

I remember my daddy pointing out a new crane that everyone was talking about. Called Goliath, it was 96 metres tall and the biggest in the whole world. In comparison, all the other cranes looked like Meccano creations. As a boy, I felt proud that the biggest crane in the world was in Ireland.

Mammy and Daddy couldn't afford a berth, so we stayed all night in the lounge as the boat heaved and rocked its way across the Irish Sea. It was packed with people who must have been in the same position as us. Daddy had made us tomato sandwiches for the journey and I remember the remnants coming up as he held me over the railings at the back of the ship when I was seasick.

We arrived into Liverpool shortly after dawn. I have in my mind a collage of multicoloured images that includes ships, motorboats, a yacht, flags and lots of activity, with big buildings and sheds in the background. I was frightened walking down the gangplank – because I could see black water lapping against the docking wall in the narrow gap between the ship and the quay and heard the ropes straining with the heave of the Mersey – but we were soon off it and on our way to the railway station.

I must have slept for most of the train journey, for I have little memory of it. From Liverpool we had to find our way to Gosport, Hampshire, in the south of England, where Margaret and Eddie were living, just five miles from Portsmouth. At one point my daddy let me stick my head out the window of the train when it was travelling at an incredible speed. I was fascinated by the way the carriages appeared to bend when the train was going around a corner, and that the sleepers on a parallel track were a blur when I looked directly down on them. I liked the feeling of the wind blowing on my face until I noticed the telegraph poles, which appeared to be very close to the track. Suddenly I knew I was about to lose my head and was paralysed with fright, but a moment later my daddy pulled me in.

We spent three happy weeks in Gosport with Margaret and Eddie. I'll never forget the ferry crossing between Gosport and Portsea – I couldn't understand why there was no bridge between the two like we had in Derry. Another thing was strange too: when we went to Mass on our first Sunday, we weren't in a proper church. To me it resembled a warehouse – I could see rafters and metal support beams. A church had holy statues and an altar, but that place was like a building site with a stage from which the priest said the Mass. I was also surprised to see him putting on his vestments. In St Mary's chapel at home, they got dressed in private in the sacristy and appeared only when a bell rang.

The thing that really stood out about that trip, though, was the constant stream of sailors in full uniform. I couldn't take my eyes off them. There were so many, and they were walking in every direction. They looked brilliant in round-rimmed white hats. I'd love to be a sailor and wear a uniform like that, I thought.

It was the only overseas holiday I had as a sighted child.

# 2

# The Troubles

The first time I became aware of the British Army was on the return journey from Gosport. As soon as we got off the train at Liverpool, I saw hundreds of soldiers and it soon became clear that they would be on the boat with us across the Irish Sea. I was so excited – it was like being in the middle of a film set. The only time I'd seen that many soldiers all together before was on television.

During the voyage, I happened upon a soldier and a young woman snuggled in the shadows of a stairway engaged in passionate kissing. My eyes nearly popped out of their sockets. At home, if a couple kissed on television, my older brothers and sisters would snigger, especially if Mammy and Daddy were there. 'Turn those dirty animals over,' Mammy would order. Someone would switch channels and everything would go back to normal. I dreaded the Playtex bra advertisement – I found it I so embarrassing, especially when a male voice explained it could 'stretch this way and that way'. My face burned and I didn't know where to look. Aboard the boat from Liverpool, though, I just stood and stared, spellbound.

When the ship docked in Belfast, the soldiers disembarked first. Orders were shouted as they formed lines. They were all carrying heavy kitbags on their backs and had their SLR rifles slung over their left shoulders. Armoured vehicles, including Land Rovers and three-ton trucks, were also pouring out of the raised bow of the ship. As I watched them march away, I stopped wanting to be a sailor and decided instead to be a soldier.

Liam picked us up in Belfast and drove us back to Derry. There had been trouble in Belfast while we were away and we went past the blackened shells of some burned-out buildings. By then, the British Army had been on the streets of Ulster for almost a year. After the trouble between the Nationalist community and the Royal Ulster Constabulary (RUC), the situation had settled down and there was relative calm in Derry.

The previous two years, though, had been turbulent: in 1969, Derry had to live through what is now known as the Battle of the Bogside, a fierce and bitter exchange between the people of my community and the police. The battle raged non-stop across three days and nights from the afternoon of 12 August until the early evening of the fourteenth. The police were overstretched and exhausted, and the British Prime Minister, Harold Wilson, responded to a request from Stormont for troops and ordered the deployment of the British Army on the streets of Derry and Belfast. Their arrival calmed things for a while and relations between the soldiers and civilians were cordial, but that intervention would have long-term consequences for the political situation and for individuals.

The Troubles seemed far away from us, but I can remember

seeing boys of fifteen or sixteen, who looked like young men to me, making their way down towards the rioting in the Bogside. They would shout to each other across the street, relaying information: 'There's a riot in Waterloo Street!' I knew people were fighting but I didn't understand why.

In time, I became aware of the religious dimension to the Troubles and, sadly, grew up believing that Protestants didn't like us and were very different people from Catholics. In truth, we have so much in common, but the Troubles drove us apart. Eventually the world began to take note, and the marches, protests and violence in Derry and elsewhere in Northern Ireland were shown on television. Our household was gripped by developments. Before, I had had no interest in the news, but now Derry was on television and I wanted to see it. I was watching, from the safety of my home, as men and youths threw stones and petrol bombs, and saw parts of my city in flames. I was too young to grasp then that it was happening because people were being denied their civil rights. The first piece of political graffiti I remember seeing was 'One Man One Vote' painted over the middle of the road that crossed our street. I read that every day and never understood what it meant.

Only a few thousand people attended the first civil rights march in Derry on 5 October 1968 – most had only a vague notion of what 'civil rights' actually meant. Derry historians now joke that if everyone who claims to have been on the first civil rights march had actually been there, the Craigavon Bridge would have collapsed into the Foyle from the weight. That evening, the shocking scenes from that first march were broadcast into our living rooms and awakened a sleeping giant: pictures of police officers attacking unarmed demonstrators instantly politicised and polarised people. My brother Martin was on the first march and he and other members of my family were on the second, a couple of weeks later, which attracted 100,000.

When my older brothers arrived home afterwards, they were talking about the trouble that had broken out around the marches. In my mind I can still see the Nationalist politician Gerry Fitt being battered by police. That they were using truncheons to beat an elected politician and other leaders of our community became a major talking point in everybody's home. And fear crept in – especially that the B Specials, an exclusively Protestant armed police reserve, would come into our area. That was a truly terrifying prospect, especially for children: the B Specials had guns. Our community had none.

On 16 July 1969, four days after my seventh birthday, the fear intensified as word spread that Sammy Devenney, an innocent man from the Bogside, had died from a terrible beating he had suffered a couple of months earlier at the hands of the police. He had been sitting in his living room with his family when they burst into his house. People were very angry, and today he is regarded as the first victim of the Northern Ireland troubles.

Soon after that, the situation began to change. Previously, policemen had regularly walked the streets of the Creggan and the Bogside. If we were playing football or swinging from a rope on a lamppost and a policeman appeared, we would grab the ball or the rope and scatter in case he decided to take our names. Respect for law and order was so ingrained in us children that we were frightened of the local bobby. Now, however, there was so much trouble. Some riots seemed to go on for days, morning, noon and night. The men in our street were organising shifts to relieve those who had been fighting throughout the night and there was talk that the authorities were going to switch off the water supply in a kind of sanction on the local community.

Few, if any, understood the significance of what was happening to our community. Eventually barricades went up, representing the effective cession from the United Kingdom of the 800-odd acres of territory that the Bogside, Creggan and Brandywell occupied. It was rebellion, and the declaration of our independence from Stormont, the bastion of political power in Northern Ireland, was empowering.

As a child I was captivated by the first pirate radio station I ever heard – Radio Free Derry. It broadcast from various locations in the Bogside and our entire community tuned into it. It was our very own BBC – Bogside, Brandywell and Creggan – radio station, and just as the British Broadcasting Corporation was an important means of communication for 10 Downing Street with the British people, Radio Free Derry fulfilled the same function inside the barricaded areas. Our government also operated out of Number 10: number 10 Westland Street. It was the home of Patrick Doherty, the legendary 'Paddy Bogside'. In hindsight, what he and the Derry Citizens Action Committee were involved in was revolution, pure and simple, and Radio Free Derry played its part. For the short time it operated, it informed the community of developments when riots were taking place. It might give out warnings and ask for help – if food and water were needed on the frontline, or people were required in particular areas to bolster resistance, or vigilantes manning the barricades wanted soup, a bowl of Irish stew or tea and buns. For us children, the best part was the record requests and the chance to hear our names on the radio.

Some days, if the wind was blowing in a south-westerly direction, we could smell smoke and CS gas – the police fired it into the Bogside in enormous quantities. Our eyes would sting and spill tears. Sometimes we saw rioters going home with their clothes dyed a pinkish red from the police water cannon. After a while, it was all my friends and I talked about.

The political developments around us also had an effect on the games we played. Before the outbreak of the Troubles, boys throughout the Creggan played 'Cowboys and Indians' and 'Japs and Americans' – 'goodies versus baddies' – largely influenced by American television series such as *Bonanza* and *The Lone Ranger*, and Second World War films about the American campaign in the South Pacific against Japan. However, after the Battle of the Bogside, we played civil rights marchers being attacked by the police; later we were the IRA against the British Army.

The day the British Army marched into Derry was tumultuous. I was too young to be in the city centre to witness their arrival, but on television I watched them march across Waterloo Square, close to the Corner Boots Store where my daddy worked. They stopped at the bottom of William Street and erected wooden barriers with barbed wire, and stood looking into the Bogside at people there looking back. Initially there was a stand-off, but very quickly their arrival was interpreted as a tacit victory for the rioters over the police, who were defeated and exhausted after three days of skirmishing. Soon there were friendly exchanges and it wasn't long before people in the Nationalist community were serving tea and buns to the soldiers.

Amazingly, the army didn't enter the no-go areas of the Creggan, the Bogside and Brandywell. A negotiated truce saw the dismantling of the barricades and their replacement with a white line that marked the demarcation boundary of Free Derry, beyond which the army did not encroach.

By the end of the year, it had been agreed that British Military Police (MPs) would assume the duties of the RUC.

Many people, including members of my own family, felt comforted, especially since their presence removed the possibility of an armed B-Special invasion. One day when the MPs were patrolling, their Land Rover stopped halfway down our street and they were offered tea and sandwiches by some of our neighbours. I was soon down around them with my mates and talking enthusiastically to them. They chatted to us for a bit and even gave us sweets. At that time, we looked on them as friends, and the neighbourhood made them feel welcome.

Until suddenly, everything changed. I know now that the political situation had made a clash between my community and the army almost inevitable. Perhaps, with the introduction of the army, if Westminster had simultaneously disbanded Stormont and imposed direct rule, the situation might have developed differently. Direct rule came eventually in the spring of 1972, but by then an unbridgeable gulf had opened between us and the soldiers.

During the early hours of 8 July 1971, the Royal Anglian Regiment shot a young man named Seamus Cusack during rioting in the Bogside. He lived in Melmore Gardens, only two streets away from us in Malin Gardens, and bled to death on his way to Letterkenny Hospital in County Donegal. Then, during more rioting that afternoon, the same regiment shot dead another young man, Desmond Beattie.

For the Nationalist community, the final straw was the introduction by the Stormont government of internment without trial, to be implemented by the army. On the night of 9 August 1971, the soldiers entered the no-go areas of Derry and Belfast and everything changed. So far the Troubles, though only a mile away in the valley of the Bogside, had seemed to be happening in another world, but now they came right into our streets. I don't know if anyone was arrested in

Malin Gardens that night, but I heard that in Leenan Gardens, the street above, a man was taken by the army. People all around were very angry and fierce rioting started. I watched the adults build barricades at the top of our street and on the main roads leading into the Creggan. Now my own street was in an area that was no-go to the army and the police.

Shooting and bombing began in earnest. I used to stand with my friends in our street and count bombs going off in the city centre. There was one day when we heard ten explode. Of course it was frightening, but also, to children, exciting: it was as if a war was going on in the distance but our street was still unscathed. Our conversations were increasingly dominated by rumours of what was happening 'down the town', meaning the city centre. Often it was said that chain stores and factories were ablaze: 'Woolworths/Littlewoods/the Essex Shirt Factory is on fire.' Sometimes the rumours were true. It became a regular occurrence.

Before long, the soft-topped Land Rovers that the MPs had driven into the Creggan and the Bogside were replaced by armoured cars. Stones and petrol bombs rained down on the soldiers, wearing full-length Perspex visors, as they faced into the Bogside.

For the first time, I felt real fear and realised my own family did too, especially my mother. She was worried because she knew some mothers whose sons had been interned. Would that happen to some of our boys? Fortunately, it didn't.

After internment was introduced, more riots erupted. I would stand at the Westway end of our street and look down towards St Joseph's Secondary School and Rosemount police barracks, where fierce fighting was taking place. At the other end of Malin Gardens, across Broadway, Demesne Gardens descended towards the wide open McGaugh's field, with its spectacular view of Derry and the Bogside. I used to sit there with my friends to watch the riots in full tilt. We saw CS gas fired from army rifles, and tracked the long, thin arch of vapour as it fell.

I remember young men driving around the Creggan estate in hijacked vehicles. Many were set on fire and left as barricades, while anything that could be used as weaponry was gathered together. Paving slabs were broken up to be hurled, and one guy took a dumper truck from a building site, then filled it with stones, bricks and anything else that could be used as a missile, and drove it to the frontline.

The rioting wasn't at our front door, but the whole community was absorbed by it. As pavements disappeared, we walked on their sand base, while the sharp crack of rifle fire and the thud of bombs were ever-present in our ears. Our town was at war.

Some barricades were made to last. At the junction of Westway and Beechwood Avenue, the barricade on the main artery into the Creggan was cemented in place. Eventually the Creggan estate had only a couple of access roads through which the arrival and departure of locals and essential services were monitored. Vigilante huts were built and manned throughout the night in case the army tried to enter the area in pre-dawn raids to intern more of us. Our street had one such hut at the junction with Broadway. If the army was spotted, the alarm was raised: the blowing of whistles, the banging of bin lids and the blaring of car horns raised a frenzied cacophony, aimed at rousing everyone to resist their advance. Sometimes there were false alarms: some vigilantes claimed to have seen soldiers, but by the time people had awakened, dressed and run to where the alarm had been raised, nothing was there. False alarms were frustrating.

On many nights the alarm was real and fierce fighting broke out. For a child, it was frightening listening to the bin lids clanging and angry voices, but worse when there were explosions and gunfire. What amazes me, though, is that in spite of the disturbances and unrest, life continued as normal. We still played football in the street, and sometimes I sat on top of the Malin Street barricades with my friends. Now and then our street gang would have its meeting in the vigilante hut, which was often left empty during the daytime. When it was raining, we'd sit in it and chat and tell jokes. It was like camping for the day.

When we played IRA and British soldiers, nobody wanted to be the army; we all wanted to be the IRA. In the end, we had to agree to take turns. One group would pretend to be an army foot patrol making its way down the street, while the others hid in the gardens waiting to ambush them; we'd pretend to open fire on each other. Once we used my brother Liam's car as an IRA getaway vehicle. We pretended to drive to another part of the estate, got out, ran round to the back of our house and 'opened fire'. We used to wear masks or balaclavas or tie handkerchiefs over our noses like the rioters did. We'd collect rubber bullets and spent tear gas canisters so that those of us playing soldiers could throw them at the others.

These were 'games', but there was another frightening reality. I remember one incident vaguely, but there must have been others. Perhaps my family tried to shield us younger ones from the horror. It happened in Dunree Gardens, three streets above ours. On the night of 26 June 1970, a house was engulfed by flames. It emerged that some members of the fledgling IRA had been making petrol bombs. Five people died, including two children, who were asleep.

As the no-go areas bedded in, the IRA became more visible.

After the introduction of internment, it was commonplace to see masked IRA patrols manning checkpoints. The rest of the world might find this incredible, but many in my community saw them as protectors. One day there was an IRA checkpoint on Broadway and half a dozen IRA men were standing on the road or hunkering by hedges. With some friends, I approached one of them. He was holding a Thompson submachine gun, and he let me hold it. I felt ten feet tall. Sometimes, even if an IRA man was wearing a balaclava, we might recognise him but we knew we shouldn't acknowledge him or shout out his name.

One of my most vivid memories is of something that occurred on Beechwood Crescent, a small, curving roadway that branched to the right at the bottom of Broadway. On the left of the crescent there was a six- or seven-foot-high wall. On the right, a terrace of small houses was occupied by pensioners – my mates and I called them 'the penshies'. From the end terrace at the bottom of the crescent, there was a clear view of the old BSR (British Sound Recording) factory on the far side of a small valley. The British Army had commandeered the site and built a number of sandbag posts that looked out towards the Creggan and the Bogside. From Beechwood Crescent there was a clear view of one particular sangar at the north-western end of the factory, close to the junction of Laburnum Terrace and Westland Street.

I was standing on the barricade at the top of Beechwood Crescent, watching a group of IRA men making their way behind the high wall. At the bottom end, two holes had been poked through the bricks and gave a clear view of the sangar; the wall offered cover for snipers. From the barricade, I watched two IRA volunteers open fire on the British Army position. It was the first and the only time I ever witnessed live rounds being fired. I don't recall if anyone was injured or killed. I hope not.

# 3

# Bloody Sunday

It was a normal Sunday. I lay in bed listening to the drone of the Servis twin-tub and the Hoover. It was one of those mornings that would have been forgotten if it hadn't been for the events later in the day.

We all knew a big civil rights march was planned for the afternoon. It had been talked about in our house, and all the others of the Creggan Estate and Bogside. My older brothers and sisters were planning to join it. The theme of the march was anti-internment, but often people were attracted as much by the camaraderie and *craic* as by the purpose of a protest. For many, it was a day out when you could enjoy an almost carnival atmosphere.

The previous week, the Parachute Regiment had been quite brutal with unarmed anti-internment demonstrators on Magilligan Strand, close to a British Army base on the edge of Lough Foyle, which was now being used as a makeshift prison. I can safely say that no one in our house anticipated violence on that march: my mother and father wouldn't have let any of their children go on it and, indeed, would not have gone themselves if they'd thought there was any danger.

I was in the street with friends, kicking a football, as our neighbours and my family began to make their way to the start of the march. After Sunday dinner, my parents and older siblings walked to the Bishop's Field, close to St Mary's chapel. Kevin and I were left with our eldest sister, Lily. She was going out with Hannis Evers, a German – later they were married. Hannis and Lily often brought Kevin and me for runs in his car, and on that particular Sunday they drove around Derry to see the march and find out what security measures had been put in place on the periphery of the Bogside, where it was to end. I remember driving past Wellworth's Store on Waterloo Place. A group of people was standing at the entrance, looking towards William Street where the marchers had originally planned to come on their way to Guildhall Square.

Eventually we went home – everything seemed quiet and low key. It was a beautiful January afternoon and I joined my friends in the street. The sun was shining, but as evening approached there was a sharp nip in the air, and we began to see people drift back into the Creggan from the march. They had gone to support the protest but weren't interested in the political rally and speeches.

I don't remember hearing gunfire that day. We saw people with tears in their eyes, but that wasn't unusual – our eyes often watered with CS gas. At first we thought there'd been a riot in town and that they'd been caught up in it. Then I heard a man say, 'There's murder down there. People have been shot dead.' I saw shock in the faces then and realised that the tears were real. It was then I knew something terrible had happened.

We walked back towards our homes, still not knowing what had happened. Passers-by were subdued. Then I spotted my uncle Willy arriving at our house. He lived in the old family home at Iskaheen, County Donegal, the birthplace of my grandfather McKinney, in the same house where my mammy and daddy had gone during the Second World War for safety. It was unusual for Uncle Willy to visit us on a Sunday, and especially on his own. Normally he would be accompanied by his wife, Auntie Brigid. And if it was a proper visit, he'd spend the whole day with us, staying for dinner and tea. Something made me afraid and I didn't dare go into the house.

Then my brother Liam arrived. He was married and living on the Lone Moor Road. He wasn't in our house long before I saw him storm back out and drive off at speed. He didn't see me – usually he'd toot the horn, smile and wave, but on that occasion his mind was elsewhere.

Eventually I plucked up the courage and went home to get my tea. I loved Sunday evenings because we always had home-made chips. But I knew from the silence in the house that something was terribly wrong. My mother's face was drawn and I could see that she had been crying. I was told that my uncle Gerard had been shot dead. Some of my brothers hadn't arrived back from the march and my parents were anxious about them, too. Not until all of their children were accounted for could they calm down.

Everyone who had been on the march brought horror stories of the shooting and killings. I sat in the middle of it all, listening to my brothers' accounts of what had happened. Some had had lucky escapes and others had witnessed shocking scenes. When the news came on, there was complete silence. By nine o'clock, we knew that thirteen people had been shot dead and as many more had been wounded.

My parents and the rest of the family had been caught by surprise at the sudden advance into the Bogside of the 1st

Battalion, the Parachute Regiment. They talked of bullets whizzing over their heads and I heard that my daddy had had to pull my mammy to the ground. Mammy said she didn't realise at first what was happening. She was wearing a new coat and the thought of having to lie on the ground didn't appeal to her. Daddy brought her to her senses when he shouted, 'They're firing live rounds! Get down!' My brother Jim, then twenty-five, had to crawl on his hands and knees down High Street to get away from the gunfire. Pearse and Noel talked about how they'd had to crouch behind a wall near the Rossville flats and how some men who ran out from behind it got shot.

Eyewitness stories were filtering into every house on the estate. When I went out later, everybody in the street was talking about it. My friends and I huddled in a corner to exchange the different stories we'd heard. Soon there were rumours that school would be cancelled tomorrow in protest over what had happened.

The next day, instead of going to school, I went with my brother Noel down into the Bogside to look at the aftermath of what people were now calling 'Bloody Sunday'. There were pools of congealed blood where people had fallen, and a huge one with a banner lying in it. There was numbed disbelief that this could have happened in our town – that so many people had been shot dead by the British Army. Crowds of young people were on street corners, but there was silence. I remember the silence.

My friends reported the gory details of how people had been killed. Stories of Bloody Sunday dominated our conversations for months to come.

The following night, after Uncle Gerard's body had been released from hospital, we went to the wake at his home in the

Waterside. Auntie Ita, his wife, was sitting in a complete daze, totally traumatised. There were people all around her, some offering water or cups of tea. I don't remember seeing the coffin, but the house was packed, as is the case at most Irish wakes. But this was a very different death. Ita had eight children and was heavily pregnant with her ninth. She had the responsibility of all those children, and now her husband was dead. It was as though her entire system had shut down.

On the evening before the funeral, the thirteen coffins were placed side by side inside the altar railings of St Mary's chapel in the Creggan. As we all went to Mass every Sunday, we might have seen the odd coffin behind the gold-coloured gates in the little chapel on the right transept of the cruciform church, but thirteen? It seemed unreal.

Gerard was buried at Iskaheen cemetery, across the border. It was raining heavily. Along the route, black flags were flying from windows and lampposts. A lonely tricolour, the green, white and orange flag of the Republic of Ireland, was flying at half-mast at the Irish Customs building, just inside the border. Despite the rain, the cemetery was thronged with what appeared to be thousands of people. Ita was carried away in a distraught state.

Three weeks after Bloody Sunday, she gave birth to a baby boy, whom she named Gerard, after the daddy he would never know. There was a photograph in the paper of her, clearly heartbroken, cradling her newborn baby.

Like all the murdered and maimed on Bloody Sunday, my uncle Gerard was a totally innocent man. He had run away as paratroopers entered Glenfada Park, firing indiscriminately into a large crowd of fleeing people. With a dozen or so others, he had gone along an alleyway and taken shelter in a small walled garden at the back of the park, looking towards the

Little Diamond and Abbey Park. Even after the crowd had fled and an eerie silence had descended, a shot rang out close to the alleyway. A paratrooper, Soldier G, was finishing off a young man called Jim Wray, who had been wounded.

The shot that executed Jim Wray must have caused the small group Uncle Gerard was with to panic. A young man, Gerard Donaghy, decided to climb over the wall and run across the entrance of the alleyway towards Abbey Park. My uncle followed him. A shot was fired, and Donaghy spun around, then collapsed to the ground. My uncle turned to his left and saw the paratrooper who had fired on young Donaghy. He raised his hands in the air, an act of surrender, and pleaded, 'Jesus! Don't shoot! Don't shoot!' Later, when the paratroopers had retreated and the fallen were being attended to, the first assumption was that Uncle Gerard had had a heart attack, as no one could find any sign of a bullet wound. Then they discovered the entry and exit sites in his sides, hidden by his limp arms.

Ita never got over Uncle Gerard's death, but she raised a family that would have made him very proud. Her husband's death must have tested her faith in God, but twenty years after Bloody Sunday, my cousin Gerard's death in a car accident almost broke it. He and his wife had been looking forward to the birth of their first baby.

I have always admired Ita and the other families of the Bloody Sunday dead and injured. Since that incident, they have shown great strength and dignity, despite the brutal way in which their loved ones were taken from them.

The impact of Bloody Sunday was far reaching. The rioting increased and people in our area became hardened and angrier. Our alienation from the British state intensified and our determination to keep the British Army out became more resolute. Young people flocked to join the IRA, to the extent that it probably couldn't cope with the influx. Dislike for all things British grew. The sense of injustice and the knowledge that a terrible wrong had been perpetrated against us was a wound that festered.

It was rumoured that the Irish government might send troops across the border. Of course, it didn't happen. There was talk of evacuations and getting the children to safe areas. And there was fear of another bloodbath. Fear, anger and mistrust took root.

A few months later, Lord Widgery's Bloody Sunday Report largely cleared the British soldiers and authorities of blame for the killings. It was the last straw. Many more young men, including some of my brothers, considered joining the IRA. Many men and women did join. The Troubles that had always seemed so near and yet so far had come to my doorstep. I was ten. I was living in the midst of war. Things had changed utterly.

# 4

# The Impact of a Rubber Bullet

The first school I attended was the Holy Child Primary School, Central Drive, Derry. It was in the heart of the Creggan estate. In the mid-1960s the Creggan, though plagued by unemployment, was a vibrant community, teeming with young families. Practising Catholics, of whom there were many at the time, adhered strictly to the Church's teaching on birth control. Consequently, large families, such as our own, were not unusual. In fact, there were so many young children in the Creggan in the mid-1960s that the Holy Child could not deal with all of them at once, so some went to school in the morning and others in the afternoon. I was among those who went in the morning.

In 1969, just as the Troubles were beginning, I was transferred to St Eugene's Boys' Primary School in the Rosemount district of Derry. It was a fifteen-minute walk from home and next door to St Joseph's Secondary School, whose grounds extended from the junction of Westway and Beechwood Avenue to Creggan Hill. St Eugene's was more popularly known as Rosemount Primary School and was quite different from the Holy Child because now I stayed all day, until three-thirty. I was nearly always one of the first to arrive in the morning because I'd take a lift from my brother Jim, who drove a van. I used to get up early so that I could leave the house with him; I felt very proud to be chauffeured to school in the highly respected vehicle of 'James Doherty, Butcher'.

After school on 3 May 1972, I was playing football in the street with some friends. Some of our neighbours, especially those with cars or gardens they took pride in, got annoyed if the ball went too close. That evening, it landed in a garden and was promptly confiscated, which brought our game to an abrupt finish. I went home around eight o'clock, and before long I was tucked up in bed and fast asleep.

Awakening on 4 May was no different from awakening on any other morning. I got up as normal, hopped from mat to mat to avoid the cold lino, washed and got dressed for school. As usual, Jim unlocked the van, I climbed in and, shortly afterwards, he dropped me off at Rosemount Primary School. I was in primary six and my teacher was Mr Eunan O'Donnell. I loved his class because he was a sports enthusiast and encouraged us to enjoy physical activity, especially football.

The day was completely normal, with nothing to suggest that my life was about to change forever. There was no music, like you hear in the movies, beginning softly and gradually getting louder, building the tension of the unfolding drama. At lunchtime, I went home as usual. There was a discussion about the new house my sister Lily had bought on the Glen Road, as she was intending to get married. It required some work and my brother Gregory, who was five years older than me, had been kept off school that day to help with painting and decorating. I'd wanted to stay off and help too, but Mammy and Daddy insisted, 'Naw, naw, Richard. You need to get back to school.'

I went down Malin Gardens, without a care in the world, turned left onto Greenwalk, right onto Beechwood Avenue, left onto Marlborough Road, and before long I was sitting in Mr O'Donnell's class. Once lessons ended and the school bell rang, I met up with some of my friends just outside our classroom. It was one of a few old prefab buildings we called 'the huts' because they were made of timber with tin roofs. They were beside the main school building, near the Helen Street entrance.

On different days we went home different ways. Sometimes we left by the main gate, which led out onto Marlborough Road – this was actually the longest way home. Sometimes I went out of the Helen Street gate, turning left onto Creggan Hill and left again at the summit onto Westway Gardens. To be honest, I was never comfortable going this way, as it took me past a heavily fortified RUC barracks with a strong military presence and an army sangar.

For the boys who lived in Lower and west Upper Creggan, the preferred way was to hop the wall between Rosemount and St Joseph's Secondary School and scurry across St Joseph's all-weather pitch, up the embankment to the back of the grass soccer pitch. From there we went through the St Joseph's canteen gate and turned left onto Westway Gardens.

Some days we squeezed through a hole in the fence surrounding the primary school football pitch. This led onto an alley behind a row of houses and shops on Beechwood Avenue and was, in fact, the most direct route to my house. Residents and shopkeepers often tried to discourage us from taking it and sometimes complained to the school authorities, who told us not to use it.

That day, my friends and I left through the St Joseph's canteen gate. I remember seeing the backs of the houses on Creggan Hill that looked out onto the St Joseph's playing fields. I remember running behind my friends up the slope between the all-weather pitch and the grass soccer field. Marlborough Hall was not far from the British Army sangar. It was a derelict building that had been firebombed during a recent riot. It had most likely been targeted because it was non-residential and was close to the Rosemount RUC station and the sangar. I went into the derelict building through an empty doorway. It was a bit eerie, but when we came home this way, we always went in to have a look at the burned rafters, collapsed floors and ceilings, and the gaping hole in the roof through which we could see the sky. I suppose it was just boys' natural curiosity.

I climbed out of a window to the back of the soccer pitch. The window was close to the sangar, which faced towards St Joseph's Secondary School and up towards the Creggan estate. The last thing I remember seeing was the army lookout post. I was ten or twelve feet away from it.

This route home from school was quite a popular one. A stream of primary school children passed that way daily, some in front of me and others behind. I wouldn't doubt for one minute that some in front of me might have thrown stones at the sangar that day. It had a corrugated roof that rattled when stones hit it. I'd done it myself. It wasn't unusual to lift a stone or brick, lob it and run like hell when you heard it banging off the sangar. The army would take a very different view, but to us children it was just a game, played in the context of the environment we were living in. Sadly, to throw a stone at the army or the police, whom we viewed as the enemy, was pretty normal.

On the afternoon of 4 May 1972, even if I had intended to throw a stone, I didn't get the chance. A soldier fired a rubber bullet, which struck me on the bridge of the nose. I didn't hear the bang. Everything went blank.

When I returned home from hospital, lots of friends came to visit me. On one occasion, fifteen children from Malin and Leenan Gardens were sitting with me in our 'good room' at the front of the house. That we were allowed to use it, the room kept for special guests, was a sign of how much my parents wanted to do everything they could to make sure I would be happy. Before I lost my sight, I would have had to beg permission to go in there.

Another day I met a group of girls we sometimes hung around with. They came from Westway, the street that ran at a right angle to the top of Malin Gardens. I don't recall their Christian names, but I know that some were from the McLaughlin, Kelly and McCrossan families. One girl, seeing me for the first time since I'd been shot, was so shocked that she gasped and put her hands over her eyes. I must have shocked all my friends – we had grown up together and spent endless hours playing in the park between Malin and Leenan Gardens – and now I was blind, having to be led.

Very soon, though, everyone was treating me in the usual way, but adjusted their behaviour to take my blindness into account. They would play football with me in the street and kick the ball towards me with instructions as to where it was. Obviously they didn't demonstrate their Georgie Best skills as they might have done when I was sighted, but it was great to feel I was still part of something I'd always been passionate about. If we played hide-and-go-seek, one of my friends would run with me and help me to find a good hiding place. In effect, they loaned me their eyes.

I decided I wanted to get back to riding a bike. My balance was perfect; the challenge was making sure I didn't crash into anything. With the help of my friends, I got up on a bike and at first I was riding into the pavement and sometimes into parked cars. Then Paul Moran, the guy who'd got the better bike at Christmas, had an idea: he'd run in front of me, calling and directing me with his voice. It was fantastic. He and Thomas Breslin ran ahead, calling, 'Come this way! Come this way!' and I just followed their voices. I cycled down Malin Gardens and around the roundabout. Sometimes I pedalled so fast they had to sprint to keep ahead of me. At the end of the day, the two lads were ready to collapse with exhaustion, but I was elated. Today I'm filled with gratitude for friends like Paul and Thomas.

As time went on, my friends realised my hearing was compensating for my blindness. Surprised by how quickly I recognised them from the tone and texture of their voices, they would try to fool me by speaking in either a deep or high-pitched voice, or with a variety of 'foreign' accents, such as Belfast, Donegal, Kerry, French, Indian, American. I could almost always tell who was who, much to their disappointment. The human voice is an amazing instrument. No matter how hard you might try to disguise it, there's almost always something that carries an individual's fingerprint, perhaps the tone, the rhythm or the musical note that everyone's has. To this day I have a file in my mind with hundreds of voices stored in it. People I haven't spoken to for several months are flabbergasted when I know them by the sound of their voice.

It doesn't always work, of course. Just as sighted people experience blanks, like 'I know you but I can't put a name to your face', so too with me. Recently I've noticed it might take me a little longer to recognise some people, particularly if I haven't met them in a long time – perhaps it's old age. Circumstances and environment often help. In certain places I expect to meet certain people, so when they come up and speak to me I'm very sharp with the voice. My friend Liam Hegarty is a director of Derry City Football Club. It's not unusual for him to pass me at the Brandywell Stadium during a match and say, 'How's it going, Richard?' That's no problem because I'd expect to meet Liam in the Brandywell at a match. The circumstance and the voice fit together. But let's say I'm walking through Westminster Cathedral in London and someone says, 'Hello, Richard.' I might not recognise Liam's voice straight away because it's out of context.

I have most difficulty with recognising voices in crowded areas with noisy backgrounds. If I'm walking down one of Derry's main arteries, Strand Road, and there's a lot of traffic, I might hear a voice clearly but not realise who it belongs to. Then I'll feel a little embarrassed – I try always to address people by their first name, and I hate having to ask, 'Who is it?' I often wonder how it looks to the person. Do they boil it down to blindness or do they think I'm getting senile?

One of my pet hates, though, is when someone approaches me and I don't recognise their voice but they persist in making me guess who they are. I offended one person when I didn't recognise his voice – thirty-seven years after we'd last met! 'What do you mean, you can't remember me? I was in primary seven with you,' he remonstrated. He'd forgotten that, quite apart from the passage of time, back then his voice hadn't even broken. It drives me around the bend when people play these games with me – it's like hearing a bad joke for the hundredth time.

Like most Irish people, I'm prone to letting out the odd

expletive without intending to be offensive. It helps, though, to be able to see on such occasions to ensure that it's not inappropriate. One day I was going to a match in the Brandywell, and as I was walking up to the gate, a man I knew well called Willie Barrett began shouting, 'Don't let that man in! It's Richard Moore – don't let him in!'

'Fake off, Willie,' I said.

'Aw, now, watch your language – Bishop Daly's listening to you.'

'Fake off, Willie!'

I walked through the gate, and Bishop Daly said, 'How are you doing, Richard?' I nearly collapsed.

# 5

# The Immediate Aftermath

After I was shot, there was, understandably, a lot of hurt and anger – not only within my family, but also within the wider community. A ten-year-old boy on his way home from school had been shot and blinded for life.

The army informed the media that I was a 'hooligan' and a stone-thrower. I knew I wasn't, and I often wondered why the soldier felt it necessary to fire a single rubber bullet on that day: did he pick me out specifically and aim at me? Was he aware of the damage he'd done? Did he ever think about me in the months and years afterwards?

Almost immediately, people were protesting about my shooting. The following morning, my oldest brother, Liam, and four members of the Rosemount and Upper Nassau Street Tenants Association were accompanied by John Hume MP to a meeting at Rosemount police barracks, where they met senior army and police officers to discuss it. They talked for almost an hour, and afterwards John Hume announced that both the British Army and the police had promised separate investigations into the matter. According to Mr Hume, the army said they would announce the outcome of their investigation within forty-eight hours.

The circumstances, though, were in contention. At the meeting, the army claimed that 'A group of about twenty young hooligans tried to remove a barricade outside the Rosemount station. Rubber bullets were fired to disperse them. One of the boys was seen to be hit and was carried away.'

Civilian eyewitnesses offered a very different version of events. Some told the media that there were boys around an army sangar that faced into the grounds of St Joseph's Secondary School. One person told the *Derry Journal* that boys were pulling at the sandbags. I don't remember sandbags. I just remember heavy sheets of corrugated iron with a single coil of barbed wire, five or six feet deep, placed before them to act as a buffer. If children were pulling at anything, it would have been the wire, for the sandbags, presumably, would have been behind the corrugated iron. Suddenly, and without warning, the soldier had fired a rubber bullet from point-blank range and felled me.

After the meeting, Liam asked, 'What could ten-year-olds do against the British Army? Richard was shot at twelve-feet range. It looked like a deliberate attempt to seriously injure him, as indeed happened. How do you tell a ten-year-old boy he'll be blind for life?'

John Hume said he had pressed the army strongly about the regulations under which rubber bullets were to be used, but had been given no satisfactory answer.

The four women in the deputation were Margaret Campbell, Mary Deehan and Mary Fisher, all from Upper Nassau Street, and Molly Cassidy from Osborne Street. They were concerned mothers who lived with their families in the area where the sangar was located. At the meeting, they had lodged a strong protest with the British Army about my injury and about the strength of the army presence in their area. They informed the waiting media that they had also outlined their protest to William Whitelaw, the British secretary of state for Northern Ireland. Margaret Campbell, who was chair of the Rosemount and Upper Nassau Street Tenants Association, said, 'It is inhuman for any adult to injure a child by firing a rubber bullet from twelve-feet range. If a father punished a child too severely, he would be prosecuted by the NSPCC. The soldier who did this dreadful deed must be brought to justice.'

The day after my shooting, a Friday, local parents kept their children home from school. Mrs Campbell told the media, 'Children have to pass thirteen army look-out posts on their way to and from school in this area. We have kept the children of the Rosemount area away from school today, and some parents do not want their children to go back to school again until there are guarantees of safe conduct and safety from attacks like this one on them.'

On Saturday, 6 May 1972, the *Daily Mirror* reported that the Northern Ireland minister of state, Lord Windlesham, had ordered an inquiry 'into how a boy was hit in the face by a rubber bullet and half blinded'. This statement is interesting on two counts. First, it meant three 'official' inquiries would be conducted into my shooting, by the army, the police and now the one ordered by Lord Windlesham. Neither I nor my family have ever been informed of the outcome of any. The second interesting point is that I was described as 'half blinded'. This is, of course, at variance with the statement my brother Liam had made. While my family was hoping against hope that my eyesight might be partially saved, some, like Liam, knew that the damage was irreparable.

The *Daily Mirror* reported that I had lost an eye and that doctors at Altnagelvin Hospital were fighting to save the other. Liam informed the press that the family wouldn't know for fourteen days whether the doctors' efforts had been successful. The newspaper reported army sources as saying, 'stone throwing lasted more than twenty-five minutes – then one rubber bullet was fired'. It revealed that the regiment involved was the 5th Light Regiment, Royal Artillery, and that a Lieutenant-Colonel David Jones had attended the meeting with John Hume, along with Superintendent William Johnson of the RUC. Mary Deehan was quoted as saying, 'The bullet hit the boy on the bridge of the nose. The ambulance was a long time coming. It is a bad area here. My little boy Desmond, who is eight, was hit by a rubber bullet the day before Richard, but not badly.'

According to the *Daily Mirror*, Lieutenant-Colonel Jones stated: 'Eleven boys began stoning one of our emplacements. They kept it up although verbal warnings were given eleven times to disperse. Then somebody wrenched away part of the barbed wire ten yards out from the emplacement. When wire is wrenched away, an emplacement becomes indefensible against bomb planting. Bearing in mind that two of my soldiers were killed a few weeks ago after wire had been moved and a bomb planted, one rubber bullet was fired. The distance between the soldier who fired and the boy was thirty feet and the shot was not deliberately aimed at the boy's eyes. Rubber bullets are not precisely aimed. They are what we call an area weapon.'

While I lay in hospital, the *Mirror* concluded, a soldier of the 5th Light Regiment was being treated for eye injuries received during stoning after I was injured.

Whether or not the soldier aimed the rubber bullet deliberately at my face, only he knows. What I will dispute, however, is Colonel Jones's assertion that I was thirty feet away. I wish I had been, for the impact would have been considerably less – I might even have seen it coming and had time to duck. All of the civilian eyewitnesses stated that I was no more than four yards away, and I remember being very close to the sangar when the bullet was discharged.

Certainly Northern Ireland, especially places like the Creggan and Rosemount, saw its fair share of violence, and after Bloody Sunday that escalated. At the time, I knew of the deaths of the soldiers Lieutenant-Colonel Jones had referred to, more human tragedy, with horrific consequences for their families, friends, loved ones and the men they served with. I would not attempt to justify the killing of anybody, but I believe it was entirely wrong to use the deaths of the soldiers to justify or mitigate the shooting and blinding of a ten-year-old boy on his way home from school.

On the day I was shot, the soldiers were standing in an enclosed sangar, protected by several layers of sandbags, barbed wire and corrugated iron. They looked out onto the grounds of St Joseph's from a porthole, which, as far as I know, was covered with mesh on the inside. It is hard for me to imagine the threat that I or the other children passing could have posed on that particular day. I do not deny that some threw stones, but as a teenager, young adult, husband, father and middle-aged man, I kept asking myself the same questions: even if children were throwing stones at the army position, was the firing of a rubber bullet and the blinding of a ten-year-old justified?

One of the things that saddens me most about the incident was that if the army had been able to prove that I was a rioter, with a photograph or film footage, they would have done so to justify their action. I think that's wrong. That I wasn't a rioter and wasn't throwing stones isn't the central issue here. If, as a ten-year-old child, you had thrown a stone through someone's window, would it give the house-owner the right to blind you? Of course not! I would expect that level of rationale from an ordinary person on the street, and, quite frankly, I would expect an even more disciplined version from a highly trained British soldier or officer.

There is no justification for shooting and blinding a child. It shouldn't be wrong because it happens to a boy on the streets of Bristol or Manchester. If it's wrong to blind a child, it doesn't matter what his religion is, or his nationality, or the political persuasion of his parents. If it's wrong, it's wrong. We can't pick and choose here: it was wrong to shoot and blind me.

Some political leaders in Britain and Northern Ireland may have attempted to justify, or even protect, the people who blinded me, but if it had happened to their child, or to one in their community or constituency, they might not have been as dogmatic. Once a community or a society begins to accept any justification for inflicting violence on children, it's on a slippery slope. It's not only the soldier who should take responsibility for my shooting, it is also those political and community leaders who, by what they say or even by their silence, are allowing a value structure to exist where the blinding of a ten-year-old boy is justifiable.

When I got out of hospital, I heard that there had been several protests to the British Army and the RUC about my shooting. The local MP, John Hume, had led delegations to police headquarters. I felt very important and special because somebody of his stature had taken up my case. In many ways, that sense of importance contributed to my recovery and my long-term acceptance of permanent blindness.

In hospital, the primary concern of the surgeons and

nursing staff was to stabilise my condition. Initially, given the severity of my injuries, they were concerned about my survival. Then there was the possibility that I might have suffered brain damage. This would require constant monitoring over a period of months.

My right eye had been so badly damaged that it had to be removed. The left one, though less damaged, was also dead. Surgeons would have removed it too, but my parents pleaded with them to leave it. They agreed, on the grounds that it wouldn't cause any harm. From my parents' perspective, it was better that the eye stayed – they harboured the simple hope that, perhaps either by a miracle or a miraculous breakthrough in optical science, my sight might one day be restored.

Now that I was home, though, the real challenge for my parents and me was to put the pieces of my life back together – in effect, to build a new future that incorporated and allowed for blindness. No one had any idea where to begin. The fact that I was only ten actually protected me from the daunting challenges that lay in the future. I was concerned only with the present, while my parents were consumed and frightened by what the future might have in store.

The first major challenge for my parents, once I was discharged from hospital, was breaking the news to me that I would never see again. In hindsight, I can recall a few awkward moments when some of my brothers tried but faltered at the last moment. I continued to assume that I couldn't see because of the bandages wrapped around my head. As the days wore on, the situation must have become increasingly difficult for my parents and my family. But I had to be told the truth.

About two weeks after I came out of hospital, four weeks after I had been shot, my brother Noel took me for a walk around our small garden. I can still remember the feel of the narrow strip of concrete that ran parallel with the clothesline, before we stepped across a low fence into our next-door neighbours' back garden and walked up and down the Bradleys' pathway. Eventually Noel broached the subject. 'Do you know what happened to you, Richard?' he asked.

'Yes,' I replied. 'I was shot by a rubber bullet.'

'Do you know what damage it caused?' he continued.

'No.'

He proceeded to explain what had happened. I'm sure we were being anxiously observed every step of the way by the family and, no doubt, by the Bradleys too, who had probably been alerted to what Noel was about to say. To this day, I'm filled with love and admiration for him: I know it took great courage, as well as sensitivity and tact, for him to be the bearer of such bad news.

I was holding his right elbow as he walked me up and down the Bradleys' and our back gardens, telling me that my right eye had been removed but that while the doctors had managed to save my left eye, it was blind. 'It means, Richard,' I heard him say, 'you will never be able to see again.'

I have no rational explanation for what happened next. I heard what he said, processed it and instantaneously accepted it. I'm sure Noel and my family were expecting a big reaction, with tears and a grieving process that included anger and depression. But it never happened.

That night, however, when I was in bed, I cried. I wasn't worrying about the future. I had no thought about employment and how I might cope. I didn't think or fret about not being able to see colours or drive a car. It was the loss of simple things – that I would never again see the faces of my mother and father filled me with sorrow. Adults might be surprised at this. Sight is such a wonderful gift that we often take for granted. I guess if you, as a sighted person, were asked what you would miss most if you lost your sight, you might think of beautiful landscapes, of the setting sun slipping under a shimmering ocean or the sky at night. I certainly miss them, but as a ten-year-old boy, it was the thought of never again seeing my mammy and daddy's faces that devastated and frightened me most.

I went to sleep and the next morning I awoke and got on with life. I'm sure that Mammy and Daddy wondered, Has it really registered with Richard what's happened to him? Did Noel tell him or did he not? I'm sure they must have been confused. Even though I was the one who had lost my eyesight, I maintain that my parents suffered as much, if not more, than I did. In many ways, I was in the eye of the storm but they had to deal with the hurricane of hurts and emotional hurdles. Years later, I learned that on the second or third night after I had been shot, my daddy returned home from the hospital and stood in the street and cried. Like most men at that time, he didn't show his emotions easily. For him to break down so publicly, in the middle of Malin Gardens, indicates the level of hurt my entire family felt. Later still, after he had passed away, I learned that while he was discussing the extent of my injuries with the surgeons at Altnagelvin Hospital, he'd asked, 'Can I give him my eyes?' The generosity of that gesture chokes me to this day.

It must also have been very difficult for my brothers and sisters. Kevin was the youngest, and he was largely overshadowed by what had happened to me. Gregory confided in me that there were times when the atmosphere in our home, after I was shot was terrible. For a time, our house was not a happy place to be. In those weeks and months, everyone was looking after me, but also looking after Mammy. She would stand crying at our back window if I was in the garden trying to kick a football. If I was out in the street with my friends, she would stand crying in the bay window as she watched me trying to join in the fun.

Some nights I awoke to discover her kneeling beside my bed. She came to pray for my well-being and often ended up in hushed sobs, begging God to show some kind of mercy by restoring my sight. I would lie still, pretending to be asleep, and listen as she watched and prayed over me. Sometimes her sadness became unbearable. To stop her, I would move in the bed as if I were beginning to wake up, and she would immediately get up and go away.

During the first two or three years after I was shot, Mammy often broke down in the house when I was out, or in the bedroom at night when she was alone with my father. Sometimes she was so upset, she had to be restrained for fear that she might hurt herself. While shielding me, the rest of the family were extremely worried about her. On one occasion, she was seen walking down William Street in the middle of the road, talking to herself. There was a fear that she was losing her mind. Even her appearance was a cause for concern. She had always been a proud woman who, in addition to ensuring that her children were neat and clean, made sure she led by example. Now, she had lost all interest in herself.

Mammy had always been a regular churchgoer before her brother's death and my shooting, and afterwards she continued to attend Mass, no doubt praying for me and for the strength to cope. She often tells the story of a woman she met one day when she was coming out of church. Mammy was in tears and the woman stopped to comfort her. She said she felt so low and so hopeless that all she wanted to do was to take me and my younger brother Kevin down to the river Foyle and jump in to end the suffering and uncertainty. Of course, the other woman pleaded with her not to do it. Whether she would actually have gone ahead had she not met the woman, I don't know – it has been known for a mother in deep depression and filled with hopeless despair to do such a thing. I feel deep sympathy and sadness for such women and their families, for I know that my own mother might well have been on the brink of suicide herself.

Looking back, I believe she suffered a breakdown, although it was never diagnosed as such. When you consider that her brother had been shot dead on 30 January and I was blinded on 4 May in the same year, you understand that her world must have imploded. Back then, there was no such thing as a trauma counsellor or other such support mechanism, just the network of immediate and extended family and, of course, our wonderful neighbours in Malin Gardens and on the Creggan estate. And for all the criticism (sometimes justified) levelled against the Catholic Church, we had wonderful priests in St Mary's parish who were always available to offer comfort. I know that my mammy and my daddy both found solace in prayer and the Church. I have no doubt that's what pulled them through, as well as their family and friends. Our entire community gave tremendous support to my family and me. It would have been difficult to survive without it.

My parents were decent people who worked hard to ensure that all their children's needs were taken care of. We were warm, safe and well fed, and they strove to give us every opportunity to get a good education and trade. Yet without warning, and through no fault of their own, for four months in 1972, the Troubles landed slap-bang in the middle of their living room and there was nothing they could do about it. Their whole world was turned upside down.

While I was the one on the receiving end of the rubber

bullet, my parents and family had to deal with the consequences of the damage it had inflicted. And Mammy and Daddy dealt with it honourably. I never heard them say an angry word about the soldier or the British Army. In fact, they went out of their way to encourage us all not to react angrily to what had happened to me. God knows, at times they had good cause to be angry. One day they received a letter from the secretary of state for Northern Ireland, William Whitelaw, intimating that they were lucky they weren't being prosecuted because their son was a rioter. On another occasion, a British newspaper published a letter from a female reader in England who stated that the woman who had lost her brother on Bloody Sunday and whose son had been blinded must have deserved it. She was implying that my mother had come from a bad family and had failed to rear me properly. That really hurt Mammy and Daddy because nothing could have been further from the truth.

Sometimes I wonder about editorial sensitivity, or insensitivity, in newspapers. Have those making decisions about what is and is not publishable become so hardened and cynical that they don't think through the consequences of cruel words, the damage they can inflict? Perhaps they do, and are happy to allow them to wound.

My parents didn't even lapse into bitterness when my sister Deirdre began a relationship with a British soldier. From the Second World War until the early 1970s, there was an American naval base in Derry and it was not unusual for a Derry woman to date and eventually marry a US sailor. With the arrival of large numbers of British soldiers in Northern Ireland, it was inevitable that the same thing would happen. And it did. However, while it was permissible for Derry women to marry US sailors, as the Troubles deepened, it was frowned upon for anyone from a Nationalist/Republican area, like the Creggan, to date and marry a British soldier. Indeed, when it was discovered that a woman was seeing one, she might be tied to a lamp-post, then tarred and feathered.

Deirdre is the youngest girl in our family, and fell in love with a British soldier. She was dating him around the time of Bloody Sunday and my shooting, so it was a difficult time for her and our family – some of my brothers were not happy. I had no problem with the idea, but I was a mere boy of ten. My parents saw the danger for her, but it was Deirdre's choice and they respected that. When it was arranged for them to go and meet him discreetly at a place outside Derry, they went.

In 1974, Deirdre and he were married, and my mammy and a few of my brothers went over to the wedding in Reading. Reflecting on this now, I am filled with amazement and admiration for both my parents. It must have been hard for them to accept Deirdre's choice but I think it shows how incredibly strong they were and also how fair-minded. My life had been traumatised by a British soldier, but they were not prepared to cast blame on the entire British Army for that action, any more than they blamed the entire British Army for the actions of the paratroopers on Bloody Sunday. The soldier Deirdre married was not responsible for the pain visited on our family, so my parents were happy to give him and Deirdre their blessing.

# 6

# American Dream

Some communities are truly blessed to have even one good general practitioner in their midst . In Derry we had more than our fair share and one of the most outstanding was Dr Raymond McClean. For a while, Raymond became involved in local politics on behalf of the Social Democratic and Labour Party (SDLP) and even served as Mayor of Derry. During the Battle of the Bogside, he set up a field hospital with nurses from the Bogside and the Creggan, treating people injured in the fighting. He later became a leading expert on the effects of CS gas, writing several reports and speaking at seminars and hearings around the world. He had been on hand to treat the first two people shot on Bloody Sunday and attended the post-mortems of the thirteen victims. After Bloody Sunday, he was elected vice-chairperson of the Bloody Sunday Appeal Committee and was sent to the US to raise funds for the families of the dead and to help spread awareness of our unfolding tragedy.

While he was visiting Massachusetts, he met with Dan

Herlihy, a Cork businessman living in the town of Worcester, who was chairman of the Committee for Justice in Northern Ireland. He told Dan about my injuries and my connection with one of the Bloody Sunday dead, my uncle Gerard McKinney. In the early winter of 1972, following his return to Derry, Dr McClean received a letter from Dan Herlihy asking if there was anything he and the people of Worcester could do to assist. I still had my left eye, so although medical opinion in Ireland was that nothing could be done, there was hope of a sort. The Massachusetts Eye and Ear Infirmary was world famous and an appointment there wouldn't do any harm. I would see one of America's leading eye specialists, who could offer a valuable second opinion. On top of this, the people of Worcester were prepared to sponsor my visit, with my parents.

I had heard of Massachusetts, but not of Worcester. When I was told we might be going to America, I was very excited, especially about the prospect of flying across the Atlantic Ocean. Then, when I realised only Mammy and Daddy would be going with me, I was upset. A few months earlier, in August 1972, I had gone with them to the French pilgrimage town of Lourdes, where St Bernadette had claimed, in 1858, to have seen a vision of the Blessed Virgin. The waters at the grotto of Lourdes are considered to have miraculous healing properties and so, with simple faith and hope, my parents brought me there. However, during our pilgrimage I really missed my younger brother Kevin, and the idea of going to America without him was too much for me. I told my mother and father that I didn't want to go unless Kevin came too. I didn't really understand that they couldn't afford to take me to America, let alone Kevin. However, between the organising committee in America and some good people in Derry and Dublin, the money was raised to bring Kevin. I adored my little brother, who, even though he was only five at the time, had been amazingly helpful to me since my blinding. He became my eyes and was always on hand if I needed anything.

Even though Lourdes had failed to produce a miracle, my parents were still hoping I'd get my eyesight back. I had begun to take the loss of it in my stride, but they had not, and would explore any chance, any faint hope, of getting it back. So, off we went to America.

We left Derry on Sunday, 7 January 1973. I was now eleven years old and was beginning to feel overawed by all the attention. Before I was blinded, I had never been on a plane, and had only once been out of Ireland – when we went to stay with Margaret in England. Since my injury, though, I'd already been to France and now America! It was all very exciting.

As I've already mentioned, the sound of the human voice was becoming increasingly important to me and one in particular is indelibly recorded in my memory. I heard it on our arrival in Boston. Shortly after we had stepped inside the terminal building, an American voice said: 'Welcome to the United States of America.' It belonged to Dan Herlihy, who, with his wife Joan, met us at Logan Airport and welcomed us into their home for the duration of our week-long visit. They were wonderful hosts and made us all feel very much at ease.

A huge number of journalists and photographers were at the airport to greet us. There was even a television crew. My mammy and daddy were very ordinary people and I was a very ordinary wee boy, but the press made us feel like celebrities. My mammy still has news clippings of my visit to Massachusetts. The *Boston Herald American* reported my arrival on 8 January and my departure on 15 January 1973, and on 11 January the *Worcester Telegram* mentioned my visit. The *Herald* sent a photographer and two journalists to cover my arrival. Photographer John Landers Jr. photographed Mammy and me. I was wearing dark shades, which I thought made me look cool. The headline reads: 'Blind Ulster Boy to Be Treated Here'. George Briggs and Arsene Davignon reported that I had arrived in Boston 'for an appointment at the Massachusetts Eye and Ear Infirmary in an effort to restore sight to one eye. According to his parents, the diagnosis has been that the right eye, blinded immediately, was beyond restoration. But there was some hope that the left eye, which failed in the intervening months, might be restored by specialists.'

One vivid memory I have of Boston and Worcester is the cold. The snow and ice were incredible. In Derry we had occasional snowfalls, but the Gulf Stream kept our climate reasonably mild. We had never (and even less so now, with the effects of global warming) had snow and ice in the quantity I remember experiencing in Boston and Worcester, and the Herlihy children turned it into a winter wonderland. One of the boys – I'm sure it was Dan Junior – placed me on his sleigh and sat behind me. I have no idea what the terrain was like. I just remember the thrill of the cold wind rushing across my face and butterflies fluttering in my stomach as the sleigh picked up speed and raced down a long and seemingly endless embankment. The Herlihys were thrilled by Kevin's and my delight, and we spent hours running back up the hill to do it over and over again.

I also got the impression that everything in America was massive. Our little fridge in Malin Gardens could have fitted two or three times into the Herlihys'. And the cartons of milk! Back home, we were still using pint-sized bottles, but in the Herlihys' home those cartons felt like gallon drums. Today most things that are available in the US are available in Ireland, but in 1973 they weren't. I felt like a little person in the land of the giants.

On the day of my visit to the Eye and Ear Infirmary, I became very nervous. I was taking my new adventure with blindness in my stride, but sometimes anxiety and dizziness preceded a panic attack, and that was how I felt as soon as we entered the hospital. Years later, I pinpointed the cause, and once I'd realised that I was always more comfortable in small, confined spaces, I never had another. It was to do with my hearing: the dizzy spells almost always occurred when I was in large open spaces or echoey places.

Bats navigate using echolocation, measuring distances by sound waves that bounce off objects. To a lesser degree, I had learned to judge distances through sound. Unlike the bat, I didn't need to emit high-pitched squeaks to orient myself in small spaces: the shuffle of my feet or the sound of my family talking elsewhere in the house helped me to establish my bearings. In big places with echoes, everything went haywire – hence my anxiety. This is the only way I can explain it to sighted people: imagine you're blindfolded and placed close to the edge of the Cliffs of Moher. With the wind howling in your ears, you are then spun around four or five times. Left to your own devices, you have to decide which way to walk. If you can imagine that, you'll understand something of the sheer terror I sometimes experienced during those panic attacks.

I never told anybody about it at the time, so when I had a dizzy attack as I walked through the hospital, I tried to contain it. I was conscious that there were strangers with my mammy and daddy and I wanted to be brave for them.

The anxiety was somewhat mitigated by a pleasant distraction. We had to follow coloured lines painted on the floor of the hospital. Blue, red, green and yellow ones led to various departments in the huge hospital. When we announced at Reception that we had an appointment with Dr Charles Regan, we were told to follow the yellow line. I laughed. I imagined the receptionist was Glinda, the Good Witch of the North, advising Dorothy to 'follow the yellow brick road' from Munchkin country to the Emerald City to see the Wizard of Oz. Dr Regan was the friendly Wizard.

Dan Herlihy had told my daddy that Dr Regan had come to prominence in August 1967 when he had rushed to save the eyesight of one of the Boston Red Sox legends, Tony Conigliaro. Two years earlier, aged twenty, Conigliaro had become the youngest man in American Baseball League history to hit thirty-two home runs in one season. In 1967, however, he was struck by a fast ball on the left cheekbone, just below the left eye socket, causing permanent damage, but Dr Regan was credited with saving his sight and making it possible for him to return to the Red Sox. Hopes were high among the adults that he might be able to do a Conigliaro job on me.

We followed the yellow line and eventually came to the famous doctor's surgery. Mammy and Daddy stayed with me throughout the examination. Dr Regan was a friendly man and I found his voice soothing and reassuring. He put me on a big therapeutic bed and carried out all manner of tests, concentrating on my left eye. I could feel his right thumb and forefinger pulling open my eyelids during various tests. One involved the use of a torch. Occasionally he would ask me, 'Is the light on?' to which I answered 'Yes' or 'No'.

There was a moment when I sensed that he and my parents were confused and, in my parents, that the confusion had ignited false hope. I heard them shuffling to the edge of their chairs in wishful astonishment. Perhaps Dr Regan was a wizard after all.

He asked me again, 'Is the light on now?'

'Yes,' I replied.

'Is it on now?'

'No.'

I was getting it right every time. Then Dr Regan phrased the question differently. 'Can you see the light?' he asked.

'No,' I replied. 'I can feel the heat.'

In later years, something similar happened to me in Derry. I was in a recording studio owned by a well-known radio presenter, Colum Arbuckle. It was located in the cellar of his house in Abercorn Road. I was standing in the technician's room, listening to music being mixed. At one point, I looked up to my left and asked Colum, 'Is that a light up there?' He got all excited and said, 'Aye, it is! Why? Can you see it?' I answered, 'No, I can feel the heat.' Colum was clearly disappointed. In an instant, the miracle of the Abercorn studio evaporated.

I spent no more than an hour with Dr Regan. By the time we had finished, he was satisfied that I wasn't going to get my eyesight back. I wasn't present when he made his pronouncement to my mammy and daddy, but I'm sure they were devastated. At that time, many people around the world, including in Ireland, believed that America had the best of everything. The US had the best specialists in the world and the best hospitals, stocked with the most up-to-date medical technology. My parents had had high hopes that maybe Dr Regan and advanced American technology would work a miracle, and their prayers would be answered. But it was not to be.

It was the following evening that I learned the result of the tests. The Worcester Area Committee for Justice in Northern Ireland had put on a dance at the Sheraton-Lincoln Inn to establish a trust fund for my education. Hundreds of people were there and Paddy Noonan's band played Irish *céilidh* music. Near the end of the evening, I was invited onto the stage with my mammy and daddy. I recall Dan Herlihy giving a speech. He had in his hand a rubber bullet and was showing it to the audience as he explained the damage it had done to me the previous year. I chuckled at one point because he described it as a 'rubber rocket'. That was a new one to me and I thought some of the American lingo was funny.

It was while I was on stage that I heard Dan tell the audience that I had met Dr Regan the previous day at the Boston Eye and Ear Infirmary but the damage was so severe that nothing could be done to restore my eyesight, even partially. I realised then that the trip, from my parents' perspective, had been unsuccessful. For some reason I can't explain, though, I wasn't disappointed. I hadn't left Ireland with the same hope as my parents. I knew I was going to see a specialist and that there was a glimmer of hope, but I hadn't had any expectations. I had already embarked on a new journey and was learning to see life in a different way. I hadn't mourned the loss of my sight, and for that I have no explanation other than the grace of my parents' prayers.

Now I was enjoying my new found celebrity status. The dinner dance that night in Worcester was amazing. I was brought around to meet everybody in the room and everyone seemed to be giving me money. I had handfuls of it! I started by putting it in my trouser pockets. When they were full, I put it in my back pockets. Eventually Dan Herlihy kindly held it for me. I was beginning to feel like the Milky Bar Kid! Back home in Derry, Friday evening was pay day for children. Our 'pay' was our pocket money. I'd be lucky to get fifty pence, let alone a pound, from my working brothers or parents. It would be given at teatime, and then began the long wait for a mobile shop that visited the Creggan on Friday nights. We called the man who drove it 'Gerry the Mobile'. He must have sold a ton of sweets on Friday evenings. Now, though, people were handing me twenty-dollar bills and more. One person gave me a small box with silver dollars in it.

Until recent times, Ireland wasn't multicultural: the big divide was between two sets of people whose differences resided in their heads. I was therefore confounded when people introduced themselves to me as one-quarter Irish. I couldn't understand it. I remember asking one guy, 'What do you mean, one-quarter Irish? How can you be one-quarter Irish?' He explained that one of his grandparents was from Ireland, two were from Italy and the other one was from Puerto Rico. So not only was he one-quarter Irish, he was also half Italian, one-quarter Puerto Rican and 100 per cent American! At the time, I thought it was weird, but now I think the mingling of various cultures and races is wonderful.

In subsequent visits to North America, I have come to realise how important heritage and background are to almost everyone. Apart from Native American culture, the history of America is very short. In Ireland we aren't excited by buildings that are a couple of centuries old, but in the United States it's different. Americans' sense of antiquity, therefore, comes with affinity to their ethnic roots.

At the end of the night, Paddy Noonan's band played the Irish national anthem, 'The Soldier's Song', and, of course, everyone stood up. When it finished, I sat down as I figured it must be the same anthem the world over, apart from 'God Save the Queen', which the BBC played at the end of its programmes every evening. Then the band struck up another tune that I didn't recognise and I remained sitting. It was my first time hearing 'The Star-Spangled Banner'. My eyes weren't working but everyone else's were, and since I was the guest of honour, they were on me. Suddenly there was a scramble to drag me to my feet.

If there was a hitch on the night, that was it. Everything else was simply brilliant. I know, too, that it was a great occasion for my mammy, daddy and Kevin, who were treated like royalty. The support they received that night in Worcester was, unquestionably, very important to them. I have no doubt it helped to cushion the disappointing news that I would never get my eyesight back. I shall always be grateful for the outpouring of kindness we received from the Herlihys, the Committee for Justice in Northern Ireland and the good people of Worcester during that wonderful week we spent in their midst.

And the celebrity status didn't end that evening. The night before we returned to Ireland, we were told that Senator Edward Kennedy had agreed to meet us at his office in Boston. He was held in high regard by the Irish and, of course, was the brother of former President John F. Kennedy. I can't remember where I was when President Kennedy was assassinated because I was only two at the time, but my parents told me that many in Ireland were in mourning because he had visited the Republic earlier that year, the first US president ever to do so. President Kennedy's picture hung proudly in many Catholic homes in Derry and across Ireland, flanked on either side by Pope John XXIII and Pope Paul VI.

My parents were thrilled to be meeting a high-profile member of the most famous political dynasty in America. Their excitement was infectious, and suddenly I was fired up too. I had no idea who Ted Kennedy was, but my daddy said to me, 'It's President Kennedy's brother you're going to meet and this man could be the American president some day too.' He never was: the mysterious events at Chappaquiddick, and the death of Mary Jo Kopechne in the early hours of 19 July 1969, frustrated any political ambitions for the White House he might have harboured.

Dan took us to meet Senator Kennedy in Boston. We drove to his office and parked in an underground car park. I was mesmerised by the very idea of cars being parked deep in the ground, underneath a multi-storey building. I remember climbing steps inside the tower block and being told that security men were standing all along the stairway. At some point I was introduced to one and he showed me his gun. I suppose all boys are fascinated by guns and I was no different.

I had the impression that about a hundred people were waiting to see Senator Kennedy after he had met me, but I seemed to have priority and the path was made easy to the room where I was introduced to him. I sat beside him and we had a wee chat. He told me he had a son called Patrick who was about my age and suggested that maybe one day I would come and stay at his home in Washington and meet Patrick. Before we parted, he wrote me a note that, to this very day, takes pride of place in my mother's home. It reads:

> To Richard Moore
> With admiration for your courage and with good wishes for you from your new friend and good friend —
> Ted Kennedy
> January 1973

My meeting with him was another block in the foundation that helped me to accept blindness and feel good about it. I reasoned that blindness didn't have to be such a bad thing when it had the same effect as Ali Baba's 'Open, Sesame'. A treasure trove of places and opportunities that a year before had been beyond my family's reach had suddenly opened up and become accessible to us. In fact, it has largely remained that way ever since.

My American experience had been so positive and so much fun that I was broken-hearted when the time came to go home. I had become very friendly with the Herlihy children and wondered how long it would be before I was sleighing again in the Boston snow. The family's kindness remains a treasured memory.

The *Boston Herald American* reported my departure and again carried a picture of me and my mammy at the airport. John McGinn wrote:

> Freckle-faced little Richard Moore, a hockey stick under one arm and a shopping bag full of souvenirs in his hand, entranced bystanders with his grin as he boarded a plane at Logan Airport last night.
>
> 'American people, they are very good,' the 11-year-old lad kept repeating in his musical Irish brogue as he headed home to Derry, Northern Ireland, with his parents and younger brother.
>
> Neither the boy nor his parents showed any sign of the disappointment they must have experienced during their brief visit to Boston.
>
> Richard, shot in the face last May by a rubber bullet fired by a British soldier in Derry, lost one eye and the sight of the other.
>
> Under the sponsorship of the Worcester Committee for Justice in Northern Ireland, the boy was brought here in hope something could be done to restore his sight.

> But last week at the Massachusetts Eye and Ear Infirmary doctors informed the boy's parents, 'There is absolutely nothing we can do.'
>
> 'When we came,' the boy's mother, Florence, said last night, 'we knew there wasn't hope for a cure, but it was our last chance.'
>
> Richard's plight, told in the *Herald American* last week, brought an outpouring of contributions from throughout New England to aid in his future education.
>
> 'Now we can afford a tutor to teach him Braille,' said his father, Liam, an unemployed shoe worker and father of 13. 'And we can buy him the guitar he's always wanted and pay a teacher to train him to play it.'
>
> And both parents exclaimed, 'Americans, such wonderful people.'

While I was staying with Dan and Joan Herlihy, they gave me a set of toy walkie-talkies. Little did they know the lifelong interest their gift would spark. Toy walkie-talkies are two-a-penny nowadays, but back then they were a rarity. The nearest we got to sending messages from one location to another was by connecting two empty cans with a piece of fish gut or thread and pulling them taut. Then we'd stand twenty or thirty feet apart to see if the sound of a voice could be carried down the line.

The Herlihy walkie-talkies were toys, so their range was no more than two or three hundred feet. They were operated by radio transmission and I could speak from our back garden to friends in the street at the front of our houses. One day, a friend and I were playing in the street with them, radioing back and forth, when a British Army foot patrol came past and confiscated my new toy. The soldier in charge said it was illegal to have them. I was devastated and went home to tell my parents. While they felt sorry for me, Mammy and Daddy resigned themselves to the loss – they weren't the kind of people who spoiled for a fight.

The next day, our house was surrounded by the army. At first we thought we were to be raided – several vehicles had pulled up outside and a number of soldiers took up positions in the gardens around. My parents were shocked when they opened the door to find a British Army major standing there. He asked courteously if he could speak to them, and they brought him into the 'good room'. He said he wanted to explain why his soldiers had taken the action the day before, and cited the security situation as the principal reason – you needed a licence to have such radios in your possession.

To us, of course, the walkie-talkies were toys that had been given to a blind boy during a visit to America. We knew nothing about that law, but the major said we could apply for a licence and even gave my parents the address they should write to. He apologised for the disappointment caused to me but hoped we would understand the difficulties the army was facing in such a troubled environment. After that he left. We never applied for the licence and I soon stopped missing the walkie-talkies.

# 7

# Learning to Live with Blindness

The American visit was important because, if nothing else, it confirmed that I was blind. Whatever the future had in store for me, I had to confront the challenges that lay ahead as a blind person. This meant dealing with the limitations of blindness. I barely even knew what they were at that stage, other than that I couldn't play football or go onto the street and mix with my friends as I once had. I'd had to learn to walk all over again, not because I'd lost the use of my legs but because I had to discover how to navigate even familiar terrain in an entirely new way. For instance, I tended not to lift my feet high enough when I stepped from the road to the pavement, and sometimes tumbled and hurt myself. I would trip over small elevations or debris in my path.

I don't know whether this was to do with the interruption of data between the eye and the brain or whether it was that, as a blind person, I was dragging my feet. In any case, I had to begin to build my knowledge in small ways that might appear insignificant to the sighted person but which were major to me.

From being a child who preferred to run rather than walk, I had to learn to move with greater care and much more slowly. If I didn't rush, I could correct myself if I was going in the wrong direction or if I encountered a step I wasn't expecting.

I also had to decide whether or not to use a white stick. When I lost my sight, all the prejudices I had about disabled people, which till then I never knew I had, came bubbling to the surface. I didn't want anyone to see me as 'handicapped' – and that's a dreadful thing to admit. I wasn't one of 'them' and I wasn't going to be treated like them. That was where my head was at that time. So I wasn't going to carry a white stick and have everyone look at me as 'one of those' blind people. I imagined people looking out their bedroom or living room windows at me and my white stick as I walked down the street, and I just didn't want that: I wanted to look 'normal'. Instead, I used the end of a fishing rod to tap my way through the streets of Lower Creggan – until one day it caught between a lamp-post and a fence and snapped. I nearly didn't find my way home. It was crazy, I suppose, but that's just the way I was. In some ways that stubbornness was a major strength for me in dealing with the situation.

So, I learned gradually to cope. I learned to walk and not to run. By feeling the fences on our street, and assisted by memory, I could soon identify the different texture and design of each fence and know which neighbour it belonged to. A lesson I learned very quickly at home was that doors are often left ajar. That's okay if you're sighted, but after a few smacks in the face I was walking with one arm straight out and the other bent at a right angle: if I missed anything with the outstretched arm, the other would act as a barrier to protect my face. In time, my parents had some of the swinging doors at home replaced with sliding ones, and that was a definite help, too.

I also learned how to feel with my feet. This may sound strange, but it's incredible how much information you can pick up from them. When you walk in combination with sight, you can take a lot for granted, and often your responses are automatic. Without sight, I had to rely on other senses and, as chiropodists and reflexologists will verify, the feet are loaded with sensitive nerve endings. I can now identify different surfaces I'm walking on and can even tell when I'm coming to the end of a pavement or steps. So, increasingly, between my hands, feet and sound, I was able to build an awareness of my environment.

Simple daily activities were no longer straightforward. When I reached for a cup of tea on a saucer that someone was handing to me, I had to do so cautiously. In the beginning, more times than I wish to remember, I would knock the cup off the saucer, spilling tea onto the carpet or a nice white linen tablecloth. People insisted that there was no harm done, but I knew better. Now I wait for the person to leave the cup and saucer on a table and let them direct my fingers to the handle. Experiences like this taught me that with blindness, you have to develop a tough skin. There are times when you will look foolish or do something embarrassing. When that happens, you just have to accept it and move on.

One of the hardest parts for me, even at that early age, was dealing with sympathy. It rankled when they openly expressed sorrow for my condition and talked about me to my companions as if I were Helen Keller, deaf as well as blind, and had somehow lost the ability to think for myself and hold a conversation. It was frustrating then, and even more so now. It's even worse when I begin a conversation with someone, then discover that they've moved away. It's only when I've delivered a sentence or two and got no response that I realise the person has already walked halfway down the bloody road!

Because I didn't receive any mobility training, I had to learn a lot of the techniques for myself – and nothing teaches you better than when you make a complete fool of yourself. During the year after I was shot, when I was just about to graduate to St Joseph's Secondary School, our class was taken on an outing to Portsalon, County Donegal, a beautiful seaside resort on the west side of Lough Swilly, about an hour's drive from Derry.

I was off the school bus and being guided from behind by one of my classmates. He was holding my arm and we were walking along the little pier at one end of Ballymastocker Bay. Suddenly there was a distraction. My friend stopped to look around and let go of me. I, of course, kept walking, not knowing that I was literally only a step from the edge of the pier, which had no railing. Next thing I'd fallen five or six feet and landed on my back in soft wet sand. Luckily the only thing hurt was my pride and, best of all, the tide was out – I can't swim.

That experience taught me an important lesson. Since then I have never allowed myself to be guided in front of someone. It's much easier for me to hold the elbow of the person I'm walking with, allowing them to lead me, rather than the other way around. While it was undeniably a major improvement to my safety, this methodology didn't always work. Once, while coming out of school, I fell down a manhole – mercifully my elbows lodged on the sides so I didn't drop all the way, but I was left dangling, trying furiously to find a foothold. On this occasion, my companion had forgotten I was blind and, again, distracted, didn't notice that he was leading me straight over a gaping hole in the pavement. Inevitably, accidents will happen and to this day they still do – it gives a whole new dimension to the expression 'finding oneself in the shit'!

So it was those small things that might seem obvious to a

blind person today – or perhaps not – that were big lessons for me. But it was generally an enjoyable learning experience, even though at times it was a bit hairy. And I've had my fair share of awkward moments. One evening quite recently, I was with my band, Midnight Hour, at the Glengannon Hotel, Dungannon, for a gig. My friend Felix Healy and I were trying to find the dressing room. He led me from a brightly lit foyer to a dining room that was in darkness. That didn't bother me, but perhaps the change of light affected Felix – and I was following him. Next thing, I collided heavily with a table. I hadn't time to give out to Felix because delft and cutlery were smashing and clattering onto the floor. It was horrendous. Have you ever been in a busy restaurant when a waiter drops a plate and it shatters to smithereens, with a crescendo of loud cracks that momentarily silences everyone? Multiply that by more than three hundred pieces.

Apparently the staff had stacked a table with everything they would need for a big function the following day. When I hit the table, the first pile toppled forward, hitting the second, and so on, in the domino effect. Of course, the noise brought the staff rushing in. Felix said that when the lights were turned on it looked like a scene from the kitchens of *Titanic* as the ship's bow was pulled under.

Perhaps they made allowances because I was blind, but the management said not a word. Felix and I can look back on the incident now and laugh. At the time, though, it wasn't funny. I was mortified when the barman came in to shovel the debris into black plastic bags.

Not all my experiences were embarrassing. Father Edward Daly, from Belleek, County Fermanagh, was a curate in the parish of St Eugene's Cathedral in Derry during the late 1960s and early 1970s. He has long been a hero to me and many in

Derry. I still remember seeing him on television, as a curate, waving a white handkerchief on Bloody Sunday as he led a group of men carrying the heavily bloodstained body of young Jackie Duddy past British paratroopers. In 1974 he was elected Bishop of Derry, and someone contacted my parents to say that he wanted to invite me to take part in his consecration ceremony. It was my daddy who told me, and I remember there was great excitement in the house. I was now in my early teens and knew it was a great honour.

Father Daly wanted me to be among the offertory procession, which would walk up the centre aisle of St Eugene's. I was to present the newly consecrated Bishop with a white stick, representing blindness, disability and all those who had been injured in the Troubles. I can't recall which of my friends led me up the aisle, but the cathedral seemed filled to capacity and I felt extremely nervous.

I look back on that day with great fondness. Even though my role was relatively small and over very quickly, it was the fact that I had been asked by such a remarkable man, for whom the people of Derry have great fondness, that made me feel so honoured. Although Bishop Daly is now retired, I am still in touch with him. I consider him a good friend.

# 8

# Music in My Life

In July 1972, at the height of the Troubles, and while Creggan was still a no-go area, my brother Martin married Anne Deane, a local Creggan girl. High unemployment and poor wages didn't allow for a big, fancy hotel wedding, such as everyone seems to have today. They were married in St Mary's chapel, and the reception was held in Anne's family home in Rinmore Gardens. It was an all-day and all-night party. No exaggeration, it was one of the best receptions I have ever attended and it has left a lasting impression on my life. Anne's brother Lorny (Lawrence) was a well-known Derry entertainer, a one-man band who sang in all the local bars. After the wedding meal, he played and everyone danced. During a break, he came to sit beside me. 'I'd love to see your guitar,' I told him – it was electric, and I really liked the sound it made.

Lorny laid it on my knee. I surprised him by lifting it and turning it around so that the bass string was at the bottom instead of the top – I'm left-handed so if I was to learn to play, I'd need one made in reverse. But it was great holding Lorny's.

'I'd love to learn to play it,' I said. The next thing I knew, my whole family was talking about it, and when my parents asked, I told them yes, I wanted to try.

A couple of weeks after the wedding, our milkman, Hugh Toland, arrived at our house. He'd heard through the grapevine that I wanted to learn the guitar. I liked Hugh a lot. He was connected to our family by marriage, nephew to Sadie, my older brother Pearse's wife, a lively, easy-going guy who always seemed happy. That day he came into the house and handed me an acoustic guitar for beginners. I couldn't believe my luck. It had a pick-up fixed into the centre where the sound hole was so I could plug it into the amplifier that came with it. Then he produced a mike stand and a microphone. Overnight I, too, had become a one-man band. But I couldn't play and couldn't sing.

That didn't stop me from standing in the front room of our house in Malin Gardens, the 'good room', showing off to all my mates who'd come round to help me make loads of noise. I sang into the microphone, plucking and strumming away, getting acquainted with my new best friend. Later that evening, my brother Marty told me that Lorny Deane had agreed to teach me. I was thrilled – Lorny's playing had inspired me to learn, and there was no one else in the world I'd have preferred as my teacher.

Lorny lived in Carnhill, another working-class housing estate a couple of miles away from where we lived, and Marty walked me there for my lessons. The distance was a challenge, and my first guitar wasn't the easiest to master. The gap between the strings and the fretboard was wide, so it was quite sore on my fingers, but I persevered. I was determined, no matter what it took, to master the instrument. Then Lorny got sick and we had to find another teacher. At least he had got me started, though: by now I was beginning to shape a few chords together, and I knew I'd eventually be able to play properly.

After Lorny, I had a few guitar teachers. One was a secondary school teacher, Paul Elder, who taught at St Peter's, at the top of the Creggan. Then there was Sean Coyle who lived on Creggan Hill, where the army had the sangar the rubber bullet had been fired from, and Frankie Robinson, from the Waterside, was a well-known country-and-western guitarist in the town. But eventually I met the teacher and the person I needed: Michael (Micky) Doherty.

He was a barber and a leader at the Rosemount Youth Centre. He helped me to master the guitar and encouraged me to develop a social life. At the youth centre, I met other young lads who played instruments, and before long we were getting together for jam sessions. Occasionally the centre organised concerts and talent shows and we were invited to play.

One snowy evening, Noel asked me if I wanted to hear the Wolfe Tones perform at the Stardust, a dance hall in the heart of the Bogside. The Wolfe Tones were at the pinnacle of their popularity in Ireland and among the Irish abroad. I walked there from the Creggan in my wellington boots, totally unaware of what was in store.

During their set, I was invited backstage. I was soaking up the atmosphere and enjoying the music when it stopped. Suddenly I was invited on to the stage – still in my wellies. The heat of the spotlights startled me as I came out from behind the curtains to be introduced to the group.

The next day, an envelope was delivered to my house. It had come from the Wolfe Tones. I must have told them I was learning the guitar but finding the one I had difficult to manage, because a handwritten note told me to buy my first professional acoustic guitar and here was the money to pay for it. Their generosity was overwhelming and I wanted to go straight to the music shop in town. That day I bought an Echo acoustic guitar, an instrument renowned for the quality of its sound and – most importantly for someone like me who would put it to the test – its sturdiness. My family and I were overwhelmed by the Wolfe Tones' generosity. In 2006 I met Tommy Burn, a band member, in the foyer of the City Hotel in Derry and took the opportunity, more than thirty years on, to thank him for his kindness.

Music was now a big part of my life, and in my lessons with Michael, I was making rapid progress, always champing at the bit to learn something new. A few months later the Wolfe Tones returned to the Stardust for another sell-out concert, and Michael arranged with his niece Carol McCamphill, a singer, for the three of us to perform during the interval. When we took to the stage, the Wolfe Tones stood to the side to watch us. I was very nervous, but I got such a rush from performing live in front of seven or eight hundred people. I was also glad that the Wolfe Tones could see that their money had been put to good use.

Because of Michael, the Rosemount Youth Centre became my hangout, and music my social outlet. It also gave me new status among my friends. People are attracted to musicians, and I stood out in the crowd because I could play the guitar. And, of course, I harboured the same hopes and dreams as other young people: some day, maybe, I'd be a star . . .

When I was thirteen, some other lads and I decided to form a band. Paul Rogan, 'Beaver' Mullan, Ned Divin, Jack McFarland and we called ourselves Dice and soon we were saving up to buy a PA system. We learned a few songs and played at concerts organised by the youth centre. We never had a hit single and didn't do too many bookings either, but we ran the odd disco in Rosemount to try to raise the money. We kept it in a milk carton, and at one point we had nearly thirty pounds. But as time went on, everybody wanted a bit, and eventually we split the money. The PA system went on the back burner. Also, cracks began to appear – we'd agree practice times but often one lad or another never made it, sometimes claiming that the army had arrested him on the way to the centre.

I'll never forget one booking Dice secured. We were due to play a New Year's Eve gig in a bar called the Pop Inn, but only Paul Rogan and I turned up. That was the night I learned that, no matter what, the show must go on. Paul and I were verging on nervous breakdowns as we took to the stage. From being a five-piece band, we were reduced to two, a drummer and guitar player. Without the others, we could do just four or five songs. And that was exactly what we did. We played the same songs all night and stretched them out as long as we could, sometimes singing ten or twelve verses when, in reality, the song had three or four. It didn't take the crowd long to realise what was happening and take pity on us as we struggled. Eventually, and to our delight, they got behind us, and before long they were out dancing and singing. I don't know if we ever got paid, but we had a good night's *craic*.

As you can imagine, that was the end of Dice. Once people stopped turning up for bookings, there was no point in continuing. It was disappointing, but – typical of my life story – something good happened almost immediately afterwards. My parents bought me a Fender Telecaster guitar. It was very expensive and I think they must have put some of the money donated in America towards it. As far as I was concerned, it was the Rolls-Royce of guitars. And they got me a proper amp for it too – I can't remember the make, but it might have been a Music Man. I now had a full professional set-up in my house.

I was gradually becoming a more accomplished player, and it was now that Michael Doherty asked if I'd like to join him in a new band he was starting with a friend of his, a singer called Jack Finley, known locally as 'Big Joker'. Of course I would – and I felt honoured that my teacher should ask me. I was fourteen when I joined the New Courtelles and we ended up playing two or three nights a week. We had different drummers coming in and out but Micky, Joker, Raymond Kelly and I were constants. As they were older than me, they treated me like a son.

We often went to Joker's house for practice. His wife Ann used to make tea and sandwiches for us and always had a special plate for me – the guys used to tease the life out of me because Ann would spoil me. I'll always be grateful to her and Joker for their kindness. As for Micky Doherty, you could go through a whole lifetime and never be so lucky as to meet someone like him. He dedicated so much time to me over the years, and I've always valued his commitment and friendship – exactly what I needed at that time, and still do today. Micky took me under his wing and, although he was older than me, we became close friends. He helped me through the crucial years when I was moving into young adulthood.

With his encouragement, I learned to play the mandolin, too. I found it relatively easy because it's so similar to the guitar. Soon I was playing both instruments in the band. We travelled all over the north-west of Ireland, playing in towns such as Coleraine, Limavady, Strabane and, of course, Derry. Getting to the various gigs was interesting because, at the height of the Troubles, there were army and police checkpoints all over the place. Sometimes we played in the British Legion Hall, popular with British soldiers. Micky and I were the only two Catholics in the band so I suppose there was always an element of risk, depending on where we played. Sectarian killings were all too common and the horrific deaths of three members of the Miami Showband, in 1975, had us on tenterhooks.

The band were on their way home to the Republic of Ireland from a gig in Banbridge, in the North, when they were stopped at a roadblock by men dressed in British Army uniforms, near Newry in South Armagh. They were asked to step out of the vehicle and line up on the side of the road. Some of the men were British soldiers from the Ulster Defence Regiment, but were also members of an illegal loyalist paramilitary organisation, the Ulster Volunteer Force (UVF). In the process of planting a bomb in the van, two of the UVF members were killed as it exploded prematurely. The remaining members of the gang opened fire on the disoriented band members, killing lead singer Fran O'Toole, guitarist Tony Geraghty and trumpeter Brian McCoy, and seriously injuring bass player Steve Travers. Saxophone player Des Lee escaped unharmed and was able to alert the authorities. The drummer, Ray Miller, wasn't travelling with the band that evening, as he had gone to stay with his family in Banbridge. Until then, musicians and entertainers could go anywhere in Northern Ireland without being targeted, but the attack on the Miami Showband changed that.

Little did I know that, thirty years later, Fate would play its part and our respective life experiences would cause our paths to cross. In early 2007, I had a phone call from a good friend of mine, the well-known Belfast promoter David Hull. He told me that the Miami Showband was re-forming and wanted to launch their Joy to the World tour with two charity concerts in Dublin and Belfast. David had suggested Children in Crossfire as a beneficiary. Eventually I met the three surviving band members, Steve Travers, Des Lee and Ray Miller, and Steve travelled with me to Tanzania in 2008 to visit Children in Crossfire projects. During the trip, Steve talked about Fran O'Toole, Tony Geraghty and Brian McCoy, and the impact on the lives of their families that these senseless killings had had. Performing with the Miami Showband at the sell-out concert in the Belfast Opera House was both a sad and a positive experience. Brian, Tony, Fran and their families were in everyone's thoughts while the band was back on stage, doing what they do best. In Steve's words, 'The sound of the music has outlived the sound of the guns.'

In the 1970s, at all the venues that the New Courtelles played, Catholic or Protestant, including the British Legion Hall, the staff and the punters made us all feel really welcome. Even when the Troubles were at their height, ordinary people – Catholics and Protestants – were really nice to each other at the music venues we attended. Big Joker Finley was a Protestant but, thank God, religion was never an issue for him or for anyone else in the band. Our music just brought people together, which made us happy. I have no doubt that many people in places like the British Legion would have known that Michael Doherty and I were Catholics, but it didn't matter. Many would have been aware, too, from the media that the British Army had blinded me. When I look back on that period, despite the horrors that were raging outside, I just remember friendliness within the band scene.

Depending on the venue, the national anthem at the end of the evening varied. If we were in the British Legion, we played 'God Save the Queen'. I never minded playing it: I'm more and more certain that the Orange and Green traditions on our island must embrace and acknowledge each other's rights.

There are two traditions and identities and both are equally legitimate; one does not have the right to impose its will on the other. Our future lies in shared respect.

Throughout my life in music, I have written the lyrics and melody of only one song. It's called 'Where?' and it's about my blindness.

*I feel the breeze blowing gently,*
*I hear the stream flowing by,*
*I hear the trees whispering softly,*
*I hear the birds singing their lullaby,*
*I smell the sweetness of the flowers,*
*I feel the warm sun against my face.*

Chorus
*Where's the blue, where's the green, where's the yellow?*
*What happened to the colours of the rainbow?*
*Where's the moon and the stars?*
*All the beauty this world of ours has to share.*

*I feel the snowflakes as they turn to water,*
*I feel the cold air as winter falls,*
*I hear the waves break against the harbour,*
*As in the distance the seagulls call,*
*I hear the fish splashing softly,*
*I feel the cold rain against my face.*

Music was and still is a very important part of my life. It provided a social outlet through which I formed great friendships, and I loved playing with Dice, which was the first of the four bands I was in. The others were the New Courtelles, Rumours and Midnight Hour.

# 9
# The Path of Education

While I was dealing with the day-to-day practicalities of blindness, the challenge for my parents was how best to prepare me for the future. This included putting the apparatus in place that would equip me for it. In the immediate aftermath of my discharge from hospital, it was decided that I should continue at Rosemount Primary School. Now, however, with the natural transition from primary to secondary school, decisions had to be made about my future education. Should I be sent to a school for the blind?

I think that many people thought I would carry on at Rosemount as a temporary arrangement. During my primary seven year, I became aware that my parents and teachers were talking about a school for the blind near Jordanstown, County Antrim. The thought of having to leave home terrified me and I panicked. Every time the school for the blind came up in conversation, I either got upset or changed the subject.

My father carried the burden of this decision. He'd had little or no formal education, so he sought and valued the advice of people whom he considered professionally qualified to help him decide what was in my best interests. The advice he was getting was that I needed to be sent to a specialist school. However, while he knew in his head that that was probably right, his heart told him otherwise. It said, 'Richard doesn't want to go away. He's been through enough. I can't send him to the school for the blind.' He was in turmoil over what he should do, but his heart was right: for me, the trauma of being sent away from home would have been greater than that of being shot.

While I was in school one day, there was a knock on the classroom door and a pupil entered. He informed the teacher that the principal wanted me to come to his office. As the boy led me down the stairs and along the corridor, I asked him if he knew why the principal wanted me. He didn't. He said he'd been walking past the office when he was nabbed and ordered to fetch me.

When I got there, I was surprised to find my daddy and one of my brothers, Bosco. I was introduced to a Mr Anderson, who turned out to be the principal of the school for the blind at Jordanstown. Panic paralysed me and I couldn't answer any of his questions. I quite simply shut down.

I was very young, but I knew instinctively what was happening. Mr Anderson was extremely friendly and warm, but I sensed that behind this façade he was on a PR mission, trying to win me over to a split from my family, friends, community and school. The thought of becoming a boarder at his establishment was torture and I was having none of it. Metaphorically speaking, they weren't going to pull the wool over my eyes. When it became clear that I wasn't to be persuaded, Mr Anderson suggested that perhaps I should visit the school for a day to see if I liked it.

A few weeks later, I went with my mother and father to Jordanstown. It was a journey I'll never forget. Inside I was panicking. During the journey I even wondered if maybe Mammy and Daddy were planning to slip off and leave me there. When we arrived, Mr Anderson had arranged for two boys, not much older than me, to take me around. They were blind, too, but I felt no connection with them. Perhaps it was because I didn't want to: I'd had my mind made up before we'd left home that morning. Even if the school was a virtual Disneyland, I wasn't going to it. It would have taken the patience of Job to sway me.

I wasn't rude as I went round the school with the boys. They were very nice and we got along reasonably well, but throughout the day I was cautious, especially with Mr Anderson. He spent most of the time with my parents and I was worried about the impression he might be making on them. What if he convinced them that this was the best place in the world for me? What if they had already gone home? The thought haunted me through every classroom and corridor, and I was relieved to meet up with them again.

I was extremely quiet as I climbed into the back of the car for the long journey back to Derry. A depression had descended on me that was darker than blindness. For what seemed like an eternity, there was a heavy silence as we drove. Then Mammy spoke. 'Liam,' she said to Daddy, 'there is no way I can send our Richard away from home to that school.'

It was music to my ears. My father readily agreed and it was as if light flooded the interior world I was learning to inhabit. For the first time in weeks, I relaxed.

But we still had to face the vexing question 'What next?' We knew that all the obstacles were not overcome. We had to convince the Education Board that I wouldn't be at a disadvantage if I stayed in Derry. Furthermore, we needed St Joseph's Secondary School to agree to take on the long-term challenge of educating me. Since schools in Derry were not equipped to deal with the blind, I don't think they were obliged then to take on the headaches I presented to traditional teaching methods.

I needed to learn certain skills, of which Braille was one so that I could read, and as I was now unable to write I had to learn to type. In retrospect, I am amazed at my daddy's foresight: he knew straight away how vital it was that I acquired these skills. He went to talk to the principal of St Joseph's, Ted Armstrong. He had a reputation for sternness, but beneath it he was a kind and compassionate man.

He considered my father's request for a while, knowing I would present a challenge to his staff and to the very culture of the school. He discussed my needs with the teachers, and agreed with them that I could go to St Joseph's. His decision came as an enormous relief to my father and me. I will be forever grateful to Ted Armstrong, to all my teachers and, indeed, the entire community of students, who created a new space for me to begin the process of learning all over again.

As soon as Daddy knew I'd been accepted, he went into the local girls' secondary school, St Mary's, and asked to speak to a Marie McCafferty, who was then coping with her first teaching post. He had been told she taught typing to the girls and asked her if she would teach me. At first, she was hesitant, perhaps lacking the confidence to take on a blind pupil. She asked Daddy to try to find someone with more experience, but if he was really stuck, she said, he could come back to her. A few weeks later, Daddy was back knocking at her door. This time she agreed.

Once the decision had been taken to let me stay at home, all the pieces were falling rapidly into place. Not only was I learning to type, but a social worker was visiting me for a few hours a week, teaching me how to read and write Braille. In fact, the local educational authority had agreed only to give me a chance in mainstream education: an educational psychologist had told my father that no one would insist on my going to the school for the blind as long as it was clear to the authorities that I was getting a proper education. 'However, if it appears Richard is at a disadvantage, he will have to go away.' That veiled threat had galvanised my father into action. Nothing was going to defeat him. I am still amazed by what he did: don't forget, he was a shoemaker, with only the most basic education, yet he saw what I needed and made sure I got it. When people ask me how I learned to deal with blindness, I tell them it was down to luck: I was lucky to have the best parents any child could have. It was as simple as that.

St Joseph's was an encouraging environment, and one of the teachers, Kevin McCallion, began to give me extra lessons after school. He lived on Inishowen Gardens, two streets below Malin Gardens, and I would walk to his house on two afternoons a week. Often, too, he came to my home to read to me – the novels and poetry I was studying for English literature, and extracts from textbooks on other subjects. He helped me with anything I found difficult, such as algebra, calculus and trigonometry, and was so generous with his time. He did everything possible to help me keep up with the rest of my class.

Miss McCafferty came to my home two afternoons a week and on Saturday mornings to work on my typing skills. In time, I developed a comfortable speed at touch typing. The highlight for me was when Miss McCafferty arranged for me to join her typing classes at St Mary's: I might not have been able to see any of the girls I was sitting among, but I had a fertile imagination and I was fully aware that I was the only boy in a room with all those girls of my own age – my 'girls alert' antenna was still working efficiently. Miss McCafferty also taught me to audio-type, and for a long time I thought that after school I might become an audio-typist.

It wasn't always plain sailing, though. There were classes I attended when all I could do was sit and listen. If the teacher was demonstrating something on the blackboard or referring to passages in our textbooks, I was at a loss. If part of the class required written work, I did my own thing. Sometimes I had a Braille book to read, but at other times I just allowed my mind to wander.

I found Braille difficult because I was learning to read and write all over again. There were days when I dreaded the arrival of Miss McGuire, the social worker who taught me. I found it really boring and slow. She insisted that I read aloud to her and it must have been extremely boring for her to have to listen to me laboriously going through each word, forcing myself not to fall asleep. While I didn't look forward to Miss McGuire's lessons, eventually I realised she'd done me a great service. She stuck with me, making sure I learned what I needed. While I'm not as fast as I could be at reading Braille, I use it every day in my work.

I spent my first two years at St Joseph's generally sitting and listening. Although I sat in the same classes as my friends, I didn't take part fully in the lessons, particularly if they involved reading from textbooks. Also, I never sat any internal exams, which normally took place at Christmas or just before the summer holidays. The bulk of my practical learning took place outside school, primarily with Kevin McCallion, Marie McCafferty and Ms McGuire. In my third year, I had an IQ test, which revealed that I was of above-average intelligence. The school decided I should begin studying for my CSE exams (Certificate of Secondary Education). By then, I'd developed an appetite for learning, and the fact that I was going to do the same subjects as the rest of my classmates gave me a wonderful lift – it made me feel 'normal', no longer different.

All my teachers were so helpful and encouraging. Many recorded their lessons on tape for me, and my classmates recorded passages from the textbooks I needed to study for the exams. Before long, I had a dedicated system in place.

I am often asked how I sat my exams and in what circumstances. In preparation, I condensed and edited the recordings into brief notes, using a small hand-held Dictaphone. I carried it everywhere and used it to revise constantly. Because of my blindness, I was allowed an extra fifteen minutes per hour in my exams. So, if an exam was two hours, I got two and a half. I sat the papers in a separate room with my manual typewriter and its rickety metal keys. There was nothing fancy back then, like word processors or laptops, and my machine would probably have driven my classmates demented with its rattle if I'd been in the same room. Also, while they read their own exam papers, mine were read to me by an examiner who sat with me throughout. Once I had listened to each question and assured him or her that I understood it, I would then begin typing my answer.

I'm happy to report that I did quite well. It was a major source of celebration, not just for my family but for our community. I was amazed when the *Derry Journal* decided to do a front-page article just after the results had been announced, with the banner headline, 'Rubber Bullet Victim Does Well'. I remember the morning that edition came out. I was sixteen, we were on our summer holidays and I was in bed.

My daddy climbed the stairs to my room and shook me awake. 'You're in the *Derry Journal* today,' he said, with obvious delight.

Of course, I, a cool teenager, pretended not to be interested. 'Yeah? What does it say?'

He read it to me with enormous pride. It was hard for me to admit it, but I was proud too – proud of my father and all he had done for me. He had not been without his critics. Shortly after I had started secondary school, someone had stopped him in the street and accused him of being selfish for not sending me to the school for the blind. I have no idea who that person was, but I'm still annoyed by their insensitivity. What right had they to be so judgemental when they knew nothing of the complexity of the situation my father was trying to deal with? I didn't discover for several years after he had died that he had fretted about what had been said. He worried that perhaps he had been selfish and that maybe he had made a decision that was not in my best interests. So he had every right to be jubilant at the acclamation offered by the *Derry Journal* headline. It vindicated his decision. I, more than anyone, know that he made the right one. He might not have been able to restore my eyesight with the gift of his own, but he gave me much more: he gave me hope and inner belief. They have sustained me throughout my life.

When I walked down the street that day, neighbours, friends and even strangers stopped me to offer congratulations – the whole community was reaching out to me yet again: 'I see you done real well at school, Richard. You should be very proud of yourself.' I was, but more than that, I was proud of my family, my teachers and all of the people of the Creggan and Derry too. Their apparently insignificant acts of kindness had been so important in giving me the strength to cope with blindness.

Until my exams, with the help of Ms McCafferty, I had been focusing on a career as an audio-typist. I had even begun a course at the North-west College of Technology – known in Derry as 'the Tech' – on Strand Road, where I was honing my skills. However, my good exam results opened new horizons. For the first time, I began to think of doing A levels and going to university – I'd be the first in my family to have a degree.

It was a big decision and involved Daddy and my teachers. I settled on two A-level subjects, history and communication studies, and returned to St Joseph's with fifteen others, the first group to study for A levels at the school. Until then, students went only as far as CSEs, then either transferred to another school or left school altogether to pursue a career.

A levels presented me with different and more difficult challenges. As pioneer students, we had to manage with the school's limited resources, which were even more limited for a blind person. But we had one great advantage: there were so few of us that our teachers were able to give us valuable individual attention.

The two-year A-level course wasn't always easy, but I enjoyed it and the time seemed to pass quickly. While it was challenging, I enjoyed the experience of focused study in specialised subjects. I sat my exams as I had the CSEs and felt reasonably confident that I had done well enough to qualify for university. Just before the results came out, though, my family and I were dealt a bitter blow.

# 10

# Family Tragedy

In Catholic areas throughout Northern Ireland, 15 August is Bonfire Night. I'm not sure why that date was chosen, but it's a holy day of obligation, the Feast of the Assumption, which probably has something to do with it. Perhaps the bonfires were a Catholic response to those that Protestants build on 12 July, to celebrate the 1690 victory of King William III at the Battle of the Boyne.

In 1978, as usual, my mates and many of the neighbourhood children had been busy collecting wood and stacking the bonfire. There was real rivalry between the streets in Lower Creggan as they tried to outdo each other. Sometimes the rivalry was such that fisticuffs might erupt, particularly if interlopers tried to steal a street's trees, tyres or bits of discarded furniture.

That day, my daddy hadn't been feeling well. The doctor was called and immediately ordered him to hospital. My brother Jim, who lived not far from the top of our street on Westway, was sent for, and I remember sitting on the stairs of our house when he arrived to ferry Daddy to Casualty. Mammy was on the phone – to Margaret, I think, to tell her that Daddy wasn't well. It was the first time we had seen Daddy ill. Until now, we had viewed him as indestructible. Often, we take those closest to us for granted, sometimes forgetting that they are human and therefore vulnerable. He was the harbour that gave us shelter and protection amid life's storms, and suddenly we were confronted with his mortality.

He must have sensed the worst: just before he left our house, he broke down and cried. I had never witnessed him crying before and it was a shock. I was filled with foreboding and anxiety. I would have given anything at that moment to make him better. My heart almost burst when I heard my mammy hug him and say, almost pleadingly, 'Liam, I'll miss you.' With that, he left the house with Jim and off they went to Altnagelvin Hospital.

At the hospital, it was discovered that Daddy had had a heart attack. He was admitted and spent ten days in the coronary care ward. It was such a relief when we heard he was being discharged. The whole family gathered to welcome him home. The ambulance men brought him as far as our front hallway and then it was over to us. We gathered around him, not sure what to do. Should he go to his bedroom or sit in front of the fire in the sitting room? Other than the time I'd spent in hospital in 1972, this was the first time, as a family, we had had to deal with serious illness.

Daddy was very weak and asked to be taken upstairs. Rather than have him exert himself, Noel carried him on his back to his bedroom. We were over-anxious, but back then there was little information. Since Daddy had had a heart attack, we thought it would be dangerous for him to exert his heart by climbing the fourteen or fifteen steps to the upstairs landing.

He took to his bed, clearly frightened and perplexed as he had never been ill before. It was new territory for him. During the next few days, I often sat on the edge of his bed and talked to him. The family was worried that he wasn't taking any exercise and I'd try to encourage him to get out of bed. Eventually he began to walk about upstairs. Often I would find him in the front bedroom, looking out onto the street. He never ventured downstairs and outside to meet with his neighbours and friends. He was, of course, extremely nervous.

One night, about a week after his discharge, while I was at the hot press where Mammy put our pyjamas, I heard Daddy breathing heavily in his room. I found him sitting on the edge of the bed, gasping for air. I asked if he was okay but already knew that he wasn't. I went downstairs and got Mammy, who again sent straight away for Jim. No one said anything, but we knew he had taken a turn for the worse.

We sat with him for a while, then sent for the ambulance. Fifteen minutes later, it arrived and Daddy was taken away.

Two days later, on Thursday, 7 September 1978, I woke up at around seven o'clock to commotion downstairs. I could hear my brother Martin's voice. My married brothers and sisters would call occasionally on their way to or from the hospital but not so early – Martin was married and no longer living at home. I had slept badly – I'd gone to the hospital the previous evening to see Daddy, but Martin had been standing guard at the door and told me that the doctors weren't allowing visitors as he needed to rest. With hindsight, I know that the family had decided to protect me and Daddy from distress. Although he was gravely ill, he was conscious, and the sight of me would have upset him.

I got up and began to walk down the stairs. When Martin spotted me, he said, 'Richard, come on down. We have something to tell you.' I was brought into the living room, where I sat beside my mammy. Daddy had died during the night. I was stunned and disbelieving. I didn't know what to say. I just sat quiet on the chair beside Mammy as it gradually sank in that my daddy was gone. He had died peacefully in his sleep.

My brothers and sisters all felt the loss in their own way, but for me a major pillar of my life was gone – the man who had seemed to know, without being told, everything I needed and had quietly gone about organising it.

I felt very sad for Mammy, too. She had lost not only her husband but also her best friend. They had loved each other through good days and bad. She had also lost the person who had taken control of so much. I'm sure her anxiety about me increased with his passing, even though I was developing a greater independence. Mothers are mothers: worry comes naturally to them.

I remember every painful moment of the next few days. We went to the hospital to accompany his remains from the mortuary chapel to our house. The coffin was carried down our steps and into the hallway, and awkwardly manoeuvred through the door of the 'best room'. During the two days of the wake, the house never seemed to empty. The kettle was constantly on the boil, while home-made buns and sandwiches were never in short supply as our neighbours kept replenishing stocks. It was the story of the five loaves and two fishes in action.

The removal was so sad. Even though Daddy was dead, there had been some comfort in having him with us at home. The poignancy of those last few minutes when we gathered around his coffin to say our final farewells will remain with me forever. Blind though I was, I saw and felt everything. We left the undertakers to close the coffin and I was walked outside and to the top of the steps, where I stood by our fence with my mother and sisters. I was conscious of a large gathering of family and friends. As the coffin emerged from the front door, deep sobs and wailing marked the beginning of my daddy's final journey. Never again would our home be blessed by his presence.

The next day, the pews on either side of the central aisle of St Mary's chapel were filled to capacity, and the transepts with the overflow. The presence of such a big crowd made us all very proud for Daddy. It was a sign of the respect and esteem in which he was held by so many people in Derry. I remember little of the Requiem Mass, as I was in a daze of grief.

One of my saddest but proudest moments was when I was selected with five of my brothers to carry Daddy's coffin down the aisle and onto the steps of the chapel's main entrance, which faced the walled city of Derry below. A century before our housing estate was built, Cecil Frances Alexander, the wife of the Anglican Bishop of Derry, was inspired by the hill of Creggan to write her famous hymn: 'There Is a Green Hill Far Away'.

There is a green hill far away,
Outside a city wall,
Where our dear Lord was crucified,
Who died to save us all.

The words capture something of the sadness of that day, for this felt to us like the sorrow of the first Good Friday.

We drove to Derry City Cemetery for the burial. A cold early autumn wind swirled around us as we stood on the exposed hill. Even now, when it's windy, I'm reminded of that sad day when we buried Daddy. Sometimes I experience it like a lament that envelops me in a wave of sorrow. During the days after my father's death, I felt the loss of my eyesight profoundly. The only visual memories I have of him date to before 4 May 1972. I have often sat around the family table as old photograph albums are taken out and the family pores over them. It hurts that I can't share the pictures and enjoy the memories with everybody else. I suppose it's a bit like that first night when I realised I'd never see Mammy and Daddy's faces again, and cried.

For weeks after the funeral, I would steal into his bedroom and sit on the edge of the bed where I had talked to him during the short time between his discharge and readmission to hospital. I would try to sense his presence by feeling the blanket and imagining pictures of when Daddy was there. It was like a photograph but through touch. It was my way of bringing back happy memories of very happy days, and remembering the advice and encouragement my father had given me over the years.

I was once asked if I would prefer to have been born blind or to have lost my eyesight when I did. I still maintain that I'm glad I had my sight for those first ten years. I'm glad that in childhood I could see my daddy and mammy, my brothers and sisters. I'm glad I was once able to see everything that goes on in the world, as well as colours and the changing seasons. I'm glad about all of that. But perhaps if I'd been born blind, the photographs wouldn't have bothered me.

# 11

# Love Is in the Air

I was studying for my CSEs when our curate, Father Frank O'Hagan, asked to see me. He was a guitar player and had just started a new folk group in our parish, St Mary's, Creggan. He invited me to join. I was delighted at the prospect and, as much as anything else, delighted to be asked. 'Yes,' I said. There were about a dozen others, ranging in age from thirteen to twenty. Most, however, were between sixteen and eighteen.

From the moment I joined, I loved it – the music and the camaraderie. One girl stood out. She had a lovely singing voice and, from the start, we became friends. Her name was Rita Page and she lived in Upper Creggan, about a mile away from my home. She and I became very friendly with another member of the group, Dessie Carton, who lived on Westway. He had a car and often picked me up to go to practice and to the Masses we played at. He'd drop Rita and me home afterwards, and often we'd hang out together in Rita's house, where we'd chat and sometimes take out the guitar and sing.

The more I got to know Rita, the more I fancied her. I

thought about asking her out, but at the time I was going out with a girl from Strathfoyle, a small housing estate north of Derry, built close to the east bank of the Foyle. We had been together for more than a year. A little later, though, we broke up, and now that I was footloose and fancy-free, I took my chances. Rita often walked me home after folk group practice, so I decided to avail myself of the opportunity to broach the subject. I felt a bit awkward and wasn't sure where Rita's head was in all of this. I still thought she saw us as just good friends, so I decided the best strategy was to invite her to a concert and see what reaction I got.

A talented and popular nine-piece band called Darts was coming to the Rialto in Derry and I was excited about going to see them. They'd had success in the British pop charts with 'Daddy Cool/The Girl Can't Help It'. Their souped-up rock 'n' roll/rhythm 'n' blues held its own in the middle of the punk-rock era. Eventually I plucked up the courage to ask Rita if she'd like to come along with me. To my delight, she said yes, and the Darts concert was our first date. From then on, our relationship developed. We began to see more and more of each other and before long we were 'going steady'. At first, we kept our relationship discreet, but after a while we felt confident enough to break the news to the rest of the folk group. Everyone was genuinely delighted for us.

Rita has always been a wonderful friend. When we first met, she was in her second year of A levels and I was beginning my first. She was doing history, too, and because she was a year ahead, she was an enormous help to me. I found A levels a major challenge, but friends, and Rita in particular, spent hours recording material, such as handouts and class notes, for me. Rita read chapter after chapter to me from course textbooks. I would have struggled to pass those exams if it hadn't been for her.

She went on to the Coleraine campus of the University of Ulster to study for a BA in history and education. A year later I followed her there to do a BSc in social administration. Rita brought me to Coleraine and back, about thirty miles from our homes. She navigated me around the university, got me to classes, made sure I had all the necessary handouts and notes, then recorded them. By the time I came to graduate, she could have sat my examinations and had another degree, she knew so much about my subject.

I was a regular visitor to Rita's home, but when she told her parents that we were going out with one another, I think her mother was initially a bit worried. It wasn't so much about the challenges my blindness would bring to the relationship as about whether we were going out for the right reasons. The one thing Rita's mother didn't want was for her daughter to have a relationship with me out of pity. That wouldn't be enough to sustain a relationship, it wouldn't be fair on me, and we would risk hurting each other unintentionally. Rita assured her parents that her interest in me was not based on pity. As she was a singer and I was a musician, we had plenty of common ground to build on.

The folk group also presented us with exciting opportunities that helped to deepen our relationship. When it was announced that the newly elected Pope John Paul II was coming to visit Ireland in September 1979, there was great excitement throughout the Catholic community. Sadly, because of the Troubles and the sectarian divide, he was unable to come to Northern Ireland. However, northern Catholics were as excited as anyone else about his visit to the Republic, especially since County Armagh was the ecclesiastical capital of all Ireland.

Father Jimmy Doherty, the parish administrator at St Mary's, was asked by the Derry diocese to look after the young people for the big youth mass planned in Galway during the Pope's visit. The folk group would take part in the singing, so we were at the heart of the preparations. As the build-up began, hundreds of young people from across the diocese came to St Mary's to sing and pray with us.

I was seventeen and in Rita's home one evening when the telephone rang. Father Jimmy was looking for me. 'Richard,' he said, 'you've been chosen to take part in the offertory procession in Galway, which will give you the opportunity to actually meet the Pope.' It was an incredible honour. A billion Catholics worldwide had been delighted at the election of the first non-Italian pope in hundreds of years, and multitudes would have given their right arm for the honour that was now being bestowed on me. I went into shock. Doubt gripped me and I kept thinking, I don't think I can go into such a big open space. I don't think I can cope with such vast crowds.

Dessie Carton was also in Rita's house that evening when Father Jimmy's call came through, and I confided my fears to him. His response was emphatic. 'Richard,' he said, 'there's no way you're going to let this pass you by. You're not only going to meet the Pope, but you're going to be meeting one of the top statesmen of the world. So make sure you accept the invitation.'

My family, of course, were ecstatic and very proud. It was an occasion of great excitement for the entire family. My parents were from humble backgrounds and I'm sure they'd never envisaged a day when one of their children would be so honoured. In fact, we considered it a great honour for the entire family. The press got hold of the story and soon articles were appearing in local and provincial papers.

When we left for Galway, the Pope had already arrived in Ireland. The excitement was almost palpable. The St Mary's folk group was travelling by minibus to Athenry, County Galway, where we were due to stay overnight. Just outside Derry we linked up with several other buses and minibuses and travelled in convoy down the west coast of Ireland. The journey was long but we entertained ourselves with singsongs, storytelling and jokes. The closer we got to Galway, the slower we progressed, for youth from all over Ireland were descending on the county for the Pope's visit the next day – there were hundreds of thousands of young people, banners held aloft and flags fluttering.

By the time we reached Athenry, a gigantic campsite had sprung up within the grounds of the Athenry Agricultural College. It was like a mini-city of tents and marquees. That night, Father Jimmy Doherty gathered us for a final practice and gave us instructions for the following day. I remember at one stage he said, 'A young girl from Derry called Teresa McDonagh is in there.' Rita told me he was pointing to a window in a nearby college building. She knew Teresa, as they both went to the same school, St Cecilia's Girls' Secondary School. Father Jimmy told us that Teresa had endured a long and difficult struggle with cancer, saying she had made the journey from Derry to meet the Pope. He suggested we should keep her in our prayers that night, asking that she would have the strength to fulfil her hope.

Father Jimmy's talk made the Pope's visit seem all the more poignant to us – and if anyone among us had been thinking of going into Athenry that evening for a pint, they decided not to. All of us were quietly praying that Teresa McDonagh would realise her dream. She was so ill that she had been flown to Galway from Derry. Years later, her family told me that John Hume had arranged the flight.

That night we had a few hours' sleep in a marquee and were roused at around five in the morning. It was still dark as we streamed out of the campsite in the direction of Galway City. We were amid a river of young people all flowing in the one direction and soon to flood Galway Racetrack, where the Pope's Mass was to be held.

Rita was to be my guide for the offertory procession and we had passes to get us into Zone A, which was just below the open-air sanctuary. We negotiated our way easily through Security, and were soon sitting at the foot of a massive altar. I had the impression that the crowds of young people were organised in a kind of horseshoe formation behind us. There was singing coming from every corner of the racetrack.

Father Michael Cleary and the Bishop of Galway, Eamon Casey, were up in the sanctuary and were helping to keep the gathering crowds entertained and in harmony. The good humour was infectious and the two men were treated with the same enthusiasm as a good warm-up act before the real star appeared. As the time approached for the Pope's arrival, everyone's excitement mounted.

Suddenly his helicopter was spotted, and the crowd went wild. Everyone stood up to cheer and wave. When the Holy Father emerged from it, it was as though someone had turned the volume even higher. The cheering and applause followed him to the top of the open-air sanctuary where he stood for a minute or two, smiling and waving. Throughout, Rita was keeping me updated on all that was happening.

Then, suddenly, a great hush descended on the gathering as everyone began to focus on the Mass. The highlight for everyone came during the Pope's homily: 'Young people of Ireland,' he exclaimed, 'I love you! Young people of Ireland, I bless you! I bless you in the name of the Lord Jesus Christ.'

Suddenly the entire gathering burst into 'He's Got the Whole World in His Hands'. The singing and cheering must have gone on for ten minutes before the Pope was able to continue with his homily and the Mass. All he could do was stand and absorb it all.

Until that moment, the morning had been dull and there had been the threat of rain, but just then the sun began to shine. I could feel its warmth on my face. John Paul II knew how to make the most of the moment. He pointed to the sky and said, 'The sun shines.' Again the crowd cheered: the Pope had interpreted it as a blessing on the occasion and on the youth of Ireland.

After the homily, the crowds settled down again and another great hush descended. The moment had arrived for the offertory procession. We had been told that when we had climbed the two flights of stairs to the altar, Rita was to guide me to within two or three steps of the Pope, then let me go forward on my own. I would carry a white stick: it was a symbol of my blindness, but I was also representing all the people who had been injured in the Northern Ireland Troubles, as I had at Bishop Daly's consecration. When Father Jimmy had asked me if I had a white stick for the offertory procession, I had told him I never used one. Then he had asked where he might get one. I told him that I'd presented the only white stick I'd ever had to Bishop Daly. 'Um,' said Father Jimmy. He went off to phone the Bishop. The stick I presented that day to the Pope was the one I'd presented to Bishop Daly.

After what seemed a long climb, I felt as though I was standing on top of a great pyramid. Just before Rita was to let go of my arm, I heard my name announced over the intercom: 'Richard Moore from Derry.' There appeared to be a delay before it was carried to the gathering below, and immediately I heard a cheer rising from a section of the crowd who seemed to be a great distance behind me. I knew it must be the Derry contingent.

Rita led me forward, then let me go. I took three steps and stopped. I knew I must be standing in the presence of Pope John Paul II. Someone to my immediate right introduced me to him. I don't know who it was, but a young male voice had spoken. The Pope, who was sitting, leaned forward, placed his right arm around my shoulders and neck, pulled me towards him and embraced me. When he saw Rita standing nearby, His Holiness smiled and beckoned her forward. He embraced her too.

The person to our right placed a tray before the Pope which he took two sets of rosary beads from and handed them to us. I then presented the white stick to the Pope. His parting words were 'God bless you,' as we turned and made our way towards the steps.

After we had descended the first flight of steps, Cardinal O'Fiaich and Bishop Casey came running towards us and almost knocked me over in their enthusiasm. They hugged us and we returned to our seats for the remainder of the Mass, almost in a trance. Rita and I knew that we had been part of something special and historic; the bond between us deepened.

Others were privileged to receive Holy Communion from the Pope, among them Teresa McDonagh. As he laid the host on her tongue, she reached forward and took hold of the Pope's right hand with both of her own. Less than six weeks later, on 11 November 1979, Teresa died. We were all thankful she had survived long enough to experience a moment that brought her great solace.

*

The St Mary's folk group had no leader, which led to all manner of disagreements about relatively simple things such as the selection of songs to be sung at services, the times and frequency of rehearsals. Eventually it disintegrated. But when one door in my life shuts, another always opens, and that was exactly what happened now.

My brother Pearse was on the parish council of the Long Tower church, which served the Bogside, Brandywell and Catholic homes within and near to the southern and eastern flanks of the old Derry walls. He asked if Rita and I might be interested in starting a folk group in his parish. Rita was very enthusiastic: both of her parents had belonged to the Long Tower parish before moving to the Creggan and still attended services there. Of all the Catholic parishes in Derry, it was by far the most historic, having been built, according to legend, on or very close to the site of the first monastery established by St Colmcille – Columba – in 546. The Long Tower chapel was built in 1784 and was the first new Catholic church in the city since the Reformation and the Plantation of Ulster. The name 'Long Tower' derives from the distinctive round towers still to be seen on ancient monastic settlements throughout Ireland today.

Pearse spoke to the chairman of the parish council, Father McLaughlin, who thought it a good idea, and we received an invitation to create a folk group for the parish. We had just turned eighteen. Our first meeting was with the parish musical director, Tony Carlin, who played the organ and was in charge of the church choir. He was well respected throughout the city and when we first went to meet him I was nervous. He turned out to be a down-to-earth, relaxed and ordinary guy who happened to have extraordinary talents, and immediately put me at ease. We became good friends.

Tony helped us to find several good young singers at local schools and initially did some work with us before handing over the running of the folk group to Rita and me. Tony Carlin taught me a lot about respect. I was in awe of his experience and superior musical ability. He was older than us and came from a well-known family with a strong tradition in music and choral singing. Alongside him, Rita and I were rookies, yet he never once made us feel inferior or inadequate. As we struggled to set up the fledgling folk group, he never imposed himself but blended into the background and made his presence felt only when asked. He respected the fact that Rita and I were the leaders of the group, accepted the hymns we chose and never failed to respond if we asked him to do something.

I owe him my gratitude for a supreme act of faith he invested in me. In 1970, he had heard the Andrew Lloyd Webber and Tim Rice album *Jesus Christ Superstar* and fallen in love with it. When the rock musical version followed and became an overnight sensation on the stages of London's West End and New York's Broadway, he decided to bring it to Derry one day and direct it. In 1984, he achieved his ambition and the show played for several nights to a packed theatre. What the public didn't know about was the faith he had placed in his lead guitarist – me! Every Thursday evening for a full year before the show opened in Derry, Tony and his brother Declan came to my home and went over the music with me from start to finish. All the other musicians could read the scores resting on their music stands, but I had to memorise every single note and know instinctively exactly where and when I was to play. At first I wondered if I could manage it, but Tony never doubted me and I put in a faultless performance night after night because of him. It was the highlight of my musical career and the greatest musical experience I have ever had. Words are simply inadequate to express the depth of my gratitude to Tony Carlin.

I have always followed Tony's example in dealing with the musicians I meet. It's so important to encourage others and, through belief in them, bring out the best in them. He also taught Rita and me the importance of respecting the person in charge of a group of musicians and singers. Good harmony is at the core of music, and the greater the harmony in a musical group, the better chance the musicians have of achieving it in their performance. The leader doesn't necessarily have to be the best musician or the most accomplished performer, but he or she must be respected until they are replaced.

We rehearsed the folk group for a few months, preparing diligently for our first Mass. Before this took place, though, we had one major hurdle to negotiate, and to us it was as daunting as Becher's Brook in the Grand National.

The administrator of the Long Tower parish was Father Michael Collins, who had a reputation on a par with his famous namesake. He projected the image of a determined military general, meticulous in his preparations for every manoeuvre, whether in peacetime or war. He came across as a stern, serious man. I wouldn't have liked to get on the wrong side of him.

Father Collins insisted on hearing the folk group before we performed in our first Mass. In the week leading up to it, we gathered at the side of the high altar, where we would be positioned during the Mass. When he arrived, he said a brief and somewhat gruff 'Hello,' then sat in a pew with a pen and notepad in hand. Rita and I were panic-stricken, but managed to compose ourselves. We were worried that maybe he wouldn't like the music, because some priests at the time didn't. Most were older men, raised in the pre-Vatican II era, who preferred traditional hymns, music and choirs. To our astonishment and relief, at the end of our rehearsal Father Collins was complimentary. He said he'd thought it was all very good, thanked and congratulated us. Rita and I went to our respective beds that night and slept easy.

With Father Collins's encouragement, the folk group began to excel. The average age of the members was between eight and twelve. Soon Rita and I decided to let them sing at concerts in the town. At Christmas, we visited hospitals and homes for the elderly to sing favourite Christmas carols. Over the years, Father Collins became a really good friend. We discovered he had a strong interest in the welfare of young people and he made himself available to help any of those in the folk group with difficulties or problems. We often went to him for his advice, which was always solid and wise.

My first impression of Father Collins taught me how easy it is to misread someone. The old adage 'never judge a book by its cover' is so true. The Catholic Church has been rightly criticised for its mishandling of priests who abused innocent children, but the media and the public shouldn't forget that the majority of the clergy, like Father Collins, are good and caring men who do their best.

The Long Tower folk group came into being in June 1980, while Derry was still in political turmoil. The following year, the hunger strikes began and the fourth hunger striker, Patsy O'Hara, was buried from the Long Tower chapel. It was a time of incredible tension. Rita and I constantly questioned whether or not it was safe to bring the children to the chapel for practice. Sometimes, at short notice, we had to cancel because of riots, shootings and bombings, which inevitably triggered increased army activity. Sometimes the roads leading to the chapel were littered with the debris of battle, the blackened shells of burnt-out cars, lorries and buses blocking our way. Even when rehearsals were cancelled, Rita and I felt it our duty to turn up in case some of the group hadn't received the message and to make sure they got home safely. We were sad that they had to cope with living in such a tough environment.

Eventually we came up with an idea to mitigate it: we would make opportunities for the group to travel to different places to get them out of the city's pressurised atmosphere. It was an extension of what Michael Doherty, my music teacher, had taught me: it was about adding a social dimension to our rehearsals and Masses. Rita and I began to arrange visits to Donegal, where we rented houses and cottages so that the folk group could come away for weekends to enjoy the tranquillity of golden Atlantic beaches and spectacular scenery. On one occasion we took them to Butlins Holiday Camp, north of Dublin, for a week. But the best and most adventurous trip was still a couple of years off.

# 12

# After University

After graduation, I was faced with a stark question: what was I to do next? For the first time since secondary school, I had no specific direction. Until now my future had been plotted out for a number of years: after CSEs I did A levels, and after A levels I went on to university. After university, I was facing the adult world and the choices were entirely my own to make.

In part, the decisions regarding my future were influenced by the compensation I received for my injuries. After I had been shot, my parents were advised to take a case against the Northern Ireland Office (NIO). It was ongoing for a number of years, but around 1976, when I was fifteen, the NIO began to make out-of-court offers to settle the case. The solicitors representing us favoured such a settlement, as they thought we might find a court case too traumatic. And, of course, they also advised that if I were to bring my case to court, there was the possibility that I might lose. Undoubtedly, the risk was there.

Intense negotiations between our solicitors and the NIO

ensued over a few weeks, and various offers were made. My daddy found the process very stressful. I became aware of this one evening when my brother Martin took me for a walk. 'Daddy is finding it very difficult to decide about the compensation. On the one hand, he wants to get as much money as possible for your future, and on the other he doesn't know how far to push it as it may end up in court.' Maybe I should help to make that decision. He was absolutely right.

By now, there had been an offer of £60,000 and I said to Martin, 'I'm happy with that.' Martin suggested I sit down with Daddy and tell him. It might make it easier for him to decide.

It was a weighty matter for a teenage boy and until then I had been happy to leave the decisions to my father, as I thought it was the right thing to do. But once I realised the turmoil he was in, I went to him and said, 'Daddy, I think you should accept the offer of sixty thousand pounds. I'd be very happy with that.' He went back to the solicitors and told them to get as much as they could, but we were now prepared to settle. In the end, they squeezed £68,000 out of the Northern Ireland Office. As I've mentioned, we were poor people, and that was a fortune to us. But when you consider that this was to do me for the rest of my life and to compensate for the loss of my eyesight, you would have to conclude that the NIO got off lightly.

What we didn't grasp was that once I had received the money, I would no longer be entitled to other benefits that, as a sighted person, I would have been able to claim. I was disqualified from unemployment benefit and denied the full university grant, entitled only to the minimum. Other students from similar socio-economic backgrounds were awarded the full amount and were allowed to sign on for unemployment benefit during the summer. If I had been unable to create a working opportunity after university, the state would have given me unemployment benefit only after I had exhausted my compensation.

It was by sheer luck, good guidance and hard work that I was able to live an independent life and not rely on the state. Many other disabled people may not have been able to cope as well as I did. I have never argued this publicly, but I always felt that the state was unjust in its double standards. The compensation offered was a small token towards helping me to live without the priceless gift of sight. Fortunately, I *was* able to get on with life and play the cards I had been dealt.

I was not able to use the compensation until I was eighteen, by which time my daddy was dead. I felt so bad about that – I would dearly have loved to send him and Mammy off on a good holiday. No one deserved it more. Instead, with one half of the money, I bought a house. I gave my mammy some money to help her out, and with the rest I went into business with my brother Pearse and his business partner, Colum McGurk. We bought a pub on Waterloo Street, in Derry, called the Castle, and two years later we bought another on the same street, the Gweedore, named after a Donegal town. At eighteen, I was probably one of the youngest publicans in Ireland.

By the time I'd finished university, I already had the pubs and agreed with Pearse and Colum that I would help to manage them. In the early stages, it was a very exciting challenge. I developed systems whereby I could run them unaided. In those days – the early 1980s – equipment for visually impaired people was basic. I had an old BBC 32K computer with an attached voice unit – a large box with an electronic voice that sounded just like one of Doctor Who's Daleks. It had none of the flexibility available nowadays in the software developed for the blind. Pearse and Colum had their own electrical and plumbing business, and I shared an office with them. At the time, the office was above the Gweedore, so whenever my computer presented limitations or broke down, I could get help from their secretary and staff, who were always willing to read to me.

At this time, my brother Jim was playing an important part in my life. He was general manager of Doherty's butchers in Derry and possessed a sound business head. He helped me enormously with running the pubs, especially in stocktaking and monitoring income and expenditure. Indeed, the discipline he taught me about good housekeeping in business has also helped me in setting up the appropriate checks and balances in running my charity, Children in Crossfire.

After a while, Pearse and Colum needed more space for their own business and decided to build premises in an industrial estate. This presented me with new challenges. Effectively, I would be working on my own and it was clear that I would need better and more up-to-date equipment. I contacted the Department of Economic Development, the Training and Employment Agency section (TEA), for advice on any support that might be available to me and an assessment of my needs.

How much would such an assessment cost? the TEA wanted to know. A local computer firm said they would be happy to carry it out free of charge, provided that, if I received a grant, I bought the equipment from them. Without that guarantee, an assessment would cost around a thousand pounds.

The TEA told me that that was too much – I'd be lucky to get that amount to buy the equipment I needed, let alone to pay for the assessment. My patience with officialdom was wearing thin. I was a self-employed blind person, I argued, trying to create employment and requiring help to run a business. To be successful, I had to instil confidence in my partners and demonstrate to others, such as my bank, that I was capable of it. The right equipment was essential.

It became clear that I was talking to a blank wall, but I wasn't going to be put off by a civil servant who appeared to have been trained in the art of advising people that they didn't have any entitlements. The more I thought about it, the more I fumed. Eventually I wrote to the British Northern Ireland minister, Richard Needham MP, outlining my situation. To my surprise, in just over a week, I received a reply: the minister had instructed his civil servants to look into the most cost-effective way to meet my needs.

Curry Barrett, an expert from the Royal National Institute for the Blind, flew from England to carry out the assessment, and calculated that the equipment I needed would cost £17,500. I went back to the TEA and asked for help to purchase it. They said that the money was still not available. So, after the minister had instructed his civil servants to find the most cost-effective way to meet my needs, I was back where I'd started. It was clear to me that someone within the TEA was blocking my reasonable request for support. (Eventually I discovered it was one particular high-ranking civil servant.) Once the minister had agreed that the expert should assess me, it had seemed pretty obvious that I would be getting the equipment. So why was I being turned down again?

Once again, I thought through my options. This wasn't just about me: it was about all disabled people, their rights and entitlements. I was a young blind adult trying to make my way in the world, and I was staggered by the lack of support from the very people who were supposed to help and encourage me.

I wanted to be a productive citizen and needed a sound foundation to build on. I was being denied that.

I turned to a wise old politician, the late Paddy Devlin of the SDLP. He listened to my predicament and immediately advised me to write to the Northern Ireland ombudsman, Maurice Hayes, who was also a boundary commissioner and permanent secretary at the Department of Health and Social Services, Northern Ireland. 'Let the ombudsman know your situation,' Paddy said, 'and get him to write to the TEA. That'll put a fire under their arse.'

His advice worked like a charm. I sent my file to the ombudsman on Friday, and on Monday morning I got a phone call from the TEA to say that the equipment would be arriving right away. My year-long battle was over. The person I dealt with in the end, Ms Meta Evans, was courteous and kind – the antithesis of what I'd encountered in my earlier dealings with the same agency.

When the equipment arrived, it enabled me, among other things, to link the tills in the bar to my computer, stock-take and place orders. Almost overnight I became self-sufficient in running my business. Both pubs were popular, but the Castle had its own unique character. Its back wall was built against the lower northern flank of the Derry walls and many of our customers joked that since the urinals were at the back, it was the only place in Derry where you could relieve yourself legally against an historic edifice. It was famous for its quiz nights and two-piece bands. The Gweedore catered for students, and emerging rock bands who wrote their own music often performed there in a dynamic atmosphere that I, too, enjoyed.

*Mammy, Daddy and my uncle Tom in their younger days, 1960.*

*Happy days at Rosemount Primary School, Derry, 1969.*

*The Moore clan outside St. Mary's chapel, Creggan, at my brother Jim's wedding to Evelyn in 1975. And, yes, the secret's out, I was a Bay City Rollers fan.*

*All spruced up for my confirmation day, 7 May 1970.*

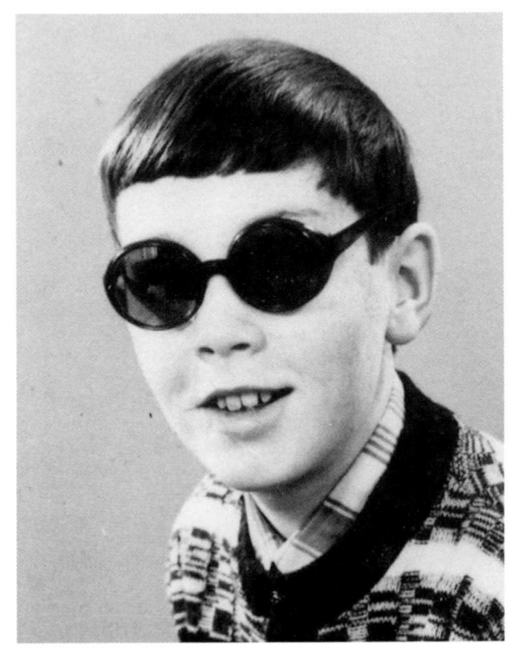

*Cool dude in the shades. After the shooting, the dark glasses became part of my identity.*

*The American dream: with my parents and Dan Herlihy in his Boston home. When we made the trip to see if top eye doctors in America could restore my sight, I never imagined it would come to pass – but more than anything I hoped for my parents' sake that it might.*

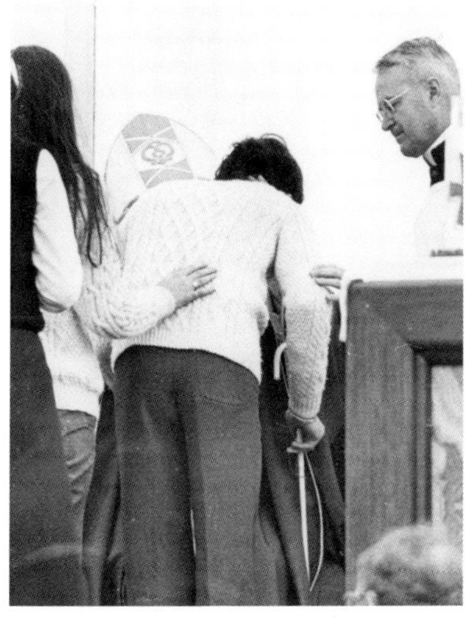

*Meeting the Pope was one of the most memorable moments of my life, and a great moment of solace for Teresa McDonagh (right) who died from cancer six weeks' later.*

*Music has always been central to my life and it's what brought myself and Rita together. From top to bottom: St Mary's Folk group, the Longtower Folk group and, looking chilled, with my band Midnight Hour.*

*Graduation Day, 1983, with Mum and Jim.*

*The bells are ringing for me and Rita. Our Wedding Day, 14 July, 1984*

*Daddy's little girls: Naoimh (left) and Enya, 1995*

*At the Ocean Road Cancer Institute in Dar es Salaam, Tanzania in 2008 – a project supported by Children in Crossfire. Where I go, my guitar comes too, and children everywhere love to join in.*

*In Ethiopia, visiting Children in Crossfire projects in 2008, with John Linehan, alias 'May Mc Fettridge', Dominic Fitzpatrick, the* Irish News *and Children in Crossfire board member Marcus O'Neill.*

*An unbelievable, exhilirating moment: welcoming the Dalai Lama at the City of Derry airport in 2007.*

*This photo reflects something I never in my wildest dreams thought would happen: Charles and myself with His Holiness the Dalai Lama at the Children in Crossfire 10th anniversary conference, Derry, July 2007.*

*I was delighted to introduce His Holiness to Rita, Naoimh and Enya. A memorable moment for all of us.*

# 13

# Going to the Chapel

A couple of years after we had founded the Long Tower folk group, Rita and I had been on a pilgrimage to Lourdes with members of my family, including my mother. While we were there, I began to think seriously about our future. We were sitting on a bus when I asked Rita if she would like to get engaged when we got back to Ireland. Admittedly, it wasn't the most romantic of settings, but she was delighted and said yes. We were both at university so we agreed that we wouldn't get married until after our graduation and one of us, at least, had a full-time job. With that in mind, we targeted 1984 as the year for the wedding and began to save whatever money we could.

We set the date of our wedding for 14 July 1984 and asked Father Collins to marry us. The folk group sang at the Mass and we invited them all to the reception. Rita's aunt Kathleen Doherty, her good friend Marie Campbell and her sister Tracy were bridsmaids, my brother Jim was best man, and Liam and Kevin were groomsmen. Pearse represented my daddy, and Rita's brother Michael represented her daddy. Our reception was held at the Strand Hotel, Ballyliffen, County Donegal, about forty-five minutes from Derry. Both Rita and I were extremely nervous, particularly during the Mass. Tony Carlin directed the folk group that day and they sounded excellent, but I think Tony was even more nervous than Rita and I were.

By the time we got to Ballyliffen, after stopping to take photographs at the Nazareth House convent in Fahan, we were completely relaxed and looking forward to the reception. I knew that this stage of the day would look after itself, as both Rita's family and my own enjoyed a good party. However, we had one more task to perform, which I was dreading, and that was the first dance. If I had been able to get someone to stand in for me at that moment, I would have been delighted. Dancing is something I simply won't and can't do. I had the brothers well warned that as soon as we went on the dance floor, they were to follow immediately so I wouldn't look as bad.

It was a fantastic day. The party went on late into the night and everyone enjoyed themselves. Because of the circumstances of my blindness, the *Derry Journal* covered the wedding, and a picture of Rita and me on our wedding day appeared on the front page the following week. When Bishop Daly saw this, he sent us a letter wishing us every happiness and success for the future. If he'd known we were getting married, he said, he would have made a point of being at the ceremony and sharing a blessing with us . I was so moved by this – I'd had no idea that he'd been keeping an eye on my progress and well-being.

To me, that letter sums up Edward Daly and shows why he was so well loved in his diocese. It gave me such a boost to receive it and sometimes, when I've felt down or depressed, I've thought about that letter and felt better. It has led me to reflect on the power we all have to encourage one another. We should never underestimate how important a letter, a phone call or a kind word can be. It might be all that's needed to give someone the little extra push they need to keep going when the odds seem stacked against them.

You'll probably think it a bit odd when I tell you that we went away on our own to the south of Ireland for only the first few days of our honeymoon, and that for the rest the entire folk group was with us! We went to Worcester, the town in Massachusetts where I had been brought as an eleven-year-old. The indefatigable Dan Herlihy and his committee had been keeping tabs on me, and when I invited him and his wife Joan to the wedding, they responded by inviting the honeymoon couple and the Long Tower folk group to Worcester for a dream holiday.

It was my first visit since 1973 and I was truly excited. The committee that had been so active back then reconvened to co-ordinate our two-week stay. Dan and Joan were still at the centre of everything, with Denis Brosnan and Pat Shaughnessy. Those four, with the other members, found homes for us to stay at, places for us to visit and the transport to move us around. They even had a few dollars in the bank from their fundraising days in the 1970s and used them to subsidise the children's airfares.

Everyone involved with the committee was clearly delighted to see that I had done so well. When we'd last met, I had been an eleven-year-old boy coming to terms with blindness. Now I was returning with my wife on our honeymoon and with the folk group we had set up. The reception party they gave us was overwhelming. It was as though they were welcoming home a war hero and all sorts of emotions raced through me. At one point I had to fight tears when I remembered that the last time I had been in Worcester, my father had been with me.

At first we stayed at Worcester State College's halls of

residence. It was ideal because it meant that the whole group was together, which gave the younger members, who had never been away from home before, an opportunity to settle and gain confidence. We spent most of our time touring and shopping in Boston, and also visited Cape Cod and Martha's Vineyard. We were in Worcester for a week, during which we gave two sell-out concerts; originally we were scheduled to do only one but demand was such that a second was arranged. It was an opportunity for me to give something back to people whose kindness and generosity had meant so much to my family and me, and the children did Derry and Ireland proud.

We performed several medleys of Irish folk and traditional songs, then some jigs, reels and several set dances. We told jokes and stories, too. I could feel the audience's affection for everyone on the stage. There is a special relationship between performers and their audience, and each audience is as individual as the next. The energy that passes between those on stage and those watching can lift a performance or crush it, and the children's confidence grew each time they were applauded. Some in the audience even whistled, and with every burst of laughter we felt as though we were riding the crest of a momentous wave. As the curtain came down, we hugged each other with sheer delight. In Derry we have a tendency to overuse the word 'brilliant', but performing for those crowds in Worcester was just that – brilliant.

We spent our second week in Plymouth, Massachusetts. While Worcester lies about forty miles inland from Boston, in the foothills of the Appalachian Mountains, Plymouth is approximately thirty-four miles south-east and on the coast, so there was renewed excitement about going to a seaside city.

Father Wren had arranged for the children to stay with families who lived on Plymouth Beach, two per host family. We would spend the day together, and at night we would split up and go to our American families. Rita and I, with Raymond Kelly, his then girlfriend Brenda Cooley and Paul McKeever, were given the run of a big house owned by Budweiser's area distributor. It had been a barn before conversion into what amounted to a luxurious mansion. We all appreciated the opportunity to have a break from the younger ones and chill out together.

As well as our visits to the beach and boat trips across Cape Cod, we recorded our first album, *Combination*, sponsored by the people of Worcester and Plymouth, a collection of Irish traditional folk songs and some of the hymns we sang in the Long Tower chapel. Rita and I had the children well prepared and, naturally, we had rehearsed the songs for the album before we had left Ireland. All of us were nervous, though, as we entered the studio, with its soundproof walls, large plate-glass windows and sound engineers watching us from behind their complex decks. When we got home, an RTÉ radio presenter played 'Carrickfergus', a track we had recorded, to the nation, and said it was 'one of the nicest renditions of "Carrickfergus"' he had ever heard.

There is an amusing story from our visit to Worcester and Plymouth. Dan Herlihy was worried that some in the US media might try to create controversy because the children had come from a conflict area of Ireland. He was worried that an unscrupulous journalist might try to get them to say something that might translate into a quarrelsome headline, perhaps causing embarrassment to the organisers or the children's hosts. It was decided, therefore, that if journalists wanted to interview anyone, Rita and I should be present. We kept reminding everyone that if we weren't around and anybody asked them about the Troubles back home, they should say they had no comment to make.

On the morning after our first night with our Plymouth hosts, one of our youngsters, Sinead, who was ten or eleven, came to me and said, 'You won't believe what happened to me last night . . .' The family she and her friend were staying with had prepared a 'big fancy dinner'. When they were all sitting around the table, the parents had asked questions about Northern Ireland. What was it like? How bad were the Troubles? What did their parents do? How did the Troubles impact on their lives? Sinead had become very uncomfortable. She told me her face got redder and redder. Eventually she'd blurted, 'No comment!'

I'm sure the family must have thought we had the children brainwashed, but clearly we hadn't explained ourselves properly and Sinead had assumed that our warning applied to anyone asking questions, when in fact we had meant only journalists. We had a word with the host family and explained to them what had happened and I know that they and Sinead had a wonderful time thereafter.

Our visit to Plymouth was such a success that the folk group went back the following year and spent the full two weeks there. Father Wren was such a lovely man and his parishioners generously supported his plan to bring us all out for a second holiday. Thereafter, the Long Tower folk group regularly went away together. We returned to the US in 1990, visiting the west coast, and also went to France. The group went from strength to strength, and almost thirty years later, it's still going strong. The children of many original members are now in the group and some current members have been with it for seventeen or eighteen years.

In 1980, Rita and I never dreamed that the invitation to

start a folk group would have such long-term resonance. Despite some very dark days in the history of our home town, our involvement with so many children has been one of the most fulfilling aspects of our lives. Through the folk group we have made wonderful friends at home and abroad, a gift of inestimable worth that money could never buy.

# 14

# Daddy's Little Girls

During the second year of our marriage, to our delight, Rita became pregnant. A few months on, though, she was rushed to hospital and lost the baby. It was a shattering blow, and when she became pregnant again, in 1988, we were on tenterhooks. On Tuesday, 7 March 1989, she gave birth to our first daughter, Naoimh. The baby was premature and was placed immediately in an incubator. We assumed that this was a precautionary measure and that in a short time all would be well and we'd have her home, so we were very shocked when the doctor in charge told us: 'She's got a good chance.'

Rita and I were thinking the same thing. 'Did he say the baby's got a good chance?' Rita asked me. Our baby was fighting for her life. Rita burst into tears. We hadn't had any idea that Naoimh was at risk.

Rita was discharged without Naoimh, and it was hard for her to come home without the baby. Our little girl spent three weeks in the paediatric intensive care unit and we went to see her every day and night. She lay in the incubator with all sorts of tubes attached to her, while all we wanted to do was lift her up and take her home. Thank God, Naoimh's strength increased every day and our joy was unbounded when we were given permission to bring her home for Easter Sunday. That was probably the most special Easter we ever experienced.

Our second daughter, Enya, was born on 22 January 1992. Thankfully, she was a full-term baby, no problems, and came home with Rita and I.

Naoimh and Enya's births were among the happiest and most emotional moments of my life. I was present when they were born, and to witness such a miracle was incredible. There was sadness too, though, because I couldn't see my two girls at the moment of their arrival. It made me reflect on my blindness, and I had to readjust to it. Until then I felt I had encountered and dealt with the challenges that blindness presented, but now I was plunged into a melancholy I hadn't previously experienced. Although I could touch and cuddle my children, I couldn't see them, and that was very hard for me.

I assumed that the birth of Enya would be easier since – I thought – I had adjusted to the fact that I couldn't see Naoimh. It wasn't, though. In fact, it was probably harder because it starkly reinforced in me the knowledge of what blindness had robbed me. I had to come to terms with the fact that this was the way it would always be. I longed to rub my eyes and see my girls for just a moment. But, of course, that couldn't happen, so as I do with most things in life, I thought about it, felt it, and moved on. To know that our baby daughters were healthy more than made up for my loss of sight. To be able to hold their hands, feel their faces and nurse them was compensation enough.

Raising babies in nappies is an experience for anyone, but

for a blind person it's even more interesting. Once when I tried to change a nappy, I wasn't sure if it was dirty – and found out the hard way that it was. Rita and her mother, Annie, had many a laugh retelling that story.

On another occasion, Rita and her mum went out shopping and left me alone minding Naoimh, who had an upset tummy at the time. I was a disaster. Even before they got home, I knew I was in a mess so I tried to cover my tracks. I took Naoimh upstairs and gave her a bath – I daren't put on a nappy until I was certain I'd cleaned her up properly.

Part of the difficulty in trying to raise children when you're blind is the need to be aware at all times of where a baby or young child is. If a child is rolling about on the floor or playing on a sofa, a sighted parent can keep an eye on them, but when you're blind, you have to develop other strategies. I had to be in physical contact with my children to be happy that they were okay. When I was on my own I was either on the floor with them or had them beside me on the sofa. I never let them crawl around the floor or sit on it without knowing exactly where they were. If I lost physical contact and the child was silent, I was in trouble. It was different when Rita was in the house. She had no difficulty sitting on the sofa and watching television while Naoimh or Enya played on the floor.

As the children got older, they began to recognise that I was different from their mammy in another way than the obvious. For a long time they didn't understand blindness and, understandably, would carry out their own little experiments and games to test me. One day Naoimh and I were in the kitchen when she suddenly went silent to see if I could find her. I couldn't. For several seconds she remained completely still. Rita was in the sitting room, and when I told her I couldn't find

Naoimh, she jumped up in a panic. When she ran into the kitchen, Naoimh was sitting on the sofa, barely breathing.

The girls were used to Rita reading them a bedtime story, and before they learned to read, I used to pretend to read to them. I would take a book and turn the pages and, if I knew the story, recite most of the text. As they got older, though, they realised what I was doing. Thereafter when they handed me a bedtime book, I'd say, 'Your daddy can't read.'

'Why not?' they'd ask.

'Because your daddy can't see.' That seemed to satisfy them.

After a day or two had passed, they would present the book again and I would repeat, 'Daddy can't read the book.'

'Why?'

'Because your daddy can't see.'

'Well, just look at the pictures.'

I could see their logic: I might not be able to read but I could surely see the pictures.

One night, Enya was adamant that I was going to read to her. I was beginning to feel desperate, then devised a strategy. 'Why don't you help me to read the book?' It worked and thus began our reading sessions whereby the children would read stories to me before they went to sleep.

I wished so much that I could read the little storybooks the children handed to me. My inadequacy hurt and I felt the sting of self-pity. At those moments I felt that I had been deprived of full parenthood. I'd have done anything to be able to sit, like any ordinary daddy, and read a simple story to my children.

At other times it was even more difficult. When Naoimh and Enya went to nursery school, there was an annual parents' day. There was always a football game for the fathers, and I wanted to be able to play. I wanted to be 'normal'. On those days, I felt it deeply, especially when the girls told me about the antics their classmates' daddies got up to.

One morning we were getting ready to leave Enya at her granny's before we went to work. Rita strapped her into her seat, then got into the driver's. I sat into the front passenger seat. Suddenly Enya insisted that I should drive. 'Your daddy can't drive the car,' Rita said.

'He can! I saw him.' Sometimes, for a laugh, I used to drive the car forward in first gear and reverse in our driveway. I could do it, of course, only if Rita or one of my brothers was sitting beside me. Enya had observed this and, naturally, assumed that I could see.

'Your daddy can only drive the car in the driveway,' Rita said.

Enya started to cry.

I struggled especially with blindness when Rita was pregnant, especially when she was very sick, with a threatened miscarriage, and had to spend long periods in bed or in hospital. She is also a worrier, like my mother, and fretted about me while she was away. Quite frankly, without her mother, Annie, I don't think we could have survived the stress. Annie came to our home, cooked for me and drove me to and from the hospital. Then, when Rita was in hospital having Enya, she looked after Naoimh and kept the housework under control. In spite of everything I've accomplished despite my blindness, I'm not a good housekeeper. I can't cook and I don't wash or iron my clothes. I know that many blind people who read this book may be thinking there's no excuse for that – and there isn't. I simply took the handy option: my family and friends were willing to help me with cooking, washing and ironing, and I was happy to let them do it.

All that Rita endured while she was carrying our two

children made us appreciate them so much that we ignored the doctors' and midwives' recommendations on where they should sleep. In the early years, we let them sleep in the bed beside us, which was great for us and for them. We loved it when they climbed in and snuggled up to us.

One day Rita and I had to meet the principal of Naoimh and Enya's nursery school, Nuala Heaney. She told us that when the girls had started the teachers had expected my blindness to be an issue. They were amazed, Nuala said, at how Naoimh had just accepted it. Rita and I were delighted, and felt vindicated in our approach to it. There's nothing in our home to indicate that I'm blind – we didn't adapt the house to suit me and have made every effort to live a normal life.

It's funny, too, how children will take a joke seriously – and you don't realise it. When the girls were small, I used to play football with them in the back garden. Once I had the ball in my hands I could place it at my feet and kick it in their direction. One day I was with Enya. It was during a period when I was travelling all over Ireland with my band Midnight Hour. Enya kicked the ball to me and asked, 'Daddy, what do you do?'

I replied, joking, of course, 'I'm a rock star.'

She asked me several times and got the same answer.

That was fine until one day she was in school and the teacher asked the children what their daddies did. The answers were as varied as the children: 'My daddy is a brickie'; 'My daddy is a manager'; 'My daddy works in the bank.' As Enya's turn got closer, the teacher observed that her face was turning from pink to crimson. When the teacher asked, 'What does your daddy do, Enya?' she blurted out, 'He's a rock star!'

Her classmates were fascinated. 'What does your daddy do in the band?' they asked, and Enya told them I played the guitar. The teacher had the bright idea of asking if Enya's daddy might come to the school and perform. Enya immediately volunteered my services and, a week or two later, I drove into the school grounds with Damien Godfrey, who played keyboard.

When we arrived at the front entrance, the teacher had all the children in Enya's class outside to greet us. As Damien and I climbed out of the van, I could hear the children's excitement and some shouted, 'There he is! The rock star!' All I could do was laugh.

With guitar and keyboard, Damien and I put on a concert. All the children and their teachers were dancing and singing, some even playing air guitar and pretending to be rock stars themselves. I learned a valuable lesson from that experience, though: you have to watch what you say to your children because it will be carried into school and, as I discovered, boomerang in your face.

When the children were in a school show, I always found it hard that I couldn't see them. It was particularly difficult when Naoimh and Enya made their First Holy Communion, because for every young Catholic girl and her parents, it's a very special day. It's almost like a wedding, as after months of preparation in school, the girls dress in white and wear a veil.

I never thought about it until the actual day of Naoimh's First Holy Communion arrived. There was great excitement in the house as Rita dressed her and I listened to the compliments she was receiving from everyone gathered to celebrate the occasion. It didn't fully register with me until we arrived in the chapel and Naoimh and her classmates were walking to the altar. Rita relayed everything to me: how lovely Naoimh and her little friends looked; how innocent and sincere they all were as they processed in pairs, hands joined. In my mind's eye, I followed her with Rita's commentary: 'Now she's halfway up the aisle. Now she's at the altar.' At that moment, my blindness hit me. I mourned the loss of my eyes and that I couldn't see my little girl making her First Holy Communion. I remembered the day I had made my own First Holy Communion in St Mary's chapel, Creggan, and here I was unable to see my own child making hers.

I listened to everybody telling me how pretty Naoimh looked in her dress, but I couldn't see her; I just had to accept that I was a human being who was blind and that blindness is, on occasion, going to make life sad. It was on Naoimh and Enya's First Holy Communion and, later, their Confirmation days that I would think of the day the British soldier had fired the rubber bullet that blinded me. Probably he had never appreciated the reverberations it would have on my everyday life. When he and his mates learned that a ten-year-old boy had been shot and blinded, they must have realised it would have a major impact on him. They will never fully appreciate what it has meant throughout my life and particularly on special days, like Naoimh and Enya's First Holy Communion and Confirmation, or their births. Those precious, magical moments have come and gone and I never saw them. I've been denied them, and that's the legacy of violence. I say this not as a personal lament, but to demonstrate the effect of war, which applies anywhere in the world. Many people, including children, have lost so much through others' violence, and too often the people who were responsible for those actions don't know the extent of the damage they caused.

# 15

# The Club

As a boy growing up in Derry, I loved soccer. My favoured team then, though, was not Derry City FC, but rather, Glasgow Celtic. There was a simple reason for this. As my interest began to blossom, Derry City FC was withering, due to a combination of the Troubles and what many suspected was sectarian politics. The advent of the Northern Ireland Civil Rights Association brought into sharp focus a deep sectarian divide within Northern Ireland. Violence erupted and contributed to heightened tension at soccer games across the Province.

Derry City FC was founded in 1928. It was preceded by Derry Celtic, but those behind it wanted it to be inclusive of and reach out to both Catholic and Protestant fans. They decided not to give it the city's official name, Londonderry, and to drop 'Celtic'. Londonderry Corporation granted permission to the club to use the Brandywell Stadium for home games, and in 1929 it entered the Irish Football League, made up of teams from across the six counties and fiercely competitive.

For the first forty years of the club's existence, there was little trouble at home fixtures, other than the traditional rivalry between teams. Then, when Linfield Football Club, a Belfast-based team known as the Blues, came to Derry, it brought with it heightened tension. Allegedly, its policy at the time of not signing Catholics mirrored the sectarianism of the highly successful Glasgow Rangers.

Sadly, with the outbreak of the Troubles, there were some disturbances involving the stoning of buses carrying visiting fans from Unionist/Loyalist parts of Belfast. With the Brandywell situated in a Nationalist and increasingly Republican stronghold on Derry's west bank, some Unionist-supported clubs expressed reluctance to play at the stadium. In 1971, the year before I was shot, the Irish Football Association declared the ground unsafe and ordered the club's home games to be played at the Showgrounds in Coleraine, some thirty miles from Derry. This meant that every week, home fans had to travel to an away game. The situation was impossible, and before long, faced with dwindling gate receipts and increased running costs, the club withdrew from the Irish League. For more than thirteen years, professional senior soccer in the city went into hibernation. As a boy, I had no home-grown soccer heroes to look up to, hence my interest in the Scottish League.

Then, for the 1985–6 season, Derry City was granted permission to join the League of Ireland's new First Division. Technically, the team would be playing in a league of a different jurisdiction. The return of senior soccer to the city was met with delight. The football famine was replaced by a football feast and almost overnight the entire city turned into a red and white army. Every home game saw the Brandywell packed, hosting up to ten thousand fans. For a while the crowds exceeded attendances at some First Division games in England.

Away games also had an enormous following, even in faraway Cork, more than three hundred miles to the south, which for most fans meant a car or bus journey: at that time, no train service linked the north-west of Ireland with Dublin and other major population centres of the Republic. The club's huge, and largely good-humoured, fan base was good news for the entire League of Ireland, which benefited considerably from the return to senior soccer of Derry City.

There was no police presence at any of the home games. The RUC were unwelcome in the entirely Republican/Nationalist stronghold of the Brandywell area, one of the original no-go areas of the Troubles. There was then no peace process, so its presence in the Brandywell would have been counterproductive. The Catholic community was so alienated from the RUC that had the police turned up to do the job that police do all over the UK and Ireland at football matches, they might have caused a riot. In fairness, the RUC did not object to Derry City providing its own stewards and taking care of crowd control. Compromise was achieved and, thankfully, in all the years since Derry's return to senior soccer, there have been no major crowd-control problems.

While most of my brothers and friends were among the new generation of fans, I didn't go to the matches as I couldn't bring myself to join a big crowd. Also, I didn't see the point in attending when I had no way of knowing what was happening. Instead I stayed at home and tuned into whichever radio station was broadcasting a live commentary. Sometimes when a big game was on and I wanted to savour something of the atmosphere, I'd get friends like Peter Cassidy and John Coyle to take me to the City Cemetery, part of which overlooks the Brandywell Stadium. I would stand with them on the embankment, away from the crowds, and enjoy the excitement that ebbed and flowed from inside the stadium as I listened on a portable radio to Richie Kelly and John Crossan commentating on BBC Radio Foyle.

Derry humour can sometimes be merciless. Friends and acquaintances rubbished my fear of crowds and teased me about defecting from the red and white army to join the ranks of non-paying spectators on 'Skint Hill', as the cemetery 'stand' became known. It was, and remains, a popular free viewing area.

In 1987, after just two seasons, Derry won the First Division and was promoted to the Premiership. To help the team bolster its chances in the top flight of Irish football, the club signed Felix Healy, a local player who had become something of a legend playing for nearby Coleraine, and who had spent some time in England with Port Vale. At the end of the 1981–2 season, he was voted Ulster Player of the Year and was among the famed 1982 Northern Ireland World Cup squad who reached the quarter-final by sensationally knocking out the host nation, Spain. He was capped four times for Northern Ireland.

Even though he was over thirty at the time of his signing for Derry, Felix Healy made a huge impact on the team, which grew in stature and confidence. During the 1988–9 season, he captained the side to a domestic treble, with Derry City FC making a clean sweep of the Premier League, the FAI Cup and the FAI League Cup. Soccer fever gripped Derry. Matches were videoed and brought for special viewings in pubs, most of which ran their own supporters' association. As the tension mounted, with the team edging towards the top of the division or reaching a cup final, songs were written.

At the time, I had a sixteen-track recording studio at my home. Because of my interest in music and sound, I had decided to develop one in my garage, which I converted into two separate soundproofed rooms. One was a 'live' room for the artist, and the other for the technician. Initially I had a four-track recording machine, but I graduated to the sixteen-track, which meant I could record sixteen instruments separately, then mix them together.

I really enjoyed experimenting, but I didn't know whether I could be a good sound engineer as sound relied so much on the volume-unit meters, which required sight to establish the right level. Was it possible to record without relying on them. In the early days, I met a musician called Clive Culbertson, from Coleraine, who also had a recording studio. He was a bass guitarist who had played with Van Morrison and was also a talented songwriter. I told him about my four-track recording machine, which was sitting in the house doing nothing because I couldn't see the VU meters. 'Of course you can use it,' he said. 'Sure I never look at the meters myself.' That was what I needed to hear. He volunteered to travel to Derry to train me. I hardly knew Clive, but he, like so many people, was so generous with his time.

Clive and I had good fun working together. He told me that often when he was recording he trusted his ears rather than the VU meters to help him determine the best levels. This gave my confidence a boost. I remember thinking, God! I can do that as well! Clive became a great mentor to me and taught me many recording techniques. He encouraged me to experiment by recording and mixing tapes, which I would bring to Coleraine for him to listen to. He often gave valuable feedback, which enabled me to improve rapidly and continue recording.

When I'd set up my studio, I advertised it locally. Before long, I was being booked by local artists, songwriters, soloists, singers and bands. Often they recorded demo tapes for their own use, perhaps for family and friends or, in the case of performers, to give out at gigs.

During the 1988–9 season, a local man, Danny Feeney, wrote 'Derry for the Cup' and I was asked to record it. I didn't know Felix Healy at the time, but he arrived down to my home to sing the song. As well as being a well-known footballer, Felix was also a talented singer who performed in the pubs and clubs in the north-west. It was the beginning of a friendship that has lasted to this day. Each time we met and talked about Derry City FC, I would say, 'I'd love to go to the Brandywell, as I love the matches.'

Felix soon grasped how big a fan I was, even though I hadn't been to a match at the Brandywell because of my fear of crowds and also because there was no commentary I could follow. He told me about Online Video, the company that recorded all the games, and mentioned the commentator, John Dunne, a popular teacher at St Joseph's Secondary School, who was considered locally to be as good as Jimmy Hill and Kenneth Wolstenholme. I knew him because he'd taught me English. Felix suggested that I should come to the Brandywell and sit beside 'Big John', as we called him, and listen to his commentary while savouring the atmosphere of the games. The only problem was that Online Video filmed and commentated from the sidelines of the pitch, so Felix needed to have a word with the Derry City manager, Jim McLaughlin, to get his permission for me to sit beside the production crew. Jim gave the green light, as did the video company and John Dunne, who said he'd be delighted to have his old pupil sitting alongside him.

My fear of crowds left me literally overnight, and I began to go to all the matches and sit listening to John Dunne's amazing commentaries. He was brilliant, hugely descriptive, very colourful and had a wonderful knowledge of the game, enabling him to read the evolving form of each team, its strengths and weaknesses, on the day. For me, it was fantastic. Now I could go to the matches, soak up the atmosphere and know exactly what was happening.

In time, local interest in Online Video pub presentations fizzled out and John was made redundant. Even so, he would still arrange to meet me at the matches, where we would sit together and he would give me my own personal commentary. To this day, if a match is not being broadcast by Radio Foyle, I can always rely on friends or family to sit beside me and talk me through the action, people like my brother Kevin, and former Derry City chief executive Jim Roddy. Now, when there's a big game, the Radio Foyle team always reserves a place for me beside their commentary box and a set of headphones so that I can know what's happening.

One year my presence proved useful to Radio Foyle. Derry were in the quarter-final of the FAI Cup and were playing against St Patrick's Athletic in Dublin. The match finished in a draw, so progress to the semi-final was down to penalties. I was in the commentary box, listening to Richie Kelly and John Crossan. Both teams started to take alternating penalties. I realised, in the excitement, that Richie had lost count. I waved to the producer, who I think was Paul McCauley, and whispered, 'Richie's got the wrong score on the penalties.'

'Are you sure?'

'Aye – he's saying it's two–one when it's actually two all.'

Paul told Richie he had the wrong score, and Richie promptly told his listeners, 'Richard Moore is here in the commentary box and is keeping us right with the penalty count. It's actually two penalties apiece, not two–one as I've previously stated.' I liked that – he was aware that listeners back in Derry who knew me would enjoy the fact that it had taken a blind man to keep him right.

I have many laughs at the Brandywell with my various helpers. On another occasion, I was sitting beside John Dunne when it dawned on me that one of my favourite Derry players, a big Scottish defender called Stuart Gauld, was having a quiet game. During a lull, I said to John, 'Stuart Gauld really hasn't featured in the match today at all, has he?'

'I know, Richard. That's because he's not on the bloody pitch!'

I laughed so much I almost fell off my seat.

Probably my most embarrassing moment with John at the Brandywell happened one Sunday afternoon after I had returned from a short trip with the folk group. We had been staying in a rented house on the outskirts of Sligo and had gone shopping on the Saturday afternoon. Rita had decided to stay in the house, and when I asked her if she wanted anything, she replied, 'Surprise me!'

When we got to Sligo town centre, I decided to stay in the minibus with Stephen Long, our bass guitarist. I asked the girls to choose something for Rita for me to bring back, and was expecting them to get me a box of chocolates or a bunch of flowers. On the way home, I asked if they'd bought me something for Rita. I heard sniggering and giggling coming from behind. Then one of the girls handed me a package, wrapped in nice paper. It felt soft, so I asked, 'What did you get?' They asked me to guess. I felt through the package and guessed it was a scarf. The laughter got louder. They then suggested I open it. I tore off the paper and lifted out what felt like silky lace material. When I held it up, Stephen nearly crashed the minibus – I'm not sure if it was from laughing or shock. In their mischief, the girls had purchased a pair of the sexiest black silk panties they could find. There was no way I was handing them to Rita, so I tossed them to the back of the minibus and forgot about them. What I didn't know was that the girls slipped them into the pocket of my coat, which was lying at the back of the bus.

The next day, I was at the Brandywell and, as usual, sitting beside John Dunne. He seemed to be developing a bit of a cold and was constantly sniffing. He asked me if I had a tissue. I checked my coat pocket and was delighted to discover what felt like a handkerchief. Without thinking, I said, 'Here, John, I have a hankie for you,' and pulled out the black silky panties and waved them at him.

'Jesus, Richard! That's a pair of knickers! I'll not be blowing my nose into them!'

I was never so embarrassed in my life – especially since there were about thirty other people within earshot. What must they have thought?

My enthusiasm for the club increased with each game I attended. I was at all of the home games at the Brandywell and went to as many away games as I could. Through time, I became friendly with the management and members of the club's board. Eventually the opportunity to become a board member presented itself. I put my name forward and was duly elected.

Money was always an issue for Derry City. The expectation of the fans was that the board would assist the management in building the best possible team on the pitch. Our challenge was to balance the books and save the club from a repetition of past financial difficulties that had almost forced Derry to fold. Now gate receipts had dropped with the fall-off of initial newfound support, so money wasn't readily available. I soon learned that there was a big difference between being a fan and being a director. As a fan, your primary interest is in knowing which players your club is buying. As a director, you want to know which players you can afford, if any, and which the club might be able to sell if it got into financial difficulties. I suppose it's like most things: when you step inside the inner chambers and are confronted with the stark realities that must be dealt with, the mystery disappears. And as you get involved in the day-to-day nuts-and-bolts operation of running an organisation, it becomes less magical and less attractive.

I certainly don't regret having become a board member of Derry City FC, for I had some really amazing experiences. The ultimate one was in 1997. By then, Felix Healy was manager and I remember standing alongside him in the last match of the Premier League Championship tournament when the final whistle blew in our match against St Patrick's Athletic. Derry had won the game and with it the title. The significance of the moment didn't escape me. There are no doubt many people who go through life without experiencing the thrill of seeing their team become champions of their country. To do so not only as a fan but as a board member was fantastic. On top of that I was standing beside the club's manager when sporting history was made. To cap it all, we were also in the FAI Cup Final a few weeks later.

The Cup Final was on 4 May 1997, which, coincidentally, was the twenty-fifth anniversary of when I was shot. By this stage, Felix Healy and I had become good friends. As we had offices in the same building, we met regularly for lunch and a chat. Before the semi-final, when we were discussing the chances of the team getting through to the final, I had mentioned to Felix the significance to me of the date the final would be played on.

Unknown to me, Felix told the players in his dressing room team talk just before the semi-final. It was a hard-fought game, but Derry emerged victorious and our hopes were high as we looked forward to the final. As a director of the club, I went to the dressing room after the game to congratulate the team. The Derry City goalkeeper, Dublin-born Tony O'Dowd, came up to me and said, 'Today's match was for you, Richard.' Apparently all the lads had agreed that they would play the semi-final for me. They wanted to ensure that the anniversary was special in some way for me.

Felix built a very good squad with limited resources. They gelled as a team, gave honestly of themselves on the pitch and worked as a tight unit, and therein lay the secret of their success. Those qualities had helped them to win the League that year and now had them just one game away from doing the League and Cup double. As players, they shared a closeness that created a bond and an understanding that were the envy of many other teams.

Derry was gripped with excitement and anticipation – the team's good fortune lifted the spirits of so many. There was a carnival atmosphere in the city and, remembering the candy stripes from my boyhood, I could see in my mind's eye hundreds of men, women and children sporting the team's colours as the big day approached. The last time Derry City had laid hands on major silverware had been in 1988–9, when Felix was captain and they had won the treble, the first and only time to date that such a feat has been achieved in Irish football.

With the League already won, the week leading up to the Cup Final saw us all in high spirits. People were even returning home from abroad to support the team. To say we were all feeling great is not overstating the reality. Everyone was talking about the game and making arrangements to travel to Dalymount Park in Dublin.

Then the unbelievable happened. Just a few days before the Cup Final, our goalkeeper, Tony O'Dowd, heard that his eighteen-year-old brother had died of a massive heart attack while training with his club, St Patrick's Athletic, in Dublin. The news was shattering for Tony and I really felt for him. His kind words to me after Derry's semi-final victory had been very touching. All I wanted to do was somehow reciprocate that kindness.

On the day of the Cup Final, we went through the motions. The team travelled to Dublin ahead of the fans. The fans followed, some leaving on Friday and Saturday to enjoy a weekend break in the capital, and many leaving Derry on Sunday morning in a convoy of coaches. Although it wasn't talked about, Tony's tragedy had sapped our enthusiasm, and the team's. Professional and semi-professional players are expected to bite the bullet and display stoicism, ruthlessly concentrating on the task in hand, but we all understood why Tony couldn't take his place for the Cup Final. He was there as a spectator.

An invisible shroud of sadness had fallen over the Derry fans. We were all aware that while the match was in progress, his brother was being waked a few miles away from the ground. We lost that match and it was no surprise: the team's heart wasn't in it. It was hard for them to concentrate knowing that Tony was hurting so badly. We all felt it. Young Declan Devine took over in goal, but it was a big task – our loss had nothing to do with him.

The day after the final, the team and many of the fans, including myself, went to the funeral in Dublin. It was one of my lowest points as a Derry City supporter, but there have been many highs. Football has given the people of Derry so much excitement and that team gave us so much pride. We are proud, too, that the Brandywell Stadium is the only one in Europe, perhaps even in the world, that doesn't have a police presence on the day of a big game. It says a lot for the discipline of the fans and the club.

If there's one thing that disappoints me about soccer, though, it's the fickleness of the fans. I believe this to be true right across the globe, and perhaps it's the case in other sports too. I became aware of it when I was a director of Derry City FC. Jim McLaughlin and Felix Healy were two of the most successful managers Derry City has ever had, and I was appalled by the abuse they endured at different times when the team wasn't performing as well as some fans expected. To make it even worse, both men were born and raised in Derry. In my view, Jim McLaughlin was the best manager the League of Ireland has ever had. In terms of the history of Derry City Football Club, it will be a long time before another manager equals the dizzy heights to which he brought the club. I know that many fans, like me, had the utmost respect for him and Felix, but a few made their lives a misery with the hurtful remarks they shouted from the terraces and on the streets. It seemed to me, at times, that some people were waiting for one or other of them to fail so that they could criticise them harshly. I was close to both men. I knew how they felt about the club and how badly bruised they were by the whole experience. It really saddened me.

# 16

# Burnout

While I had a passionate interest in music and the bars were a wonderful place to gain work experience, I gradually became dissatisfied and realised that, in the long term, the pub trade wasn't for me. Whenever I had the opportunity, I found myself getting more and more involved in charitable causes and on issues of justice. One day I had a call from someone in Dublin that redirected my life. Don Mullan had grown up in Leenan Gardens, the street above my own. I remembered him as a good goalkeeper who I had taken shots against both before and after I was blinded. (I'm certain I scored as many goals against him without my sight as I did when I could see!)

Don told me that an international group was coming to Ireland and that he had been asked to arrange a visit to the North; he said he'd like them to meet me. As we talked, I offered to help him organise a full itinerary in Derry, to include meetings with various political viewpoints and victims of the Troubles. It was the first of several such visits and I really enjoyed meeting people from across the world – Asia, Africa,

Latin America, Europe and the US – who brought their own stories and perspectives to my life.

Over time, my friendship with Don developed and soon he was inviting me to Dublin and around Ireland to participate in events he was setting up with an organisation called AFrI (Action From Ireland), of which he was director. In the late 1980s and early 1990s, Don established a now well-known annual famine walk from Louisburgh to Doolough, County Mayo, in memory of a ten-mile hike undertaken by starving peasants in 1849, during Ireland's Great Hunger. The walks, while recalling an historic incident, were primarily about highlighting injustice and human rights violations in our world today. Rita and I used to bring a busload from Derry, mainly members of the folk group, and often took part ourselves. In 1992, Archbishop Desmond Tutu, from South Africa, and his wife Leah led the walk. He had come to open a small Famine Centre in Louisburgh and the folk group had learned several South African hymns, which were also rousing songs of protest. The Tutus were moved by the singing, and the walk was unforgettable. We thought of the trek undertaken by scores of poor and hungry people on a cold winter's day in 1849. Several died from exposure, and folk memory recalls a terrible storm.

The Doolough Valley is situated between the Sheefry Hills and Mweelrea Mountains. It is, I am told, one of the most spectacular valleys in Europe, with its beautiful deep, dark lake which the sun seldom shines upon because of the towering hills that enclose it. The narrow valley acts as a wind tunnel during storms. The day we brought the folk group there for Archbishop Tutu's walk, the wind was positively dangerous. People were being blown off their feet, and two had to go to hospital. We had no option but to put all the children in the bus and drive them to Louisburgh for shelter. But when we left that day, we were acutely aware of the horror that had befallen some of our own people a century and a half earlier, and of the suffering endured by so many during South Africa's apartheid years.

Through this and other experiences with AFrI, I began to feel a calling to work in world development issues. I was confronted with the terrible truth that people were dying of hunger, were caught up in war and were on the receiving end of terrible injustices. I found that I wanted to make a difference. I began by organising the itineraries of international groups visiting Northern Ireland and joining in with AFrI events. Little by little, I spent more and more of my time on charity work rather than running my business.

Around this time, Don asked me to meet a group visiting Derry led by a friend of his, Adi Roche. I thought I was going to meet a man – I'd assumed that Adi was short for Adrian. When I arrived in the Waterside and went into the Everglades Hotel lobby, a woman approached me and asked if I was Richard Moore. I was momentarily flummoxed when she introduced herself as Adi! She was with another woman, Anne Norman, with whom she had founded the Chernobyl Children's Project, their response to the horrific physical and genetic injuries suffered by the people of Belarus following the world's worst nuclear disaster: the meltdown of the Chernobyl nuclear reactor on 26 April 1986. In the immediate aftermath, mothers gave birth to children with grotesque abnormalities, directly linked to dangerously high levels of radiation. The land, too, had been contaminated, requiring evacuation and abandonment. Some people refused to leave their farms and continued to cultivate radioactive ground, which contaminated the food chain. Radiation is invisible and Chernobyl remains, quite simply, the world's greatest nuclear nightmare; its effects will be felt for hundreds, if not thousands, of years. It is a warning to humanity about the damage we are doing to the earth and its long-term ability to sustain human life unless we drastically change our ways of interacting with nature.

I will always respect Adi Roche and Anne Norman for having founded such an important humanitarian organisation. Meeting them, hearing about their work and being a part of their campaign were important factors in shaping my thinking over those years. The Chernobyl Children's Project had branches all over Ireland, and they encouraged me to establish one in Derry. My first volunteer helper was Alex McLaughlin from Temple Grove, Derry. We were joined by two solicitors, Des Doherty and Greg McCartney, then by Martin Roberts and Kathleen O'Donnell. In 1996, Kathleen took over running the project and all these years later the Derry branch is still active.

From the day I was shot, I managed to direct my life in a positive way. I enjoyed everything I did and my life was very full. From education to work, marriage to parenthood, charity work to bands and sport, I was kept extremely busy.

But all of these things required commitment, and I didn't realise I was burning the candle at both ends. Quite often I was working an eighteen-hour day, although I never saw it as work. I had my day job in the bars, meetings with Derry City FC, the Northern Ireland Disability Council in Belfast, the Chernobyl Children's Project, plus the folk group and my band. I should have seen the crash coming, but I didn't. One night on stage at the Fort Royal in Ballymena with Midnight Hour, I realised I was having trouble focusing. I couldn't visualise where I was standing. Everything in my mind's eye was blurred. It was clearly the beginning of a panic attack, and I spent the rest of the gig trying to suppress the symptoms. When I came off stage I was in a state of complete exhaustion. The following night, the band was playing in Cookstown, but by then anxiety had taken hold: I simply couldn't face the idea of walking onto a stage. The thought of getting on, let alone getting off, paralysed me. I asked another guitarist to stand in for me, and on Monday morning I phoned the band members to tell them I was leaving.

It was a big shock for them. I was the leader, the guy who ran the band, dealt with venue managers, collected and distributed the money. I organised the PA, the road crew and for the lads to be at the pick-up points every week when we were travelling to gigs. In effect, I was the glue that held it all together. Everyone was disappointed that I had to go, but they understood my situation and wished me luck for the future.

Even though I'd left the band, things didn't improve – in fact, I felt worse. I was having panic attacks. I constantly had a feeling of nerves in my stomach. Some of my old fears and phobias returned. I felt exhausted but couldn't sleep. There were nights I was going to bed at eleven and waking up again at two. I couldn't concentrate at work, as I was always tired.

One of the hardest things was not playing in a band at the weekend. I was used to coming home from work on a Friday, having a quick bite to eat, then heading out to play. All of a sudden, I was at home with nothing to do but sit in front of the TV. For most people it was normal to relax like that at the weekend, but for me it wasn't. My mind was running at a hundred miles per hour even though I had made the decision to slow down.

As the days turned into months, my chronic inability to unwind, coupled with sleep deprivation, left me mentally exhausted. I couldn't understand what was happening to me. I wanted to cry, but for no particular reason. I felt I was losing my mind.

It all came to a head one Saturday night when Derry City were playing in a local derby against our Donegal neighbours, Finn Harps. Normally I'd have been looking forward to a match like that, but I didn't want to go and was feeling worse by the minute. Eventually I went to stand at my front door to get some fresh air. Rita followed me. 'What's wrong, Richard?' she asked.

I broke down. 'I don't know. I just can't get rid of these feelings of anxiety and stress.'

The next day, I went to see Dr Raymond McClean. I explained to him how I was feeling and that I couldn't understand why. I wanted him to send me for a blood test or tell me a virus was going around that I'd been unfortunate enough to pick up. On the other hand, I was so exhausted I'd have been happy if he'd just prescribed a pill to make me feel normal.

The first thing Dr McClean said was, 'Richard, let's list out your various jobs.' By the time I finished telling him about everything I was involved in and responsible for, he said, 'And you're surprised about feeling the way you feel?' He explained that he could prescribe a course of medicine for me, but he didn't think that was what I needed: I was pushing myself too hard and needed to cut back on my workload. It was impossible to continue working eighteen hours a day without burning myself out. I had to learn how to relax and enjoy doing nothing. He recommended long walks by the sea and said I should learn to meditate.

It was sound advice, and I carried it out almost to the letter. I started walking with my brothers Noel and Jim. I signed myself up to a transcendental meditation course. Within a month, I was sleeping properly. I couldn't believe it. I was getting about eight hours' sleep each night, which allowed me to function normally during the day without feeling constantly exhausted.

Dr McClean had said it would be approximately two years before my energy levels were restored to normal. Throughout that time, Felix Healy was a tremendous support. When I explained to him how I was feeling, he told me he'd gone through the same experience. He called me regularly, offered good advice and was always available for a chat.

I'd discovered that I needed to look after myself. It was a timely lesson, and one I'd needed to learn.

# 17

# The Choctaw 'Trail of Tears'

My involvement in the AFrI Great Famine walks, the visits to Derry of international visitors, the experience of being shot and the support and generosity I received from my community, family, teachers, students and friends had all led me to develop a global awareness and a need for change. I was wondering what I wanted to do with the rest of my life. Since my involvement with the Long Tower folk group, I had always been an organiser and fundraiser. Setting up itineraries for visitors and sharing my own story were second nature to me, but I wanted to do more. I could feel the desire growing steadily within me, but what I wanted to do, and how I might go about it, still weren't clear.

Shortly before Christmas 1991, Don Mullan and his wife Margaret paid us a visit. The previous year, Don had made a fascinating connection with the Choctaw nation of Oklahoma whom he had invited to lead the annual AFrI famine walk. In 1847, the Choctaw had learned of the suffering of the Irish during the Great Hunger and from their meagre resources had donated $170 towards famine relief in Ireland. Just sixteen years before, in 1831, they had been forcibly removed from their ancestral lands in Mississippi to Oklahoma, five hundred miles away, during which they had lost almost half of their people. This was the first infamous 'Trail of Tears' that Native American tribes suffered during their clearances to so-called 'reservations'.

The chief of the Oklahoma Choctaw had led the AFrI walk in 1990 and the media response had been encouraging. There was national coverage, and Worldwide Television News had broadcast the story of the Choctaw and Irish link to more than forty countries.

At school, the year of Christopher Columbus's 'discovery' of America had been drummed into our heads: 'In fourteen hundred and ninety-two, Columbus sailed the ocean blue.' The year 1992, therefore, was the five hundredth anniversary. The original inhabitants of the great continent hadn't been awaiting discovery by a European explorer who unexpectedly stumbled on islands off its east coast (the West Indies) while testing the hypothesis that Earth was round.

Don and AFrI came up with the idea of using the anniversary to take the Choctaw–Irish link to another level. He was planning a walk in support of those starving in Somalia, and wanted to re-create the Choctaw Indians' Trail of Tears. On this occasion, the walk would be in reverse: it would originate in the Choctaw reservation in Oklahoma and walk back to Mississippi. Symbolically it would emphasise that Native America had existed, with its own thriving history, culture and traditions, long before it was 'discovered' by the European. It would culminate at the two-thousand-year-old Choctaw Nanih Waiya, meaning 'Productive Mound'. Nanih Waiya is the Choctaws' most sacred site, situated close to the town of Philadelphia, Mississippi. It is their 'Mother Mound' and legend has it that the Choctaw people emerged on to Earth from it.

To many Native American people, their environment was sacred, to be treated with care and reverence. The lands also contained the sacred remains of their ancestors, whose spirits inhabited the rivers, mountains and forests. Removing the Choctaw from their home was like separating them from their soul. They had hugged and kissed their trees before they embarked, at gunpoint, upon their Trail of Tears.

Don and I were agreed that there was no point in being interested in history for its own sake. It was important that we learned its lessons and applied them to present-day reality. The purpose behind re-enacting the Choctaw Trail of Tears was threefold: first, it would, during this five hundredth anniversary year, recall a dreadful injustice perpetrated on the Choctaw and all other Native Americans; second, it would be a means of expressing Irish gratitude for the Choctaws' humanity during the Great Famine; and third, it would highlight the fact that others still suffered similar injustices across the globe, despite all the technological advances and potential of the twentieth century.

I was particularly saddened by the thought of children dying because they did not have access to basic necessities like food, water, shelter and medicine. At this time, the famine in Somalia was at its height and the walk would be an important focus. However, through its South American contacts, AFrI was also aware that Indian nations in Brazil were now similarly threatened by logging companies that were increasingly encroaching on their traditional lands as they devoured thousands of acres of the rainforest the native people had coexisted respectfully with for millennia. Those who resisted were being killed or beaten, while others were coerced to move away from their ancestral lands. AFrI had invited representatives of Brazilian Indians to join in the walk.

Straight away, I committed myself to taking part in the second half of the walk, from Arkansas to Philadelphia, Mississippi, and rounded up four volunteers from Derry: my younger brother Kevin, Felix Healy, Don Stewart, a bass player in Midnight Hour, and Paul McKeever. We helped each other with the fundraising and with the training we had to do to get ourselves physically ready for the walk.

However, when the time came to leave, I had lost my enthusiasm for the venture to the extent that if I could have pulled out, I would have. As the day for departure loomed, I began to regret ever having agreed to go on the walk. It would be my first time away from home without Rita and the children – just the thought of it made me homesick even before I left. The mind can behave in strange ways when one is under pressure and, crazy as it might sound, I was actually hoping that some sort of disaster would crop up and save me from having to go. But I couldn't let my brother and my friends down. And now I'm so glad I persevered: that walk proved to be a turning point in my life.

The minute Paul McKeever picked me up, the *craic* started and I relaxed. As well as being a superb pianist and drummer, he's a practical joker. He had us laughing all the way from Derry to Dublin Airport. During that fun-filled drive to Dublin, we discovered that Felix Healy, fearless on the field of play, had a phobia of flying. That exercised our minds for a good part of the journey. Poor Felix! We made light of plane crashes and what might happen if the plane got into trouble. He became more and more petrified. It took three flights to get to Arkansas, and I was sitting beside him when we departed

Ireland and climbed to thirty thousand feet. Suddenly we hit an air pocket and the plane must have dropped a thousand feet. I was convinced he'd wet himself – and I'm glad he was there, because if he hadn't been, *I* might have wet myself.

We arrived in Arkansas after two long-haul flights and a bus journey. My first impression of Arkansas was the distinctive accent – that long southern drawl, so different from the northern and western states. At first I thought it was a put-on – it's the kind of accent we tried to imitate as kids when we pretended to be Americans. I honestly didn't know people really talked like that until I arrived there. On our first evening I was sitting in the hotel lobby with Paul and Don. We decided to order a pizza, which was delivered by a young woman. She approached the hotel receptionist with a question that, in Arkansas slang, amounts to a greeting like 'How's it going?': 'Where were y'all?'

When the receptionist replied, 'I was outside sucking myself some weed,' I couldn't believe what I was hearing. I felt as if I was watching a Tennessee Williams play. I'm sure the Americans found our Derry accents equally entertaining, but we had many laughs over the southern drawl.

The walk was a real challenge. Although we'd done some training, we still ended up with blisters. I learned that you can literally walk them off your feet, provided, of course, you can ignore the pain. We were very lucky in that one of the walkers, Sheila Foy, from Edenderry, County Offaly, was a nurse: she spent many hours attending to our ailments, but everyone on that walk helped to make it an enjoyable and unforgettable experience: Michael Connolly (Monaghan), Jennifer Deegan (Dublin), Padraic Donlon (Meath), Michael Dowling (Cork), Padraic Drohan (Dublin), Sheila Foy (Offaly), Felix Healy (Derry), the Reverend Walter Hegarty (Limerick), P. J. Kennedy

(Clare), Paul McKeever (Derry), Liam McNeill (Dublin), Kevin Moore (Derry), Richard Moore (Derry), Don Mullan (Derry), Colin Morrison (Dublin), Martin Nolan (Dublin), Catherine Nolan (Dublin), Donnacha O'Dulaing (Dublin), Jim Rogers (Mayo), Don Stewart (Derry) and Declan White (Dublin). Also, we had a dedicated driver in Eoin Dinan, from Dublin, a gentle and generous person. He was always ready with refreshments along the walk and, best of all, a ride back to our hotel at the end of each day.

We had a set distance to accomplish daily in order to reach our destination on time, so we would set off very early in an attempt to beat the searing heat of the Mississippi delta. We rose at about five and were on the road by six, in time to witness sunrise over the ancient land of the Choctaw. By midday, we had the walk for that day broken and usually found a diner or were driven to our hotel for lunch, where we hung out until about three o'clock before we began on the last two or three hours of the day's quota.

There were some great characters among the Irish doing the walk. Father Walter Hegarty was in his late sixties or early seventies and amazingly fit. Originally from County Donegal, he had been a married man with a large family but had joined the Dominican order after his wife had died. He had a dry sense of humour with a wonderful delivery in his droll Donegal accent. Kevin White was also in his sixties, the son-in-law of Sean MacBride, the Irish Nobel Peace Prize winner and co-founder of Amnesty International.

It is amazing what you learn about yourself on such a long pilgrimage. Physically I was able to walk an average of fifteen miles a day, but then I encountered a barrier. Psychologically, my energy seemed to drain and I hit a near insurmountable wall. There were a few days when we had to cover nineteen miles and the last three or four were sheer agony, especially with blisters. I was never as delighted to see anyone as I was to see Eoin with his cups of ice-cold water at the end of each day. At that moment I felt if ever a man deserved to be canonised while he was still alive, Eoin Dinan would be top of my list!

The highlight of the walk for me was the arrival of a small group of people from Latin America. They were led by a truly remarkable Irish Holy Ghost missionary priest, Father Pat Clarke from Dublin. He inspired me enormously. His entire life is given up to the world's poor, particularly in Brazil. He was recently the subject of a documentary film on RTÉ by the freelance television and radio journalist Anne Daly. Pat showed me the immense power and strength of gentleness – a central tenet in Buddhism – and also gave me an insight into the core values of the truly religious: humility and compassion. To look at him you would never have suspected he was a priest and some might criticise him for this. To me, though, he was a giant.

Father Pat and his group were on their way to Ireland to a joint AFrI and Trócaire conference on the plight of indigenous people around the world. They had decided to join us because many South American Indians were enduring today at the hands of logging and other companies who put profit before people what the Choctaw had suffered during the nineteenth century. Their delegation included Sister Rebecca, an American nun who was defending the rights of Brazilian Indians; Bishop Apparecido José Dias, whose role within the Brazilian hierarchy was to minister to Brazil's indigenous peoples, Colin Karai Tataendi, a spiritual leader of the Guarani Indians in São Paulo state, and Karana Baniwa, an Amazonian Indian. Bishop Dias had had to thumb a lift on part of his journey to meet up with us.

Neither Colin Karai Tataendi nor Karana Baniwa spoke English, but their stories, translated by Father Pat and Sister Rebecca, about the loggers and land grabbers were heartbreaking. They were appealing to the moral conscience of humanity in the face of powerful political and economic forces supported by the military, paramilitaries and private armies. I was amazed that colonialism is still such a force. While sovereign European governments may not be laying claim to lands across the globe, the natural resources in those areas are being colonised by profit-driven commercial interests and vulnerable people, like the Guarani and Amazonian Indians, have little defence against the onslaught.

While the walk was sometimes tough, I loved having the space to think and have deep conversations with the others. As the two weeks progressed, I listened to Father Pat and Sister Rebecca share their experiences. From them I heard at first hand how people were being forced to live in poverty. They had come respectively from communities in Ireland and America with excellent amenities, but they were prepared to give up those comforts to live among the people and communities they wanted to help. And they did it in the most unassuming way, not looking for thanks or notice.

I learned a lot about myself during that trip, but I also had to acquire new skills. It was the first time I had stayed alone in a hotel and I had to look after myself. Sighted people take packing and unpacking suitcases for granted, but both can pose a major challenge to the blind person. And I had never had to think about it before. Here I was, twenty years after I'd been blinded, and for the first time I had to do things for myself. To start with, I lifted my belongings out of the case and left them down in different parts of the room, but I soon realised I couldn't remember where I'd put everything. 'Out of sight, out of mind' – how true. So I developed routines around packing my clothes and toiletries to avoid the problem of remembering where they were each morning and night. It was good for me, and that trip ignited in me the passion for international travel that would soon dominate my life.

I really enjoyed being away from the pressures of my business. There were long periods, particularly during the last five or six miles of a day's walk, when endurance required focus, and we plodded on in silence. During this time, I found myself thinking more and more about my future. Instinctively, as we neared our final destination of the Choctaw sacred mound, Nanih Waiya, I knew that I wouldn't continue in the pub trade for the rest of my life. I had come to the conclusion that even though it gave me a comfortable lifestyle and the freedom to play in the band, I needed more.

I wanted something meaningful in my life that would be more rewarding than material gain, and wondered if I could turn my own experience into something positive so that I could help others in different parts of the world. I had been shot and blinded, but I had had my family, community and friends around me, and many great opportunities had come my way. Thousands of children in other parts of the world might have their eyesight, but none of the things I had.

Despite my loss, I was blessed. I had grown up to be a confident man, able to articulate my needs and rights as a disabled person. It had to be possible for me to use my abilities to raise issues on behalf of vulnerable people in other parts of the world. But as well as talking the talk, I wanted to walk the walk. I could use my story and skills to help raise resources for international projects to support people across the globe. After all, my family and I had benefited from the generosity and kindness of others during our hour of need. I had only to think of Dan Herlihy, the people of Worcester and all they had done when, on the far side of the Atlantic Ocean, they'd heard of my plight and the distress of my parents. Or, indeed, the endless support I had received, and still do, from the local Derry community.

One morning, we were at a hotel on the edge of Lake Teokata, Mississippi. It was a beautiful place, with a gentle breeze dispersing the usual atmospheric mugginess. Don Mullan and I hadn't left with the rest of the group because we were doing some interviews with the local press. Over breakfast I said to him, 'I'd really love to spend the rest of my life doing work like this.' It was an honourable aspiration, but I knew I'd have to be sensible about taking it further. I was a married man with a wife and two children and I needed a job like anybody else. But I also knew that if I ever found work in the charity sector, I'd give it 150 per cent and sell off my business to dedicate as much time as I could to it.

Don listened, then promised to help in any way he could. After that we went to meet the local press.

That evening, after dinner, Paul McKeever brought me onto the lake in a canoe. He let me paddle it for a bit, but I was useless at it and all we seemed to do was go around in circles. He, however, was more successful and we made headway until we began to explore the entrances to some of the little creeks that flowed into the lake. It was then we discovered that some trees grew branches below the surface of the water. Before we knew it, we were stuck, unable to move forwards or back.

I couldn't swim and wasn't wearing a life jacket so I began to feel nervous, but Paul was laughing. Unknown to me, many of the walkers, including all of the Derry lads and the veteran RTÉ presenter Donnacha O'Dulaing, were watching our progress from the hotel balcony. Seeing our predicament, they burst into convulsions and caused quite a stir as they jeered us. It was all we needed. Paul said, 'That's it, f *** them! One way or another we're out of here.' I turned in the direction of the shouting and gave the fingers as Paul poked with his paddle, mumbling expletives under his breath as the ridicule continued.

It took all of ten minutes to dislodge the boat. I found myself thinking about how the Choctaw in their heyday must have glided effortlessly along Lake Teokata as they fished and ferried one another from bank to bank. Soon Paul was nonchalantly paddling us back to shore, pretending not to know what all the fuss was about, but I was glad to feel my feet back on terra firma and promised myself I'd never do that again.

One of the really nice things about the walk was how we got friendly with a variety of Mississippi people. We stayed at the Lake Teokata hotel for about three days, and on our last night a couple of locals joined us for a few drinks. I got the guitar out and we had a singsong, sitting beside the lake. As midnight approached and our new friends took their leave, one of our group reported that a number of pedal boats were tied up about a hundred metres to our right.

There were about eight of us and, like mischievous schoolboys, we decided we'd avail ourselves of the find. My promise to myself after the canoe episode went out of the window as I rationalised that pedal boats sit flat in the water and therefore are less likely to capsize. In darkness, we pushed four of the boats onto the lake. I sat alongside Don Mullan and we pedalled as if we were setting off on the Tour de France. The other boats were close behind, but because we knew we probably shouldn't be doing this we were silent, apart from the odd suppressed chuckle.

By the time Don and I reached the middle of the lake, we had left the rest of the group behind. It was a beautiful night. Everything was so still, the silence broken only by night wildlife – crickets, owls and a dog barking in the distance. Don and I stopped pedalling and sat back with our heads tilted towards the night sky to enjoy the tranquillity.

When I was young, I used to love gazing at the stars, the fathomless expanse of the universe. I remember wondering what might be happening somewhere else in space and whether there were such things as aliens or Martians. Even when I was a child, looking at the stars made me thoughtful and reflective. Don began to describe for me everything he could see that night above Lake Teokata.

I had never before understood the dimensions of the cosmos and our place within it, so he explained that the sun was the nearest star to the earth and that the planets of our solar system were recognisable by their reflected light. He described some of the great constellations to me, such as Orion, Andromeda and, my favourite, the Starry Plough, or as the Americans prefer to call it, the Big Dipper. I remember the Starry Plough well and can plot it on a piece of paper, the seven stars that make the shape of a pot with a handle. I had been taught as a boy how to use the two outer stars on the edge of the pot to locate the Northern Star. Don told me that the lake was so peaceful the stars were reflected on its surface. It was one of those unforgettable magical moments that leave an indelible mark on your memory. To be honest, it would have been so romantic if Don had been a woman – but he wasn't!

The next thing we heard was a stern male southern drawl: 'Who's out there? You're not supposed to be on the lake after dark. It's dangerous so get back to the shore immediately.' Everyone remained silent, thinking that the caller couldn't see us in the dark. We were all wondering what the 'danger' might be. Were there crocodiles and other predators lurking within striking distance?

The caller turned on a powerful spotlight, which picked up a couple of the boats. Don and I were just beyond its reach and were determined not to put up with the embarrassment of being told off. 'Right, let's start pedalling,' Don whispered, and he somehow managed to steer us around the side of the hotel so we weren't caught. We jumped out of the pedal boat, pulled it on to the lakeside and ran for cover like two convicts who had just escaped San Quentin. We scurried around the perimeter of the hotel, joined our six companions, who were being upbraided by the night porter, and asked innocently, 'What's wrong here?' We had such a laugh later – the others had had to eat humble pie, but we enjoyed bragging about our escape.

A couple of days before the end of the walk, Don had to make contact with the Mississippi Choctaw to plan our arrival at Nanih Waiya. He hired a car and I accompanied him on the drive to their reservation. All went well at the meeting, and Don was on a high as we left because the Mississippi Choctaw had invited us to an annual tribal gathering at which there would be traditional dancing, games, costumes and food. They had also agreed to mark our arrival at Nanih Waiya with a sacred ceremonial blessing. Don was chatting excitedly as he pulled out of the reservation and turned left onto the two-way highway. Suddenly he went silent. Then he said, 'Richard, there's a juggernaut driving straight for us on the wrong side of the road!'

For a second, I was confused. Then the penny dropped. 'Don,' I blurted, 'do you not think that maybe you're on the wrong side of the road?'

'Jesus! You're right!' I felt my seat-belt lock as he

accelerated frantically and pulled the car over to the right-hand lane just before we were completely taken out.

We laughed nervously after the big truck had passed, its horn bellowing with derision. 'Bloody hell,' I joked. 'It took a blind man to keep you on the right side of the road and in the process I saved your life and mine!'

He laughed and told me that even if we'd been knocked into eternity, it would have been by the right truck. We were, after all, in Bible-belt territory and the driver of the juggernaut had a big sign above his cab that read: 'I'll take you to the Kingdom of God.' It made the trip up the creek with Paul seem like a picnic.

That evening, over dinner, we learned that a big Nashville country-and-western band had come to town. The Mississippi folk were excited about it and we caught the buzz. We travelled into the countryside and eventually came to a massive barn with capacity for a thousand people. Felix, Paul, Don Stewart and I were especially intrigued, as we had all been involved in the band scene back home. Here the locals were big into country-and-western, especially the modern variety, which you didn't really hear in Ireland until the arrival of Garth Brooks. Also, the packed audience encompassed all generations, from teenagers to couples in their sixties.

There were several bars, serving mainly beer, and scores of long tables hugging the barn's side walls. In the middle, the dance floor was on fire with energy as old and young jived and line-danced the night away to the Jack Robertson Band's music. They were all dressed for the occasion: cowboy hats, cravats, studded boots, decorated blouses and skirts. The only things that seemed to be missing were hip holsters and Colt revolvers.

By now we had had many evening singsongs with Paul

McKeever on piano or keyboard, Don Stewart and myself on guitar. Many in our group were by then in awe of Felix Healy's voice. Word went around that a large Irish contingent was in attendance and Jack Robertson invited us all on stage to be greeted by the big crowd. While we were there, we lobbied Jack to invite Felix to sing a few songs. The audience hollered and applauded as Felix walked to the mike. Next thing, the band struck up a combination of songs including Elvis's 'American Trilogy' and the Billy Ray Cyrus song, 'Achy Breaky Heart'. Felix went down an absolute storm, with everyone up on their feet and swinging. They absolutely loved him and shouted for an encore. Felix was brilliant that night and we all felt very proud of him.

I thoroughly enjoyed our walk through Mississippi. Those of us from Derry had a natural affinity with the black civil rights movement, which had inspired our own, and we were very conscious of the American South's history of segregation and white supremacy. The movie *Mississippi Burning* tells the story of the disappearance and murder of three young white civil rights activists at the hands of the Ku Klux Klan. In one scene, their car is found in a swamp on a Choctaw reservation. I was jolted when a local person told us that a dirt track to our right led to the swamp where the Klan had disposed of the activists' car.

The recent history of American racism still resonated in some of the areas we passed through. One evening we were in a hotel in Greenville, Mississippi. A piano in the foyer acted as a magnet, and Paul McKeever began to play. A fantastic singsong developed – Felix, again, was in top form – and the favourite of our group was 'An American Trilogy'. During our stay there, a young receptionist simply couldn't do enough for us. She was on duty that evening, and we sensed that all of the guests and staff were really enjoying our impromptu performance. However, when we went up to get the keys to our rooms and asked her if she'd enjoyed the music, she stunned me with her response: 'Oh, yes, I really did,' she said, 'until you started to sing that nigger music.' We knew that Mississippi had its history, but it was a shock to hear such a young woman come out with a comment like that.

Despite that negativity, though, the walk was a wonderful experience and the Choctaw people were very friendly and welcoming. On the last day we enjoyed the traditional dancing, singing and food they arranged for us at Nanih Waiya – a great finish to a fantastic few weeks.

# 18

# Children in Crossfire

In January 1996 I had a call from Don Mullan. He had just returned from a meeting with Allo Donnelly, the chief executive of an international relief and development organisation. Allo wanted Concern Universal to set up an office in Ireland, and Don came highly recommended as someone who might be interested in taking this on. He couldn't, though, because he was fully committed elsewhere. However, he hadn't forgotten our conversations during the Trail of Tears walk in 1992, when I had expressed the desire to be involved one day in the kind of work he was doing, so he had suggested that I might be interested.

He gave me Allo's number, and from the moment I called him, there was a rapport between us. We met first in Dublin, where we discussed some of my ideas, and he invited me to come to Chatham, near London, in a few weeks' time, where the Concern Universal offices were then situated. He wanted me to make a presentation to the organisation's board about my background and experience and why I wanted to work in the development sector.

I used the intervening time to think out clearly what I wanted to do, and eventually decided to set up an organisation called Children in Crossfire. I would love to say that the name was totally original, but it wasn't. In 1974, I had appeared with some of my friends from the Creggan in a documentary called *Children in Crossfire.* In 1982, there was a follow-up film looking at how the children in the first had progressed in the intervening years, also called *Children in Crossfire.* I felt that the name would be perfect for the organisation because it captured much of what we would be about. I wanted to develop a charity that would focus on children – not just those caught in war, but children who were gripped in the crossfire of poverty and injustice globally.

I travelled to London, made my presentation and, a few days later, had a call from Allo giving me the thumb's-up. In September 1996, Children in Crossfire was born.

During the early days, Allo visited me many times. He was such an inspirational person. On many nights I sat spellbound, listening to his experiences of Africa and knowing I had made the right decision to get involved. Over the last twelve years, Children in Crossfire and Concern Universal have worked successfully in partnership with communities in Africa, Asia and South America, tackling some of the issues brought about by poverty. I am extremely grateful to Don McLeish, Allo Donnelly, Ian Williams and the other staff and board members of Concern Universal for giving me the opportunity to create and develop Children in Crossfire. In many ways, the seed of Children in Crossfire was sown within Concern Universal. The Children in Crossfire board, staff, volunteers and supporters have been instrumental in helping it to grow and flourish with their hard work.

Working with Children in Crossfire, I am privileged to visit other parts of the world and, more importantly, meet people whom I've learned about through the various justice and peace campaigns I've worked on over the years. Often they are some of the poorest people in the world, but they inspired me to begin the work I'm doing within a movement to build a better world.

The first trip I ever made to a developing country was in 1999, when I went to Malawi in East Africa. I travelled with my colleague Brídín Flanagan, who was then a Children in Crossfire fundraising co-ordinator, and Ian Williams, the executive director of Concern Universal. I was nervous about going, and the night before I left home, I didn't sleep. I knew that a whole new chapter in my life was about to open.

We arrived in Blantyre Airport after a long flight. I was expecting to feel a stifling or even suffocating heat as I left the plane, but I stepped out into a comfortable temperature and pleasantly low humidity. The airport was small and it wasn't long before we had been processed through Immigration and had collected our baggage. Gerry Carthy, a Kildare man, was waiting to pick us up. He was then Concern Universal's country director in Malawi.

As we drove to Gerry's house, he described the landscape and scenes we were passing through. I could feel that we were on a tarmacked road which scores of dirt tracks branched from. There was a lot of hustle and bustle, and the cacophony of sound increased as we got closer to Blantyre, which is Malawi's second largest city. From the passenger seat at the front of Gerry's jeep, with the window down, I could hear that we were overtaking heavy lorries and smell their exhaust fumes.

Gerry painted a vibrant picture of the endless stream of humanity on the road. Most were walking, barefoot. Some were on bicycles. Others were pulling or pushing large wooden carts mounted on car wheels, laden with goods for the city's many markets, which were full of people selling all sorts of vegetables, fruit and herbs. Africans carry everything on their heads – a cage of chickens, bread or firewood. They balance their load on a kind of skullcap with raised edges, called a *nkhata*. I imagined the markets of Blantyre to be a real melting pot of myriad activities, and sometimes the sounds struck me as chaotic.

While I was affected by the poverty and difficulties the poor faced, that first visit was a gentle introduction in comparison to my next visit two years later. I returned to Malawi in 2001. Samson Halu, an Ethiopian, was looking after the projects supported by Children in Crossfire and had lived in Malawi for several years. I had met him during my first trip. Lately he had been alerting us to a developing famine. His warnings were reinforced by increased media reports. The combination of unusually heavy rain in 2000 and a drought in 2001 meant that food resources were reaching a critical level. The government had allegedly sold off reserve stocks, such as maize, so by late September/earlyOctober the country was in trouble: on average, 130 people were dying each day from lack of food and hunger-related illnesses.

Once I realised how critical the situation was, I contacted my cousin Seamus McKinney, who worked for a widely read regional newspaper, the *Irish News*. Could he ask his editor to run an appeal on behalf of the people of Malawi, highlighting the developing famine? Seamus arranged for me to meet his bosses.

I travelled to Belfast with my colleague, Ursula Moore. We met with Jim Fitzpatrick, the chairman of the *Irish News*, his son Dominic, the managing director, Noel Doran, the newspaper's chief editor, Joanne Daly, head of marketing, journalist Maeve Connolly, and Hugh Russell, the well-known photographer. I told them about Children in Crossfire's work in Malawi and what I had recently found during my field trip. I emphasised how critical the situation was and that international help was urgently needed. It was vital that humanitarian organisations such as Children in Crossfire got to work immediately. While we couldn't save the lives of everyone in the famine-stricken areas, we could at least help to save some, and I felt a compelling responsibility to do what little I could. I appealed to Jim, Dominic and the rest of the team to get behind Children in Crossfire.

It was the start of a wonderful friendship between myself, the Fitzpatrick family and the *Irish News*. Dominic said that the newspaper would like to get behind the appeal, and in the subsequent days we discussed the best approach. He agreed to send a photographer and journalist with me and John Ryan McLaughlin, Children in Crossfire's head of community fundraising. I suggested to Dominic that he should come too: once he had seen the situation and the work of the charity for himself, he would be more committed to helping us, both now and in the future. I also asked if I could invite John Linehan, better known as May McFettridge, the character he portrays during his hilarious performances. While most people see only his funny side, I knew him to be compassionate and caring too.

I had first been introduced to John around 1997 by a friend, Maureen Lindburg, and part of my strategy in establishing Children in Crossfire was to invite various celebrities to draw public attention to it. I had always loved John's sense of humour and I'll never forget my first meeting with him in Belfast. We met in a pub and John made the mistake of asking me how I had lost my eyesight.

It was the ideal opening. I decided to push the boat out and tell him the full story. I was hoping that by the end he'd have so much sympathy for me that he couldn't refuse to get involved with Children in Crossfire. I gave him an A-to-Z blow-by-blow account of what had happened. I must have gone on for thirty minutes. Eventually, when I ran out of steam, I paused for his response. After a moment's silence, he said: 'Holy God! I only asked what happened to you. I didn't expect the Gettysburg Address!'

I nearly fell off my chair laughing, and so did Maureen. It was the last thing I'd expected after my tear-jerking tale, which was what made it so funny. But that's John Linehan and that's what makes him so special. In the months and years since that meeting, I have discovered he has a heart of gold. We became, and remain, great friends. And what was more, he became one of our greatest supporters, making himself available wherever possible and often at great cost to himself.

I knew that if I could persuade John to come to Malawi with us, he would be a powerful ambassador for the charity on his return. Thankfully, Dominic had no objections, so John travelled with us to the famine-stricken area. The *Irish News* covered the entire cost of the trip, which I was very grateful for.

Before we left, I met with John, Maeve and Hugh to brief them on what I had found on my recent trip. I told them it was possible the situation there had deteriorated and that we should be prepared for heartrending sights and sounds. We also discussed the role each of us would assume on our return.

At the end of October 2001, we flew to Malawi for four days. First, we visited a distribution centre in the Dedza district of the country where people gathered to receive a quantity of soya bean mix for their families. Each bag weighed a kilo and was about the size of the sealed packet you'd find inside a family-size cornflakes box. That had to last each family for a month. Water was added to the mix and turned it into a sort of porridge. This was their lifeline. Guidelines for distribution had been agreed with villagers and their chiefs and involved weighing children. If they registered below a certain weight, their family was considered to be in a critical condition and, therefore eligible for relief.

We were all shocked by what we witnessed. Many people who were turned away seemed borderline and none had any excess body fat that might increase their chance of survival. It was clear that within weeks the same people would qualify for relief – if, indeed, relief was available by then. About six hundred people were sitting quietly in a nearby field, awaiting assessment and, hopefully, food. Some had walked long distances to get there. Many hadn't eaten for several days. It was heartbreaking when they found their journey had been in vain and that they did not qualify for the soya bean mix. When they noticed Dominic, John and me, they came to us and began to plead for help.

'Can you help us?'

'Can you give us food?'

'What are you here for, if you cannot do that?'

Dominic spoke loudly and clearly so that as many people as possible could hear him: 'We cannot promise you food today. In fact, we cannot promise you anything today. But what we will promise you is that very soon we will be back in Ireland and we will make sure that your story is heard by our people and we promise we will try to get you help.'

Meanwhile, a man was walking around with a small paper bag, scouring the ground for seeds that might have fallen from the bags during distribution. It was a real culture shock: we had come from a throwaway society to a place where literally every little grain mattered. The hardest part for us all to cope with was the children. Unlike their parents, they didn't seem to know how close to death they were inching. Some were running around, still smiling and acting like children, yet they had no food. As we left, we passed people walking along the dirt tracks barefoot, carrying the bags of soya bean mix on their head or under their arms and, in some cases, on the handlebars of bicycles. They were the lucky ones.

The next day we drove to the village of Ajibu. I will never forget what we encountered there until I die. It was probably ten miles from the main road, but because we were travelling on dirt tracks, our progress was slow. When we eventually got there, we discovered forty-two of around five hundred villagers had died from hunger in the previous week. That included twenty-four children and amounted to almost 10 per cent of the population.

We stood outside a mud hut where, a few days earlier, an entire family of seven had died within two hours. In desperation, they had walked into the bush, picked poisonous berries and eaten them; their agony had traumatised their neighbours and friends. Villagers escorted us to the cemetery along a narrow laneway. Five minutes later, we stood beside rows of freshly dug graves. There were no headstones, only small gatherings of rocks. Some graves had four rocks, others six and one had seven; the number of stones indicated how many people had been laid to rest in each grave. Each day a new grave was opened and whoever had died was buried in it. There was no such thing as a family plot.

I had the strangest feeling standing at these modern-day famine graves. During the early 1990s, when I was taking part in the famine walks, I had visited some of the mass famine graves from the Great Hunger of 1845–9. They were part of Ireland's tragic history. Now, at the beginning of the twenty-first century, I was standing at a new famine grave. I felt as if I had one foot in the past and the other in the present. For the first time I could empathise with how Irish people must have felt when they were burying loved ones who had died from hunger. It is incomprehensible that a century and a half since the Great Irish Famine, in a world that considers itself modernised and advanced, the scandal and sheer injustice of hunger, poverty, pain and all the suffering that accompanies famine is all too real. I was totally overwhelmed.

Coming away from the graveyard, I walked with local village women, most of whom could speak English. I told them that what we had found was horrific. One woman replied with words I have often quoted since and which will remain with me forever: 'There is one thing worse than dying from hunger. It's watching your children die from hunger.'

When we left Ajibu, we were all very quiet. I was particularly conscious of John Linehan's silence, for his sense of humour was what kept us going during those four days. For at least an hour, nobody spoke and I sensed that tears were being shed.

On the third day, we visited a small rural hospital in the Theola district of Malawi. In famine, people don't die only from hunger. Most deaths are caused by hunger-related disease. The body's immune system begins to fail so that vomiting and diarrhoea become life-threatening, with typhoid and cholera never far away. At the hospital, we came across a baby girl named Clare. To our group she looked no more than six months old, but the doctors told us that she was a year and a half. Her mother had died from HIV/AIDS at the age of twenty-one, and Clare's situation was equally dire as she had been born with the virus. For the same reason, half the children at the hospital were not expected to survive.

Dominic, John, JR and our two newspaper colleagues, Hugh and Maeve, were shocked by the conditions we found at the Theola hospital, which were less than basic. There were few comfortable beds such as we are used to seeing in the Western world. Instead, people lay on the floor, some with only a mat for comfort. In one of the villages Hugh befriended a wee boy, whom he called Frank. Frank followed Hugh everywhere, partly because of his camera – all children in Africa seem fascinated by them. Hugh was so taken with Frank that he would have given him the shirt off his back. He shared a lot with the child, and I have no doubt that Frank remains an important memory for him.

When we left Malawi, we were determined that we would all do our very best to help the people we had encountered by bringing their story to the people of Ireland as soon as we could. Less than a week after our return, the entire management and staff of the *Irish News* were committed to helping Children in Crossfire save lives in Malawi. Their campaign began with a wrap-around cover for the paper that carried a full-page photograph of a child we had met during our visit. Inside, several pages were devoted to telling the story, in words and pictures, of famine-stricken Malawi. Over four days, the newspaper made the appeal on behalf of Children in Crossfire, so all of our staff were briefed and ready to respond to any public enquiries and, we hoped, donations that might follow.

This was new territory and we didn't know what to expect. We weren't even sure what we might hope to achieve by way of a target. I remember discussing with Dominic whether we should set it at £25,000. We decided against this in case we fell short and were disappointed. Inwardly I was hoping for £10,000 or £15,000.

From the minute our office opened on the first day of the appeal, the phone was ringing with people donating money. We were almost overwhelmed. Then, on the second day, the mail began to arrive in quantities we had never previously experienced. On the third day, there was even more. Within three weeks, the appeal had surpassed all our expectations. Public donations reached close to £250,000. Through Irish Aid, the development agency of the Irish government, we received a further €750,000.

I telephoned Samson, project manager in Malawi, and told him the good news. He could hardly believe it and I heard hope and excitement in his voice. We discussed how best we could use the resources we now had, and over the next six months we fed somewhere in the region of 190,000 people in the area we had visited. We also purchased a drilling rig to assist communities in locating sources of clean water.

In January 2002, the rains arrived in Malawi and the situation improved dramatically. Normally there is one harvest per year, but in some areas it was possible, due to the condition of the soil, to have a second. This was known as winter cropping and we had been able to help with this, so I was delighted to see that the project was successful. In a global context it was but a drop in the ocean, but everyone involved in trying to help save lives among the people we had met during our visit felt heartened. For some, at least, we had made a difference.

Dominic Fitzpatrick and I decided we had to let *Irish News* readers know how their money had been spent and the successes it had achieved. As part of the emergency appeal, Children in Crossfire held a fundraising golf tournament and dinner in Belfast. More than a hundred golfers played and were joined by their partners in the evening. It was near the end that

I discovered the then deputy first minister for Northern Ireland, Mark Durkan, was there. The last time he and I had been in touch was several years before when he had invited the Long Tower folk group to sing at his wedding. Now he told me he'd be happy to help Children in Crossfire in whatever way he could; all we had to do was ask. So I did: would he be willing to travel to Malawi on behalf of Children in Crossfire, then tell *Irish News* readers how their money had been spent? He agreed straight away.

In January 2002, Mark, his wife Jackie, my colleague Ursula Moore and I left for Malawi. It was my second visit in less than four months. Samson Halu met us and brought us to the Theola and Dedza districts. Malawi was more or less as it had been on my first visit in 1999. People were smiling, food was growing, the rains had come and I could feel that despite the ongoing challenges of being a poor country, a corner had been turned. At least for now people were safe, and I felt a deep satisfaction at the small contribution everyone involved in helping Children in Crossfire had made.

Mark saw the drilling rig bought by *Irish News* readers pumping clean water from deep below the ground. It had the capacity to drill an average of two hundred wells each year, with a maximum total of a thousand, some of which would be capable of producing enough clean water over thirty years for up to two thousand people.

With the rain, the dusty tracks we had driven along in early November were now muddy. The vehicle slid back and forth as we travelled out to the villages and rural hospitals we had helped. From time to time it got stuck, and I smiled at the thought of Mark Durkan, deputy first minister of Northern Ireland, out shoving and pushing, sometimes digging with his bare hands, to get our wagon moving again. His visit to

Malawi was very positive and worthwhile. It enabled us to feed back news to all our donors of how their efforts had made a difference to the lives of fellow human beings – people they would never meet in this life, but some of whom they had undoubtedly saved.

Over the past twelve years I have visited other developing countries, such as Tanzania and Ethiopia in East Africa, The Gambia and Ghana in West Africa and Bangladesh in Asia, and have met so many warm and friendly people. Despite the difficulties they face in their daily lives, they somehow find happiness and joy in living. All of the cultures I have encountered are rich and vibrant. I especially love the music of Africa, Asia and Latin America. Music is important because it gives me the colour and atmosphere of a country. I know that in Africa they wear very colourful clothes, but I can't appreciate them. However, through their music, especially the four-part harmony for which Africa is famous, I see beauty beyond colour in their voices and rhythm.

The unrelenting grind that people in the so-called 'third world' or 'majority world' must endure has affected me deeply, but I have had many positive experiences. I have met people of great dignity, determination and humanity, and discovered how the kindness and generosity of ordinary people in Ireland and elsewhere benefit others directly. It has all inspired me to continue with the work. No matter how small a donation might be, together we can change people's lives.

# 19

# Meeting the Dalai Lama

One day when I was working at the Children in Crossfire office I had a phone call from a Helena Schlindwein. She wanted to know if I'd be interested in becoming a member of a committee that was making plans for a forthcoming visit to the Derry area by His Holiness the Fourteenth Dalai Lama of Tibet. She told me that it was being sponsored by the World Council of Christian Churches and was still a year away. However, since the Dalai Lama had expressed the wish to meet victims on all sides of the conflict in the North of Ireland, it was important to begin making the arrangements now. The committee would be inviting a small group of about thirty victims, and since I had been blinded in the Troubles, I might be able to help in developing a process sensitive to the needs of victims across the entire community.

Over the year, the committee met quietly to plan for the visit, which was set for 20 October 2001. The venue was to be St Columb's Park House in the Waterside area of Derry. The Dalai Lama, we were told, had several engagements on that day. He would spend two hours with the victims, then attend a tree-planting ceremony in the grounds of St Columb's Park House, which had nothing to do with us.

My knowledge of Tibet's history and the Chinese occupation was limited. I was aware that His Holiness, many monks and refugees had fled their land for the safety of India. Other than that, I knew that he was considered a man of peace and reconciliation, for which he had won the Nobel Peace Prize. As his visit approached, I got more and more excited.

On the day of the Dalai Lama's visit, we gathered early. As the thirty victims of the Troubles arrived with the committee members, the excitement grew. The chairperson, Maureen Hetherington, was extremely nervous: we were gathering together people from different political and religious sides of the conflict. However, as soon as the Dalai Lama arrived in the room, any tensions, anxieties or fears that had been present in advance evaporated. His Holiness has an aura of happiness around him and when he smiles he emits positive energy. I sensed an immediate wave of relaxation flow over us. I heard him laughing and sensed the warmth of his smile.

When he eventually sat down, he spoke personally to everyone present. It is always interesting to hear people from a different culture speak a language they aren't fluent in. I'll never forget his question: 'What is your complaint?'

'Tell me your complaint,' he would say to people. If an Irish or British person asked such a direct question, it might be considered offensive, but because he was speaking in his second, or perhaps even third, language, everyone present knew what he was trying to convey.

Those present began to tell their stories to His Holiness. He listened intently and offered some words of advice and comfort. I remember one woman, towards the end of the session, saying, 'Your Holiness, you have helped me today because for years I couldn't forgive the men who killed my husband.' She had felt that by forgiving his killers she would be betraying her husband. It was a heartfelt and moving moment in which I realised what a powerful influence for good the Dalai Lama is in the world.

I was taken by his logic and the simplicity of his explanations. He had spoken about the power of forgiveness and had addressed the issue of betrayal. It was clear that as the woman had listened to him speak about how it is possible to forgive without betraying the memory of your loved one, she had found solace and peace.

Then came my turn: 'What is your complaint?'

I told my story briefly, adding that I had always forgiven the soldier who shot me. I also told His Holiness that I had taken great encouragement from his message of forgiveness and compassion: I had come to realise, I said, that forgiveness is a gift primarily to myself, and that sometimes I didn't understand my ability to forgive but that I had found freedom in it.

His Holiness responded, 'You might be blind, but you can see further than people with eyesight.'

'Your Holiness,' I said, 'I wonder could you phone up my wife and tell her that?' The room erupted and, above the chuckles, I could hear the Dalai Lama leading the laughter, which set me off too.

When the meeting ended, we all stood up to say our goodbye to him. We were all under the impression that you could not touch him above the shoulders, but he soon put paid to that idea. He hugged everyone. When he came to me he grabbed my arms, stood still for a second or two, then gave me a hug. I thought that that would be my last contact with him. I'd understood that he would have lunch in a room set aside for him and his entourage and that the rest of us would eventually drift away. But His Holiness decided he would have lunch with everyone and, to my amazement, I was placed beside him at the table.

It was one of the most extraordinary experiences of my life. The Dalai Lama insisted on serving me my lunch. He filled my plate with food and poured my drink. He handed me my knife and fork and throughout lunch kept asking me, 'Are you okay, Richard? Do you want some more food or drink?'

During lunch, His Holiness asked me to elaborate on what exactly had happened to me, then told me a little about where he was based in Dharamsala, India, and about the Tibetan refugee children who lived there. He asked me if I would be interested in coming to his monastery to talk to them because he thought it would be good for them to hear my story and that I had forgiven the soldier who had blinded me. I told him that I'd love to.

Then, out of the blue, he asked, 'Do you know what I look like?'

'No, Your Holiness.'

He took my hands and insisted that I feel his face and bald head.

I am aware that some visually impaired people do this to try to develop a sense of people they are comfortable with, but I never have. However, when the Dalai Lama asks, you don't refuse, so I felt his head. The only thing I could think of saying was, 'God, Your Holiness. You have a big nose!' He burst into laughter and so did I.

At the end of the meal, I stood up, thinking we were finished, that once we had said goodbye, that would be it: after all, our guest was about to conclude his visit with the tree-planting ceremony. I was also conscious that I shouldn't be hogging the limelight. The Dalai Lama stood up too and expressed his gratitude to everyone for sharing their stories with him, then said goodbye. He walked towards us all and I stood back, but he took my hand and led me towards the door. Before he left the room, I thanked him and said goodbye, but he wasn't having that. 'Come! Come!' He pulled me outside and across the grass to where the tree-planting was to take place.

At this stage, I was totally bewildered and besotted by the man. There were lots of journalists from the newspapers, radio and television awaiting his arrival. One asked His Holiness, 'How do you think your visit went here today?'

I was flabbergasted when he responded, 'Don't ask me. Ask him.' He was pointing at me, apparently, and continued, 'It's people like him you should be talking to.'

I had to say something, so I said, 'It's been a very positive visit and we've got tremendous encouragement from His Holiness. We appreciated His Holiness putting the victims first and I think it was a very worthwhile experience for all involved.'

I was still feeling a bit awkward at having been dragged into the centre of attention, and when a radio interviewer distracted the Dalai Lama with an impromptu interview, I decided to disappear. Maureen Hetherington was close by and I asked her to take me back to St Columb's Park House. I meant to walk towards the vehicle His Holiness was travelling in and position myself there to say a final goodbye.

Suddenly I heard footsteps running behind me and a voice calling, 'Wait on your friend. Wait on your friend.' It was His Holiness. I couldn't believe what was happening to me. Here I was, being chased by the Dalai Lama, who was describing me as his friend!

After we had finally said goodbye and he had left, I returned to St Columb's Park House and sat down to catch my breath. Even now, some years later, when I think about that extraordinary day, I am filled with a warm glow. At the time of writing, I still haven't followed through on the Dalai Lama's invitation to visit him in Dharamsala, but I intend to do so.

The day after his visit to Derry, I was due to speak at a public event at the City Hall, Belfast, at which His Holiness was also speaking. I left Derry early with Father Maningi, who was visiting from Tanzania, Don McLeish, chairperson of Children in Crossfire, and Maureen Hetherington. We arrived in Belfast about nine-thirty a.m. Next to the main auditorium there was a room where about a hundred people had gathered, awaiting the arrival of the Dalai Lama. Several dignitaries, including the victims' minister, Adam Ingram, were among them. When His Holiness arrived, I was standing in the middle of the room. He spotted me, made a beeline for me, took both my hands, put them on his face and said, 'It is your friend.' I was speechless.

His Holiness insisted that I sit beside him in the room and asked what time I had left home to get to Belfast. I said I'd got up at about six, and he responded, 'I get up at three-thirty and then I meditate.' I asked him was he looking forward to the day's events and if he was tired from all the travelling he had been doing. He replied, 'No, I feel very good.'

Just then one of his minders interrupted: 'Your Holiness, can I introduce you to the minister, Adam Ingram?' I still have a chuckle at that because I think – in all honesty – His Holiness would have sat chatting to me but for that interruption.

He had made me feel very special in the same way that Bishop Daly, Ted Kennedy and the Pope had. My encounter with the Dalai Lama was another step along the road to accepting, and continuing to accept, blindness and its consequences.

For the tenth anniversary of Children in Crossfire, I invited His Holiness to be the keynote speaker at a conference reflecting on global issues affecting the children of the world. I was amazed when he accepted almost immediately.

# 20

# 'Do You See Darkness?'

When I speak in schools, particularly primary schools, I find that children are fascinated by blindness. I can understand this for I was, too, as a child. I remember once seeing a blind man walking along a street in Derry. I wondered what it must be like for him, and when I got home I closed my eyes and groped my way around the house, using my hands as buffers. One benefit of having had sight is that I can relate to children in a way that they understand because they, as I once did, tend to close their eyes and think that that is blindness. I suppose, in some ways, it is.

The main questions children ask me are: 'Do you see darkness? Are you looking into blackness?' They are puzzled when I tell them that isn't the case at all. The mind's eye, or imagination, is an incredible thing. I visualise everything without even trying. So when I'm in a room or walking along a street, noises help me paint pictures in my mind. All the sounds I hear, including echoes, converge to create pictures. And because I once could see, I also imagine in colour.

I might not be correct, but when I'm sitting on a sofa, for example, I'll imagine it to be a particular colour. Leather, for example, often evokes dark brown. Depending on the type of wood on a floor, I might see it as either a grainy brown or light brown. I can see windows in my mind's eye, for often that is where external sounds are coming from. Therefore, depending on the time of day, I would imagine it as bright or dark. If I go into a room where there are no windows, I generally imagine this as a dark room. If I hear a bird fly past, I immediately imagine the bird – I might see a thrush when in fact it's a swallow. I can tell if a bird is big or small by the sound of its wings. Swans, because of their wingspan, tend to make a great swoosh with each flap.

I don't have to concentrate or make an effort to conjure up these images. It happens without any thought. What I see may not resemble what you might see if we were in the same room, but I'm able to visualise my environment, which helps me to create a context for wherever I am.

In the years immediately after I was blinded, I found it important to listen to how companions described scenery around me. Now it's less important because I see through sound. When I stand on a hilltop overlooking a spectacular view, or near the edge of a cliff with waves at its foot, I no longer need anyone to describe to me what they see. I'm already seeing it through my hearing and no matter if, or how often, they describe it to me, I will still revert to the images in my mind's eye, created by sound.

As a blind person, I was always searching for a suitable hobby. Eventually, through my brother Liam, I discovered Citizen's Band radio. In the late 1970s, CB radios were being brought into Ireland from America. As with the Herlihy walkie-talkies, they were illegal in Northern Ireland, which, of course, made using them even more exciting.

I remember sitting in Liam's car one evening outside his house. He had a CB radio wired into it and we were talking to people in other parts of Derry and beyond, with what sounded like really fancy names they called their 'handle'. It was all part of the CB language code. I recall names like 'Beverly Hills Babe', 'Southern Comfort', 'Lady Queen', 'Beauty Queen' and 'Queen of Sheba'. I was also intrigued by the fancy names tagged to familiar places around Derry. The Creggan estate where I lived was known as 'Beverly Hills', and Gobnascale in the Waterside was 'Galveston'. Eventually, of course, I bought a CB radio, and my handle was 'Hi-Fi'.

CB radio enables you to move onto sidebands through which you can transmit to other CB radio operators in different parts of the world. Atmospheric conditions, known as 'skip', play a big part in determining the range of transmission. When these were good it was possible to talk to operators all over Europe and, on a really good day, across America. Through my chats with them I learned I could become a qualified 'amateur radio operator'. In my spare time, I studied and eventually sat the exam, passed and received a B licence, which allowed me to operate on local frequencies. Later I took an exam for an MI3 licence, which, when I passed, allowed me to transmit all over the world on a variety of amateur bands.

I bought all the necessary equipment. I had a big 20-metre beam aerial, which sat on top of a tower with a rotator that turned the aerial to face the direction in which you wanted to transmit. If I wished to transmit to North America, I pointed the aerial due west. If I wanted to transmit to Brazil, I faced it south-west, and so on. Europe, of course, was due east.

This introduced me to a whole new community and over

the years I had some really interesting conversations with people in Brazil, Australia, South Africa, Barbados, other parts of the Caribbean and islands in the Mediterranean. One evening I made contact with someone in Tel Aviv, Israel.

I loved this period of my life. Being a radio operator was so interesting. It's a great hobby for a blind person because all you need is your microphone, your radio and the ability to talk, which as anybody who knows me will tell you, has never been a problem for me!

In 1997, a group of us, including some members of the folk group and, of course, Rita, Naoimh and Enya, holidayed in France at a caravan campsite. One day someone came up with the idea of hiring bikes and going for a cycle down to the beach. I was excited at the possibility of a tandem, but when we got to the bicycle shop they didn't have one. Undeterred, I decided to hire an ordinary bike and the plan was that Orla Mc Swine and Ursula Moore would be assigned to help me. One would cycle slightly in front and the other slightly behind. I would respond to their instructions, just as I had with Paul Moran many years before in Malin Gardens.

I was delighted when I managed to cycle down to the beach with no major problems, and when we got back to the campsite, I wasn't for giving up and decided to cycle around it. Many different European nationalities were staying there, some of whom, I'm sure, would have found the idea of a blind man riding a bike hilarious while others might not.

Orla, Ursula and a few others were with me. The more I cycled, the more my confidence grew and at times I was actually overtaking them. At one point, I came flying around a corner and started heading down a hill on a gravel track. Suddenly I lost control and went off into a grass verge. I had no idea where I was and my two companions seemed to have disappeared.

Several German tourists were outside their caravans, having just set up beautifully adorned tables for a barbecue they were in the process of cooking. Some were standing while others were sitting with an early evening beer – to be confronted by a madman bearing down on them. According to my friends, I was heading straight for them at around twenty miles per hour. Orla and Ursula told me that the Germans were totally bewildered – I'd have paid to see the shock on their faces. In the nick of time, my two friends rediscovered their voices and shouted, 'Turn left. For God's sake, turn left!' I swerved and ended up as a crumpled heap in the bushes.

When my friends caught up, they were relieved to discover I was okay. Out of relief, we all started laughing, but I'm sure the poor Germans must have been wondering if they'd picked the right campsite for their holiday.

Another summer we all went to Florida and took a day trip to Wet 'n' Wild, a fun park themed around water. I can't swim and have a real phobia about my head going under water, so I was naturally apprehensive. As the day progressed, my female companions prevailed on me to join them on various slides and rides. The first was a gentle and enjoyable experience, which made me more confident and therefore agreeable to more daring adventures. A snaking slide, with water flowing down it, poured itself and you into a pool below. I agreed to go down it on the condition that three or four people would be waiting at the bottom to catch me. Then there was a slide that involved sitting into a large rubber ring that made its way along a river of rapids. I managed them all without falling off and had so much fun in the process that I wanted to keep ascending the ladder of risk. I began to go on bigger, faster and bumpier rides.

The largest slide in the park was called, I think, the Summit Plummet. The management boasted that it was the highest water slide in North America. It was a nearly vertical drop of seventy-six feet and involved climbing numerous flights of stairs. When you got to the top, you lay on your back, crossed your arms over your chest and, with a gentle nudge from the attendant, became an ever-faster projectile hurtling at breathtaking speed towards the bottom. The slide was so high that none of our group had the nerve to take it on. The required body position, which resembled that of a corpse in a coffin, was enough to give anyone the jitters.

We had a fantastic day at Wet 'n' Wild and were all feeling very satisfied as the first of us made our way back to the lockers to change our clothes. Five or ten minutes later, Máiréad Gallagher, Maria Clarke and Deborah Clifford arrived into our locker room, pumped up for having conquered their fear of the Summit Plummet. 'Richard, you should do it. You'd love it. It's brilliant!'

Naoimh and Enya kept saying, 'Go ahead, Daddy! Give it a go!'

I could feel the nerves building in my stomach and instinct was telling me not to. But my head reasoned, 'God knows when I'll next be in Florida. If I don't do it now, I might never get the chance again.' Another voice in my head remonstrated, 'You've had a great day. Forget about it. It's only a slide.'

Crazy though it might seem, I pulled off my shirt and shouted, 'Okay, I'm gonna do it! I'm gonna do it!' In my excitement, I turned to grab one of my female companions by the waist.

A male American voice asked, 'You're going to do what?'

I was lucky I didn't end up with a broken nose. All I could do was apologise, much to the amusement of our group, who were falling around the locker room in fits of laughter.

After that I would have looked a real wuss if I'd backed out, so I was determined to follow through. The entire group accompanied me back to the big slide to witness my performance and reaction. The three who had already done it, Máiréad, Maria and Deborah, agreed to be at the bottom with Naoimh and Enya to collect the remnants. Ursula Moore and Sarah Gallagher, Máiréad's twin sister, agreed to accompany me to the top.

We climbed the endless flights of stairs, on the way meeting people coming back because the view from the top was too frightening – 'No way! No way!' There was a guy just in front of me who told me, 'This is the second time for me going on this slide and the first was like having an enema. Don't forget to cross your legs as well as your arms – and remember, you don't slow down until you hit the water.'

My God! I thought. What have I got myself into?

The three of us continued our climb. The whole way up, Sarah was encouraging me: 'It's no problem. Don't be worrying.' She was actually dancing on the way up and clicking her fingers to the music playing in the background. The plan was that when we got to the top, Sarah would go first to alert those at the bottom that I was next. Ursula would follow me. But at the top Sarah's confidence momentarily deserted her when she saw the drop. She looked over the edge and all I could hear her say was, 'I can't do it. I can't do it.' So that left me.

I could feel the nerves in my stomach tightening, but I was determined not to back out. I simply switched my mind off: 'It lasts for about thirty seconds and I'm not going to think about it.'

There was a bar across the top of the slide to hold on to while you manoeuvred yourself into position. I lay back and the attendant told me to place my arms across my chest. It felt ominously like making the sign of the cross before being executed or going for an operation. Some people push themselves over the edge. Others need a nudge. The attendant asked me if I wanted to push myself over. I told him, 'If you wait for me to do it, you'll be standing all night.'

Then I heard him call to the people below, 'Blind man coming down! Blind man coming down!' With that, he placed his hands on my shoulders and pushed me over. And what a thrill!

I don't think my body touched the slide the whole way down, but I made the fatal mistake of not crossing my legs. My swimming shorts disappeared up my backside and the water battered my groin relentlessly. After I'd hit the water and been pulled from the depths by my friends, I couldn't stand up straight for several minutes. I felt like a footballer who had forgotten to protect himself before a free kick cannoned into his bits.

That sensation soon passed, though, and I never regretted the experience. It was, quite simply, fantastic.

Our whole group had been nervous as I plummeted from the summit, knowing how anxious I was about being submerged in water. Deborah, Máiréad and Maria were standing close to the bottom, waiting for me, and when I had come flying down the slide, they'd jumped into the water to help. At first after they'd caught me there was silence as they'd looked at my face and wondered, How is he? But when they realised I'd loved it, they gave me a big cheer and several pats on the back.

Thereafter, I never looked back. When next we went on holidays to Disneyland or Universal Studios, I was head of the queue to try out all the roller-coasters. For years before, I'd often hide from the Florida or Californian sun, sipping a Coke, while the rest of the group tried out all the rides. Not any more! The Summit Plummet had introduced me to a mental trick that helped me overcome my fears. I reasoned that since nothing terrible had gone wrong in several thousand rides before mine, and since each ride lasted about a minute and thirty seconds, nothing much could go terribly wrong this time. I learned to close my mind and just explore whether I enjoyed the ride or not.

My first roller-coaster was Space Mountain in Disneyland. I remember stepping into the carriage and the safety bars settling on my shoulders. It was a narrow spacecraft-type vehicle, so there was no one else beside me. I remember thinking, Oh God! Why am I doing this? Then it slowly began to move and gradually rose higher and higher. The next thing I remember is the sensation of my brain being squashed against the back of my skull. We shot from nought to sixty m.p.h. within two seconds. At the end of it, I was totally energised and and went straight back for another go.

When I went to Six Flags in Los Angeles, I rode all the roller-coasters. One of the biggest, Goliath, had incredible G force. Now I'm a total convert. I love roller-coasters.

Blindness can be fun. I seldom miss an opportunity when I can use mine to make people laugh, sometimes at the expense of others. One such occasion presented itself several years ago in Dublin, in the early stages of my friendship with Don Mullan. He and I were having lunch in a hotel. It was a fairly generous lunch after which I asked Don to bring me to the gents. He placed me facing the urinals, but I needed to use a cubicle. He led me to one and I closed the door. So picture the scene. I am in a cubicle and Don is standing outside waiting for me. I realised he was beginning to feel uncomfortable when he said, 'Hurry up, Richard, in case somebody comes in.'

Just then I heard the door of the gents open. A guy came in and went to the urinals. However, he was conscious of a man shuffling close to the cubicles and apparently glanced uncomfortably over his shoulder once or twice at Don. Don clearly felt the need to say something: 'Don't mind me, I'm waiting for someone. Isn't that right, Richard?'

I couldn't miss the opportunity. I remained completely still and silent. The guy peeing had looked at Don as he spoke, but with no response from me, the pressure increased. In desperation, Don pleaded, 'For Christ's sake, Richard, isn't that right?' By now I was ready to burst out laughing, but I managed to contain myself.

At this point I heard the guy zip up his trousers. He didn't wait to wash his hands. As he made a hasty retreat I heard him say to Don, 'I know all about it. You're in for an early lunch!' I'll leave it to you to decipher what he meant, but as soon as I heard the door close, I collapsed into hysterical laughter. I laughed even more when I heard Don protest, 'You bastard!' I could almost feel the steam and heat coming off his red cheeks!

I had another experience around public toilets some time later. On this occasion, the pressure was on me.

I went for the day to Belfast with two friends from the Long Tower folk group, Brídín Murphy and Maria Clarke. It was a beautiful warm day and we visited a couple of pubs during the afternoon. Eventually we found ourselves sipping beers outside a bar called the Cutters Wharf. Nearby I could hear water falling, similar to a lock on a canal.

I've never been a heavy drinker. The most I enjoy is a couple of glasses of dry white wine if I'm out for dinner. That day, however, Brídín, Maria and I were having so much fun that I was now into my third or fourth beer, much more than I would normally drink, and I was happily inebriated. At a certain point, though, I realised I needed to relieve myself. My dilemma, of course, was that I was with two young women, both in their early twenties, and I was embarrassed to ask them. Back then, some fifteen years ago, there were few disabled toilets. I'm not even sure if legislation had been passed to make them compulsory in public places.

In any case, the sound of the running water nearby was becoming torturous, and eventually my discomfort became so unbearable I had to ask my two female companions for help. They were certainly not going to take me into the gents, so they decided the only thing they could do was take me to the ladies. Maria went in first to ensure that the coast was clear. After a couple of scouting missions, she came out and said, 'Come on, quickly, Richard.' So I ran with Maria into the ladies' toilet and closed the cubicle.

I had just begun to pee when I heard Maria announce in a whispered panic, 'Richard, stay still. There's someone coming!' I was, of course, feeling tipsy, and that combined with the fact that I was in a ladies' toilet made me giggle.

Obviously the woman who had come in to use the toilet heard me. She said nothing to Maria, who was pretending to wash her hands, but next thing we knew, she was coming back with a member of staff. Maria whispered, 'Richard, don't come out!'

Two seconds later, I heard the woman announce, 'There's a gentleman in that cubicle.' Suddenly there was loud knocking on the door and a voice demanded, 'Excuse me. Identify yourself.'

At this stage, I had a decision to make. Should I open the

door and identify myself or stay quiet? I also had Maria's instructions lodged in my mind. I decided to remain quiet.

I then realised that if the women decided to look under the door, they would see my shoes and know that a man was in the cubicle, so I stood on the toilet seat. Then I realised my head might be visible above the door, so I got down on my hunkers. And still the banging continued and the voice demanded: 'Identify yourself! Identify yourself!'

By now I had stopped giggling and for some silly reason I thought I was in real trouble. My heart was pounding. However, eventually the two women left and Maria hissed, 'Quick, Richard. Out!'

We ran from the ladies' toilets, through the pub and outside, where we plonked ourselves on the bench beside Brídín, who, of course, was oblivious to our adventure. Maria was too embarrassed to look back to see if we were being watched from inside, but our escape didn't go unnoticed. Brídín pointed out that there was a trail of toilet paper attached to my shoe that led right to the ladies' toilet.

# 21

# Journey into the Past

I'm not exactly sure when I first began to think about the soldier who shot me and what it might be like to meet him, but the seed of the idea might have germinated not long after I was shot. I have no clear answer as to why I wanted to meet him. The only thing I can say with certainty is that being blinded by a rubber bullet was one of the most significant events of my life and it involved two people: the soldier and me.

I had been curious for many years about him. I knew nothing about him: not his name, his age or his rank. I didn't know how he felt about firing the rubber bullet or, indeed, why he had fired it. These were questions that exercised my mind during quiet moments, as I lay awake at night or travelling alone on a bus or train. While I was curious and hoped to find answers to these questions in the future, I never made any determined efforts to meet the man. However, I indicated during various television and radio interviews over the years, in Ireland and the UK, that I wanted to.

As the years passed, particularly the twentieth and twenty-fifth anniversaries of my shooting, the idea of meeting the soldier became more and more important to me. Thankfully, the Northern Ireland Peace Process, underpinned by paramilitary ceasefires and British demilitarisation, began to act like a poultice, slowly draining away the poison that had festered over three decades of bitter political and religious strife. Voices that had often barked with bitterness sounded softer and more reasonable, and in spite of inevitable difficulties and setbacks, people who had once appeared to be intractable enemies began to open up to one another. As the level of trust evolved on both sides, so did my desire to find the soldier. I hoped that the new climate of developing friendships between the communities of Northern Ireland, between Northern Ireland and the Republic of Ireland and between Ireland and Britain might correspondingly provide him with enough reassurance that it would be safe for him to come forward and meet me.

Many times in my thoughts I wondered where in the world he might live, if, indeed, he was still alive. I wondered if he was married and had children. I wondered, too, if he ever thought about the young boy he had blinded in Derry in 1972. Did he ever wonder what had happened to me and how I had turned out? There were times when I wondered if he was still a soldier patrolling the streets of Derry or elsewhere in Northern Ireland. I didn't even know if he was English or Irish. I wasn't obsessive in my curiosity but all those thoughts and questions would exercise me from time to time.

You may be surprised to learn that when I did think about the soldier, it was never with anger. I felt no resentment or hatred towards him. This is something I find hard to explain and I fully acknowledge that individuals and families on all sides of the Troubles who have been injured or bereaved may not feel as I do. My acceptance of blindness and my lack of bitterness or self-pity made it easier on my family, particularly my mother, who, in that four-month period in 1972, had had to cope with the loss of her brother and then with her son being blinded. The trauma of both incidents had unleashed a deluge of stress on a harmonious and loving home. I have no doubt that my blinding sent my father to an early grave and resulted in my mother's breakdown. In the circumstances, therefore, I readily acknowledge that bitterness was an option, but it was one I chose not to take. To some, that might seem irrational and inconceivable. It didn't feel irrational to me.

Despite their sorrow, my parents never once displayed any bitterness or anger towards the soldier, and that, to me, is the key to my own acceptance of blindness and lack of bitterness. My mother often tells a story about a day when she was walking to Mass at our local chapel, St Mary's, with a neighbour. As they came out of Malin Gardens and turned right onto Creggan Broadway, they encountered a British Army foot patrol walking towards them. One of the soldiers said courteously as he passed, 'Good morning, ma'ams.' My mother reciprocated with equal courtesy.

The woman walking beside her was taken aback. When they had passed the patrol, she asked, 'How can you speak to him? Those were the guys that blinded your son!'

My mother replied, '*He* didn't blind my son, so why should I have any anger towards him?' Undoubtedly, I had absorbed her attitude.

My parents lived their religious beliefs with quiet dignity and preached them without words, so when I think about not having any hatred and anger, I think about my parents. Who and what I am today I owe primarily to them. They were good Catholics, who practised their religion with fervour and deep faith. Their belief in a loving God and, in particular, the example of Jesus on the cross, convinced them that forgiveness was the key to inner peace. Consequently, while it must have been difficult for them, they had already forgiven the soldier and bore him no grudge.

I believe they didn't have it in them to be bitter or angry. All they were concerned about was their children, one of whom was now blind, and making sure that we were all given every chance of making it in the world. They were particularly concerned about helping me to survive what had happened and they firmly held onto the hope that some day I might get my eyesight back.

Over the years, a couple of journalists had attempted to find the soldier who had blinded me. I'm not sure how hard they tried, but I recall an American coming back to me and saying she had reached an impenetrable wall. Then, around 2001, the situation began to change. At the Children in Crossfire fundraising dinner in Belfast, organised by the *Irish News* in aid of the people of Malawi, I was introduced to a documentary film director, Brendan Byrne, of Hotshot Films. He was a friend of Dominic Fitzpatrick, the managing director of the *Irish News*, sponsors of the event. After we had chatted for a while, Brendan asked if I'd be interested in meeting him again to discuss the possibility of him making a documentary film about my story.

We had a couple of meetings thereafter. I told him about a fundraising trip I had made to Newport Beach, California, with my colleague Ursula Moore. JR's uncle, Monsignor Bill McLaughlin, was parish priest at Our Lady Queen of Angels Church there and arranged for me to speak about Children in Crossfire at all Sunday Masses during our visit.

At the end of one service I was approached by a man who

asked, 'Would you mind telling me the nature of your injuries?' The directness of the question caught me off guard. To be honest, I didn't know the full nature of my injuries. I knew only that I had lost my right eye and couldn't see with the left.

The man, while courteous, continued to probe with a series of in-depth questions in an attempt to ascertain the full extent of the damage. When he realised I was a bit fazed by his questioning, he introduced himself as Dr Ed Wong and explained that he specialised in eyesight. Then he stunned me: 'Depending on the nature of your injuries, there might be a possibility of you getting your eyesight back through artificial means.' I knew I was in a very wealthy part of America and that many successful people lived in that parish, so if this doctor lived there, he was probably a leader in his field. He said he'd like to see me again before I returned to Ireland.

A few days later, Dr Wong explained to me that technology was available to allow a small camera, the size of a pea, to be connected to the brain. He was working on new instruments that would improve its performance considerably. Surgeons could insert a tiny electrical circuit into the skull near the vortex that sent electrode signals to the part of the brain that controls eyesight. The tiny circuit board had hundreds of electrodes through which electric pulses were transmitted to the brain from the tiny camera located on a specially designed pair of glasses. While in its infancy, the technology had already proven that the process was capable of creating images.

He told me that surgeons were in the process of developing laser technology to vastly increase the information capacity being transmitted to the brain. While the technology was limited at present, resulting in a limited interplay between shadows and light, it was hoped that, in time, images via laser would make it possible for the brain to receive and interpret moving objects in colour.

As you can imagine, I was intrigued and began to contemplate something I had never thought about before – that I might recover my sight. But at the same time I was very cautious. Indeed, Ed was too: he didn't want to raise my hopes unrealistically. The technology was at the very early stages of development and he didn't know whether the vortex of my brain was functioning normally. He explained that if it had been damaged in the shooting, there was little chance of the technology working for me.

I returned to Ireland in such a relaxed state that I forgot about my consultation with Dr Wong. Such is my contentment with my blindness that I didn't even bother to find out whether or not the vortex of my brain was working. Some people might think I was afraid to know so I pushed it to the back of my mind. Quite honestly, I didn't even make that decision. While in some respects my encounter with Dr Wong opened up the possibility of eventually getting some form of eyesight, it wasn't something I was desperate to achieve – and that's how I feel today. Yes, of course I'd love to have my eyesight back. I'd love to be able to see for all of the reasons I've outlined. But for me, blindness – obviously I can't and don't speak for other blind people – is not such a terrible option.

Brendan Byrne listened with interest when I told him about my encounter with Ed Wong. I also told him, as I had other journalists, about my desire to meet the soldier some day. And I told him about my passion for Children in Crossfire, which, after all, had brought us together at the fundraising dinner in Belfast. After our meeting, he approached BBC Northern Ireland to see if they would be interested in my story. Several weeks later he called to say that he had the go-ahead and the funding to make the documentary.

Brendan and I had several conversations about the soldier. Naturally, he saw the possibility of my meeting him as a pivotal element of the documentary and, no doubt, so too did the BBC. However, I told Brendan that if he managed to find the man, we had to proceed with sensitivity and care. The soldier had to understand that I had wanted to meet him since long before the documentary had been mooted, as a fellow human being, not as an adversary or enemy. Even if Brendan succeeded in discovering who he was, there was always the possibility that he might not be able to film our meeting: if the soldier agreed to see me, he might not want cameras around. I also wanted to make sure that, whoever and wherever he was, he knew I wasn't making contact because of the documentary.

I worked with Brendan on the film for more than a year, including a journey to the US and Canada, during which we explored the new technology into helping blind people regain some semblance of sight. While I did not have a desperate need to get my eyesight back, I was curious to find out more about artificial eyesight, so when Brendan presented me with the opportunity, through the documentary, to go to America and learn more, I was excited. However, the more I learned about the subject and the type of sight it provides, the more I realised it wasn't for me. The process involved invasive surgery on the brain and would produce confusing images and shadows, which, in my view, wasn't sight.

We also went to Africa to film projects in Malawi supported by Children in Crossfire. Throughout, Brendan updated me on the progress he was making in trying to find the British soldier. It was very slow and I wondered if he, too, might hit that impenetrable wall.

I had given Brendan all the information I had collected about the incident. From this, we knew the regiment the soldier had been attached to, the 5th Light Regiment, Royal Artillery. We also knew that his unit had been located in Rosemount, Derry, at the time I was shot. This considerably narrowed down our focus to about eighty serving soldiers – but we were trying to unravel the circumstances of an event that had happened more than thirty years before.

Hotshot Films, through one of their researchers, Derryman Joe McCauley, made contact with former soldiers in the British Army who had served in Derry in 1972. Some remembered the incident in which a ten-year-old boy had been shot and blinded, but not who had fired the rubber bullet.

I spoke to a few soldiers myself in my quest to find the man who had blinded me. An ex-soldier at the British Army's Veterans Association invited me to England to attend one of their functions so that I might ask publicly for help in finding the soldier. I did not, however, go ahead with this, partly because I wasn't sure if it was the right approach to take.

Eventually, Joe McCauley had a breakthrough. One of the soldiers he had been communicating with came up with a version of a name, but it was unclear: the man he spoke to wasn't sure of the exact pronunciation of the soldier's surname. At least it was something to go on. In a last-ditch effort, Hotshot Films decided to hire a private detective who had been a member of the Northern Ireland security services. Through additional confidential enquiries, they gained access to documents that included a list of names of the soldiers who had been in the unit in May 1972. One of the names on the list corresponded closely to the one they had been given. The man's whereabouts were eventually established and the private detective, who had a letter addressed to the soldier from me, approached him.

While we were 99 per cent certain we had the right man, we still needed confirmation from the soldier himself. My understanding was that the private detective explained he was there because a documentary was being made about a man in Northern Ireland. This man had been shot and blinded as a ten-year-old boy in Derry in 1972. He then asked, 'Are you the soldier who fired the rubber bullet?' The soldier confirmed that he was. Once this was established, my letter was handed to him. I had spent several weeks formulating in my mind exactly what I wanted to say, and in the end I tried to convince him that I had no motive other than reaching out to him in friendship and forgiveness.

When he opened the envelope, Charles read:

> Dear Charles,
>
> I realise that this letter may come as a shock to you. However, I sincerely hope that you will give it your utmost consideration. While it is not easy for me to write this letter I also understand that it is possibly not easy for you to read.
>
> I will start by introducing myself. My name is Richard Moore and I live in Derry, Northern Ireland. Thirty-three years ago on 4th May 1972 I think we came across each other for the first time. I was 10 years old then. Whilst on my way home from school I was shot and blinded by a rubber bullet. I am glad to say that I have never allowed this experience to hinder me or make me feel bitter in any way.
>
> As you are probably aware by now, not only from the first two paragraphs of this letter but from the person who so kindly has delivered it into your hand, it is my understanding that you are the soldier that fired the rubber

bullet. I genuinely have no concept of how a letter like this would impact on you. However, I would like to reassure you that it is not my aim or motive to make you feel bad or guilty in any way. Also, I would like you to know that you have absolutely nothing to fear from me.

Sure being shot, and blindness itself, has had a major effect on me and my family. I won't try to pretend to you that it didn't. The person I am, the work that I do, the life that I have has been as a direct result of that day. However, I was able to adjust to my situation very quickly and I soon got on with rebuilding my life. I would not have been able to do this if it were not for the support that I received from my family, friends and the people of the Creggan estate where I lived.

Since being shot I feel my life has been a very positive and interesting experience. I am a very happy and contented blind person. I would like to share a little bit of my story with you. The reason why I want to do this is to give you a sense of the type of person I am and why I want to meet you. I fully understand and respect that you probably don't want to meet me. You have got on with the rest of your life too and I do not want in any way to interrupt that. I appreciate that you may have put the whole incident behind you and have no desire to re-visit it but I hope that you are open to meeting me.

After I was shot I eventually returned to the Rosemount Primary School. I then went to St Joseph's Secondary School where I did my O levels and A levels. Eventually I qualified from the New University of Ulster with a degree in 1983. I met my wife Rita whilst doing my A levels. We married in 1984 and have two beautiful daughters. Naoimh is 16 and Enya is 13 years old. I also learned the guitar and became self-employed as a publican. I became actively involved in a variety of community issues and groups.

However, today I am the director of a relief and development organisation called Children in Crossfire. We support projects throughout the world in Africa, Asia and South America. We work with some of the poorest communities on this planet and I must say that it is extremely rewarding work. I also believe that I ended up in this line of work as a direct result of my life experience.

So, why do I want to meet you? I can answer that question but not entirely. From the day I was shot I can honestly say that I have never felt a moment's bitterness towards you. I really can't explain this myself as it seems illogical but that's how it is. As I am sure you can appreciate, the most significant thing to happen to me in my life is being shot and blinded. There was only one other person directly involved that day and that's you. I would therefore like to meet you in order to complete that circle. So instead of all these years just thinking about it, to really meet you in the flesh and get a sense of the sort of person you are.

I believe I am a very balanced, confident person who has learned to deal with blindness and its effects very well. I genuinely don't need to meet you out of some kind of desperation. I just would like to meet you and you never know we might even become friends!

At the moment I am the subject of a BBC documentary. This documentary, which is still being filmed, is focusing on various aspects of my life, my work, interests etc. Also, it is exploring the possibility that I might be able to get my eyesight back through artificial means. It was through the making of this documentary and my expressed desire to meet you that you were discovered. However, I must emphasise that the documentary is not my motivation and I am not writing to ask you to take part. In fact, quite the opposite. I am happy to meet you where you want, when you want and I will respect your wishes totally to remain anonymous. Since I was a young teenager I have always said that I would like to meet the soldier who shot me and now I can't believe after all these years that you are sitting reading my letter.

Charles, I hope you will say yes to me. I am confident you won't regret it in any way. Northern Ireland was a difficult place in 1972 and the subsequent years for everyone. Many people from all sides have suffered as a result of the Troubles. I genuinely believe that no one has a franchise on suffering. Everyone was affected by it. However, sadly, I also believe that when people find themselves in unusual circumstances they sometimes do unusual things. Well, I don't think that anyone could dispute that Northern Ireland was an unusual place. I also realise that not everyone feels like me and I fully respect that. However, notwithstanding the difficulties, it is important that we learn from the past. That we do not allow the hurts and hatreds of the past to be handed on to our children.

If you decide not to meet me I will respect your wishes entirely. I often wondered over the years if you ever thought about me or even knew that I wanted to meet you. Now at least I know for certain you are aware of my desire. The rest is up to you. However, if you do agree to meet me privately I think the significance of such a meeting should not be underestimated. In Northern Ireland at the moment we are in the process of building peace. It is not going to be easy. There are many thousands of people out there who have been so badly hurt by the troubles. I think the fact that you and I are prepared to meet, put the past behind us, not allowing our experience to have a negative effect on our future, is a very strong message.

I have enclosed my address, telephone numbers and my e-mail address. Please feel free to contact me in whatever way you prefer. You might even wish to communicate initially via a third party, that's fine by me. If you do decide to write then the most private way is by e-mail. My computer talks and I am able to access my e-mails independently.

Finally, thanks for reading this letter and I look forward to your response if, and when, it comes.

Richard Moore

Within three weeks, I had a response. It was delivered by Brendan and his camera crew on 26 September 2005. I was delighted, simply because the soldier had replied. Some of the words he had used seemed insensitive, and Rita became angry when she read the letter, but I could also sense that there was a degree of compassion which, I believed, made room to build on.

Rita was upset because she felt that the soldier appeared to have little regret over what had happened. When I let my children, Naoimh and Enya, read the letter and asked their opinion, Naoimh told me straight up that she didn't like him. I was saddened by all of this because I wanted my connection with the soldier to be a positive one for my entire family. I wanted Rita and our children, as well as myself, to grow to like him.

I was now in the middle of a roller-coaster of emotions. On the one hand, I didn't regret having reached out to offer the soldier forgiveness and friendship. On the other, I began to doubt that I was doing the right thing. Was I raking over old coals? Was I reopening old wounds? At one stage I wondered if I was simply creating the opportunity for the soldier who had blinded me to attempt to publicly justify what had happened. How would my wider family feel about that? I also saw that it all had the potential to collapse around me. But I still wanted to do it. I knew now that it would take time and I was determined not to let the documentary get in the way of a healing process I had envisaged long before the film had ever been discussed.

I found it interesting that the soldier's letter bore no address. Neither had he signed it. Understandably he was cautious, perhaps even on advice from a lawyer. I didn't know, but I could understand why he might frame his letter in a way that would limit my ability to snare him if, indeed, that had been my long-term intention. Of course it wasn't, but it would take him a while to realise this and I therefore needed to be patient. I felt his second paragraph was revealing. He admitted that he wasn't sure who would be reading his letter. It appeared, on balance, that he was more inclined to present his case. I still saw positives in the letter and wanted to build on them. Undeterred, I chose to forge ahead.

In difficult situations, I take time out to ponder. By nature, I'm a thinker and spend time weighing pros and cons. This was one of the most difficult situations I'd had to cope with and I was feeling churned up inside. I was trying to manage a complex emotional process, and at the same time I was an integral part of it. I was very quiet throughout the day and wanted to be alone with my thoughts. That night, I felt the need to talk to someone I trusted.

I was lucky enough to be surrounded by good friends who

always gave me solid advice. Just as family and close friends had been an important part of my ability to deal with being shot and with blindness, such friendship and support were vital after I had discovered the soldier. They affirmed my decision to keep going. I realised I couldn't expect the first letter back from the soldier to be the answer to all our prayers or, indeed, the perfect response. It was going to be a long process.

The evening I received the letter, I phoned Don Mullan. He asked me how I felt about it and I told him I wasn't sure. 'Do you want to hear it?' I asked, and when he said he did, I called Naoimh and asked her to read it to him. As I listened to the innocence in her voice and the weight of the words she was conveying, I had to breathe deeply to keep myself in check. The letter had been read to me earlier by one of Brendan's documentary crew, but it was a whole different experience listening to it read aloud by my young daughter.

> Dear Richard,
>
> I very much welcomed receiving your letter, though I must say I was certainly a little surprised, as I never knew that you wished to meet me. I had hoped to reply a little earlier, but various recent events and a number of attempts at trying to produce exactly what I wanted to say by way of response has resulted in this delay!
>
> I am most certainly happy for a meeting to take place as having read your letter I am in absolutely no doubt that you are indeed an extremely well balanced person, and all the reasons you give for wishing to meet seem to me to be totally positive. May I suggest that as you are happy to travel we get together in Edinburgh sometime in late October or mid to late November. At present I am a little uncomfortable with putting my home address at the top of

this letter (not that I have any reservations about you knowing it) but I have no idea who else may read it. Can I therefore ask that you reply via our contact giving some suggested dates and I will let you know which are the most convenient from my viewpoint.

From what you say it is clear to me that despite your blindness you have made a great success of your life, and the charity you currently direct attempting to alleviate the suffering of children throughout the world is a very worthy cause, and one I would certainly like to hear more about. It seems strange that you say 'I also believe that I ended up in this line of work as a direct result of my life experience', the starting point of which was the terrible injuries you suffered as a result of being struck by the rubber bullet fired by me on the 4th of May 1972.

I feel I must at least give you some idea of the background to this tragedy from my perspective, though I entirely accept that your view may be very different. As we are both aware 1972 was certainly an extremely violent time in Northern Ireland for very many people with almost daily shootings, bombings, sectarian murders, etc. The Army had people being very seriously injured, or killed, on an almost daily basis between January and the late summer of that year. The one event of that period I do remember in great detail was a bomb blast that killed two of the soldiers in my own organization. Regarding the events leading up to the 4th of May, I cannot recall when, but sometime before that date I was ordered to protect Rosemount police station with a detachment of soldiers. In reality it was more like a small fort than a police station, and there was no likelihood of members of the public visiting it, or police leaving it to walk the streets! We were certainly shot at daily, and a number of fairly crude homemade nail and petrol bombs were thrown over the wire, few of which fortunately functioned. Various other unpleasant incidents occurred which also kept us very busy. The incidents that took place during the night of the 3rd and during the day of the 4th of May were much the same, though frankly with the passage of some 33 years I certainly cannot remember exactly what happened and when. However I eventually fired a rubber bullet and you were tragically the recipient. I believed at the time that the action I took in the circumstances prevailing was justified. The subsequent Military and Civil Police enquiries also believe that firing the rubber bullet was justified. I therefore did not feel any guilt at the time, nor do now. However as soon as I found out how seriously you were injured, I felt deep shock, great regret and great sadness, and had I had the luxury of knowing what the outcome was to be, I most certainly would not have fired. Very large numbers of rubber bullets were fired at that time and the ones I saw hit people appeared to have little or no effect. The shock has obviously gone, but the sadness and regret, though somewhat faded with the passage of time, are still there. And with the advantage of hindsight I wish I had not taken the action I did.

It will be good to meet you and have a chance to talk. I also very much hope and pray, that perhaps there is a possibility using state of the art technologies, of you recovering your sight.

I look forward to hearing from you.

As Naoimh read the letter, I suddenly felt the magnitude of what was happening. So many thoughts and memories were racing through my head. When she had finished, I thanked her and asked her to close the door after her. As soon as I heard her leave, I started to cry.

At that moment I preferred to be alone: I didn't want Rita or the girls to see me in such a state. I was anxious to carry them forward with me in the process – if they saw me hurt, their instinct would have been to protect me by rejecting the soldier and encouraging me to end the process. Painful though it might be, I wasn't ready to do that and still felt I had a long way to go before I knew the wisdom or folly of it.

I don't know why I cried that evening on the telephone with Don. Maybe I was feeling sorry for myself, for despite my upbeat nature, tragedy is interwoven throughout my story. I certainly cried because of some of the things Charles had said that I found more than a little insensitive. But I cried most of all because it is sad to hear a sixteen-year-old girl reading a letter aloud from the man who had blinded her daddy. The innocence of her voice, in contrast to the seriousness of the letter, was all too much for me at that moment.

In an attempt to make sense of it all before I slept that night, I decided to articulate some of my thoughts and emotions – I needed to clarify them and get them out of my head. When I came off the phone from Don, I went to my computer and wrote.

> *26 September 2005*
> Today I received the long-awaited letter from Charles, the soldier that blinded me. I am not sure how I feel. I am delighted that he has decided to write to me and agreed to meet me. However, there were parts of the letter which I just found difficult to listen to. On one hand, I always knew the soldier would have his own version of what

happened. I understood that if he was to live with himself and the actions that he carried out then he would need to justify to himself what he had done, perhaps to let himself off the hook. Whilst, on the other hand, in my mind anyway, it is impossible for anyone to justify firing a rubber bullet at a 10-year-old boy wearing a school bag on his way home from school. The challenge for me is allowing these two thought processes to exist side by side. Can I do that? I don't really know at this stage. However, I think I should try.

I have embarked on a journey, maybe I didn't realise how difficult this journey would be at times, but I know now. Today I am filled with emotion. I just couldn't wait for the camera crew to leave so that I could be left alone with my thoughts.

Many thoughts went through my mind whilst listening to the letter being read to me. I thought of my mother and father, what they had to go through, the hurts and mental anguish which brought my mother to breaking point. I also thought about the many adjustments I had to make and still have to make in my life. The countless Christmas mornings and times in the lives of my children when I was denied seeing their smiles, their funny faces, excitement in their eyes and so on. Then there are my brothers and sisters and what they went through. Their lives also changed forever.

However, I think the saddest part of the letter came at the end when he wrote, 'The shock is obviously gone but the sadness and regret, though somewhat faded with the passage of time, are still there and with the advantage of hindsight I wish I had not taken the action I did.'

I can't explain it but that sentence brought me to a

place that I never thought I would go. I think for the first time in 33 years I was hurt.

I decided to ring my close friend Don Mullan. I always trusted Don's judgement on many things but in particular this issue. On this occasion I just wanted to get his angle or his perspective on the letter. What happened next I didn't expect and couldn't prevent. Whilst I was on the phone to Don my daughter Naoimh entered the room, and I asked her to read the letter over the phone to Don. With the combination of the sense of emotion I was already feeling and Naoimh, my daughter, relaying the words of the soldier to Don, when she handed the phone back and left the room I broke down and started to cry with Don. I never did this before.

To say I cried because of one thing or even the letter itself would be wrong. I cried because at last I was connecting at a human level with the man who had played such a significant part in my life. I cried because it is sad. A 10-year-old boy did lose his eyesight and life can be cruel. I cried because my children have only known their daddy to be blind and that is not fair. I cried because no child should ever have to read a letter like that. I cried because I heard two things in the letter which are, and will always be, hard for me to deal with: he did not feel guilty then and does not feel guilty now, and yes I probably felt a little bit sorry for myself too. However, I think I cried most of all because I needed to let go of all that emotion and because I'm not as strong as sometimes I think I am. I now know that before this process is finished there will be more tears but I will be stronger as a result of it.

In spite of everything, the most important thing for me was

that the soldier had responded. While he didn't sign the letter, I knew, for the first time in thirty-three years, what his name was. And he had expressed the desire that we might meet one day. This, more than anything, was a step forward.

That night and over the next few days, I realised that the soldier and I were, at long last, going to meet. I also realised that there was no way I could allow Brendan to film and potentially jeopardise the meeting. It was an awkward dilemma, for Brendan had helped me to track the soldier down and I knew that my meeting the man was an integral part of the documentary. It was essential, however, that he understood that I wasn't meeting him as a publicity stunt. I gathered from the letter that Charles had wanted to present his case to me and I felt that at our first meeting, a camera and other ears would be too intrusive for both of us. A camera crew would stilt the meeting, make it awkward and less natural, and might even corral us into reactive positions regarding the shooting. In front of a camera, Charles might feel compelled to justify his actions, and for me that wouldn't achieve anything. In fact, if that were to happen, it would give out altogether the wrong message of what I was about.

I wanted the meeting to be a positive experience for us both and hoped it might help others to deal with their hurts. I had no idea what Charles might say, and while I felt strong enough to deal with most of it, I was concerned by Rita and my children's reaction and worried that it might compound the pain that they and others, especially my wider family, and possibly people injured during the Troubles, had felt. After all, I believed my father's life had been shortened by the trauma and my mother and siblings had had to carry an enormous burden of hurt. I wasn't going to allow a situation to develop that would traumatise them again, thirty-three years on.

Through the international experience I had gathered with Children in Crossfire and the cross-community work I was involved with in Northern Ireland, I had gained an insight into the sensitivities and difficulties that might arise. I worked – and still do – with a woman called Maureen Hetherington, who was the co-ordinator of the Junction, a peace and reconciliation centre in Derry, and another community worker, Eamon Dean of the Holywell Trust, on the fringes of their peace projects. Part of their work involved bringing together ex-paramilitaries, ex-British soldiers and victims of state and paramilitary violence. Their work meant taking major risks, so I had a good understanding of the challenges and pitfalls in facilitating such a delicate process. If I were to meet the soldier, those issues might arise. To have a television camera stuck in the middle might damage any possibility of friendship irreparably, and I couldn't allow that to happen.

Thankfully, I trusted Brendan Byrne as a film-maker and considered him an honourable man who was genuine about what he was trying to achieve with this documentary. He was disappointed when I told him that he and his crew would not be present at my first meeting with the soldier, but I knew he understood where I was coming from.

What transpired next is best described as a complicated series of negotiations during which I was anxious to meet Brendan's wish list for the documentary, but also not to compromise an important personal process that would continue, I hoped, long after the BBC had broadcast the film. I felt frustrated that Hotshot Films was the broker between the soldier and me and that the only way I could communicate with him was through them. I was not in control of a situation of enormous importance to me. Apart from his letter, I didn't know what Charles was thinking. Was he wondering if I wanted to expose him simply to get a bit of publicity for myself? I knew he had my letter in which I had outlined my aims, but I was still worried. Understandably, Hotshot Films had assured the soldier that I wouldn't be contacting him directly.

However, as piggy in the middle, I was finding the entire process increasingly stressful. At one stage in the autumn of 2005, I decided not to meet the soldier after all. Trying to keep everybody happy was too complicated. Maybe another opportunity might present itself some time in the future. At least somebody now knew his name and address, and he had acknowledged that he had discharged the rubber bullet that had blinded me. To protect the integrity of the process, I was prepared to give up for the moment my lifelong desire to meet the man.

Once I had made that decision, the tension left me, and so did the acute headaches to which I am sometimes prone. Thankfully, the emotional roller-coaster that I was on began to level out. With that weight off my shoulders, balance and contentment returned to my life. I'm so grateful to Don and another very good friend of mine Father Paul Farren for listening to me endlessly during this time. I couldn't have dealt with it without them.

At the end of October, I went to Guatemala on a trek to fundraise for the charity. When I returned to Derry, I was a whole lot fitter than I had been when I'd left, but I was also determined that I was never going to camp again in my life! Guatemala was a great experience and great fun, but my back was killing me and the sleepless nights had taken their toll. After the long-haul overnight flights back to Ireland, the first thing I did when I got home was to fill the bath and soak for an hour in steaming hot water. I had dozed off when my mobile phone startled me. It was Maureen Hetherington.

'Richard, do you know the Dalai Lama's in Belfast today?' she said excitedly. 'I have two tickets to hear him speak in the Waterfront. Would you like to go?'

In seconds, my exhaustion was forgotten. Sleep or no sleep, there was no way I was going to miss His Holiness the Dalai Lama.

Because of my previous encounter with him, I was just happy to be in the audience and to listen to his talk. I was taken aback, though, when His Holiness began to talk about his encounter with me a few years earlier. He recalled that the last time he was in Ireland he had met a man who had been shot and blinded but had forgiven the person responsible. I sat there, thinking, That's me he's talking about! Part of me wanted to jump out of my seat and shout, 'Your Holiness, it's me! I'm here!' Of course, he had no idea I was in the audience.

When his talk was finished and he had left the stage, Maureen and I got up to leave. Just then, one of the Dalai Lama's party, who was in the audience, approached me and asked, 'You're the person he was talking about, aren't you?' She asked me to wait, as she said His Holiness would surely want to meet me once he knew I was present. Maureen and I waited in the main auditorium, which was quickly emptying. The woman returned and breathlessly exclaimed, 'He was about to drive away, but when he heard you were here, he jumped out and he is waiting downstairs to greet you!'

She and Maureen led me downstairs to meet the Dalai Lama for a second time. As soon as he saw me, he embraced me with a great bear-hug and I told him how delighted I was to meet him again. He draped a ceremonial white silk *kata* scarf around my shoulders and we spent five or ten minutes chatting. I told him I'd found out the name of the soldier, that we had exchanged letters and that I was hoping to meet him some day, hopefully soon.

I said goodbye to His Holiness, then went back with Maureen to her car for the ninety-minute drive to Derry. We were both elated by what had transpired and I was still in awe that one of the great global icons, a man revered by Tibetan Buddhists as their god-king, would not only remember me but had been clearly delighted to see me once more. Again, he had invited me to visit him in Dharamsala to tell my story to Tibetan refugee children.

During that journey back to Derry, I had an insight that galvanised my determination to meet the soldier. My story had made such an impression on His Holiness that, five years later, he not only remembered our first encounter but also thought it worthy of public mention. At that moment, I knew I had to make a concerted effort to meet Charles. I considered contacting him directly, even if it meant breaking confidence, but I hoped it wouldn't come to that.

The following day, I telephoned Brendan Byrne and the private detective Brendan had engaged to find Charles. I was now very anxious to meet the soldier and asked them to please get in touch with him. Brendan told me to forget about the documentary and filming. As far as he was concerned, he wanted to help me meet Charles. That came as a huge relief. I told Brendan I wasn't ruling out the possibility of being filmed with Charles at some stage, but I needed to meet him privately first, and if that went well and he was comfortable, our next encounter could be filmed. I was amazed at how quickly and easily all the obstacles that had seemed to exist had literally vanished overnight. If it hadn't been for that timely encounter with His Holiness the Dalai Lama, I don't think I would have made those calls. I can't help feeling that all of this was more than just a coincidence. I believe the energy of His Holiness had an important part to play in clearing that path.

I didn't hear anything for a couple of days, but eventually Brendan called with a date. Charles had agreed to meet me on Saturday, 14 January 2006. I let it be known that I was happy for him to choose the venue, and the only request I made was that he would be alone also. Charles suggested the Hilton Hotel at Edinburgh Airport and we agreed to meet there at twelve o'clock some two weeks hence. At last, the meeting was going to happen.

When Rita and my closest friends heard that I was going to meet him on my own, they were nervous, but I sensed there was nothing to be afraid of. Undeterred, I pushed on, determined to come face to face with the man who had plunged me into darkness. I had often wondered what I would say if I met him or what I hoped to get out of such a meeting. Well, this was the real deal: I was going to meet him. As the days passed, what I wanted to achieve became clearer. Certainly I wanted him to know that I didn't hate him, but I also wanted him to acknowledge some of the hurt his action had caused. I didn't expect him to say sorry, but to hear him say he understood the pain would be enough. I also knew that after I had met him, I might see things differently. I was grateful for my resilience: since my shooting, I have always bounced back from setbacks. I thanked God, then as now, for that attribute.

# 22

# Meeting the Soldier

In preparation for meeting Charles, I talked to my family and close friends. I was mulling over what I hoped to achieve. I didn't want Charles to feel he was there to be accountable to me. I had made up my mind that no matter what he was like, whether he was a very nice man or completely the opposite, I had forgiven him unconditionally and I wanted him to know this. I knew little about him, other than that he had retired from the army as a major.

I also told myself I wasn't going to Edinburgh with the expectation of an apology, although that would help to mitigate the suffering he had caused. I wasn't going to ask him to explain his actions on 4 May 1972; I wasn't going to put him in the dock or revisit the evidence. I was meeting him, first and foremost, because I wanted him to know that I totally forgave him and hoped that perhaps our shared experience might help others with forgiveness and reconciliation. Even if nothing dramatic came of our encounter, I wanted us to meet as two human beings whose lives had intersected through an act of violence during a tragic period of modern Irish history.

I was realistic enough to know that the soldier and I could not meet without talking about the events of 4 May 1972. In truth, there were some questions I wanted to ask him about the incident, but I also wanted to make the space for him to share his story with me. Equally, I needed him to accord me the same respect and provide me with the space to share my story with him.

I hoped that if we could trust each other and he understood that I wasn't coming from a position of anger or hatred, we might be able to discuss the hurts that had resulted from my shooting. Perhaps naïvely, I felt it would help me and my family if I heard him articulate an understanding of the pain his action had caused.

On a practical level, I was going to a meeting as both facilitator and participant, and I didn't know if I could manage that. How would I feel when he walked into the room? Would I start crying? I hoped not. Almost everything depended on the kind of man he was, on his reaction to me and on what buttons he would press inside me. Much was unknown.

As the day approached, I worried about my family. My experience of being shot and blinded had affected them too, and I needed the support of my family, my mother and siblings for what I was about to do. I needed them to come with me, at least emotionally. I needed to know I had the backing of the people who meant most to me in the entire world.

Also, I had to think about and be sensitive to other victims who had lost life and limbs in more than three decades of the Troubles. One morning before I went to meet the soldier, I was at home getting ready for work and listening to Radio Ulster. A news item concerned a woman in Belfast whose husband had been shot and killed by a plastic bullet fired by the security forces. I felt guilty that I was going to meet the guy who had fired a rubber bullet at me. The last thing I wanted to do was to hurt people who, like this woman, were still looking for justice for loved ones killed or injured during the conflict. I supported her quest for truth and justice; she was entitled to them as a basic human right.

With all these things on my mind, I decided, the day before I went to meet Charles, to visit my daddy's grave in the City Cemetery. As I stood beside it and talked quietly to him, I asked him for understanding and for the strength and support that I would need the following day. I asked him to be with me on the journey and hoped he felt I was doing the right thing. Then I went to visit my mammy. I had kept her updated on developments with the soldier, so she was aware of what I was about to do. If I had thought for one minute that she was uncomfortable with the idea or didn't want me to follow through, I would have found it hard to continue. But 'Old Flo', as we call her, never let me down. She made me a cup of tea and when we were sitting together, I told her, 'Mammy, I'm going to Scotland tomorrow to see the soldier who shot me.'

'Who's going with you?' I told her I was going on my own. 'Jesus, Mary and St Joseph! Are you wise?' Her primary concern was that I would be okay.

When I asked her how she felt about my meeting him, she pondered for a few seconds. 'Ah, well. Sure he's only a human being too.'

'I might bring him to meet you some day.'

Without missing a beat, she said, 'Richard, if you're happy with that, then I'm happy with it too.' Old Flo never fails to amaze me. Her strength and forgiveness are incredible. In all honesty, if – God forbid – someone blinded either Naoimh or Enya, I don't know if I could be as forgiving as she is.

I asked her for a photograph of her and my daddy together, as I wanted to show it to the soldier if the opportunity presented itself. Actually, I wanted it in my pocket so that I had a sense of their presence with me during the meeting. I intended to bring a photograph of Rita, Naoimh and Enya for the same reason. I wanted the soldier to see my children and in some way to realise that behind me and around me there were ordinary people and that I didn't live in isolation.

Rita and the girls knew that I wanted to leave for my meeting with the minimum of fuss. The evening before, we discussed whether or not they should all get up in the morning to see me off, but I didn't want that. I was afraid it would be too emotional for me. The more ordinary the day, the more in control I would be when I eventually met the soldier.

On Saturday, 14 January 2006, my mobile phone alarm woke me at five o'clock and I got up to prepare for my journey to Belfast International Airport. I had agreed with Brendan Byrne and Hotshot Films that they could film me leaving home and accompany me to the airport, but from there I was on my own and there would be no cameras. As I left the house, Brendan and the crew were waiting outside. The airport was an hour-and-a-half's drive and my flight was at eight-thirty.

Through my work with Children in Crossfire, I had travelled long distances all over the world. Today I was going to Scotland on a forty-five-minute flight, but it felt like the longest journey of my life. I didn't know anything about my destination or how I would feel at the end of the trip.

A gentle rain and mist followed us for most of the drive. I could hear the windscreen wipers making quiet sweeps. There was harmony in the soothing sound as we drove towards

Belfast. Brendan and the camera crew were in the car with me and interviewed me on the way to the airport. Strangely, this allowed me to focus on the meeting. Brendan asked me loads of probing questions about how I felt and what I wanted to say to the soldier, which helped me to organise my thoughts. I prayed for strength and felt sure that my father was with me in spirit.

As I made my way to the aircraft, I realised that I was feeling reasonably relaxed and positive. Indeed, I was actually looking forward to the experience. It was almost surreal. Even though it seemed a long time since I had first learned the soldier's name, I was still incredulous. 'Is this a dream?' I asked myself. 'Is this really happening? Am I actually meeting the guy who fired the rubber bullet?'

The flight landed at Edinburgh Airport on time. Good people seemed to surround me that day. I was escorted off the plane and brought to a taxi rank. My driver very kindly conducted me into the foyer of the Hilton Hotel and passed me on to the receptionist. She, in turn, led me to a comfortable sofa by a coffee table. A minute or two later, a porter approached and asked if I'd like a wee cup of tea. Of course, neither he nor the receptionist had any idea of the significance of this particular day in my life, yet their kindness added to it.

'I'd love a cup of tea and a biscuit,' I told the porter. He was soon back, placed the tray on the coffee table and proceeded to arrange the delft and cutlery for me. He asked if I'd like him to pour the tea, and directed my hand to where the biscuits were. When I went to pay him, he said he'd sort that out when I was finished. Ten minutes later, he was back, asking if I'd like a wee top-up. His thoughtfulness and friendship meant a lot to me. I was in a strange place, in Scotland on my own, and it was so nice that someone was treating me as I was used to being treated by people in Derry. It reinforced my belief that, no matter where you go, the world is full of good people.

I was *in situ* an hour and forty-five minutes before Charles was due to arrive, so I spent the time making phone calls. The first person I rang was Rita, to let her know I had arrived safely. Then I spoke to my mother. I could tell she was still concerned that I was alone: she asked where I was and who was around, but seemed to relax when I told her I was sitting safely in the foyer of the Hilton Hotel. I told her not to worry about anything, and explained that when the soldier arrived, I would be switching off my mobile phone, but as soon as the meeting was over, I'd give her a call.

Once I'd made contact with home, I relaxed. I had my talking-book machine with me, so I put on the headphones and started listening to *Freedom in Exile* by His Holiness the Fourteenth Dalai Lama of Tibet, though to be honest, I couldn't concentrate on it: I was too excited.

There were moments while I waited for the arrival of the soldier when I wondered if he had already come into the hotel and was watching me from a distance to make sure that I was alone. I wondered if he, too, was nervous. I even wondered if he might come in, look around and then decide, 'No! I can't do this.' How would I know if that were the case? I decided that if he didn't show by lunch-time, I'd order something to eat and head back to the airport in the late afternoon, as my flight was in the early evening. Instinctively, though, I knew he would come.

At about eleven-fifty, I heard footsteps approach the area where I was sitting and a mature, cultured British voice said, 'Hello, Richard. It's Charles.'

I stood up to shake his hand. 'Hello, Charles. Good to meet

you. Thanks very much for coming to see me.' The thirty-three-year wait was over.

With that, we launched into ice-breakers such as the time of my flight, when I had arrived and how long I'd been waiting. Charles said that if he'd known I was in so early, he would have come sooner. After that, the best way to describe the conversation is that it was like being on a first date. Sometimes we fumbled as we talked over each other, then politely apologised and waited for the other to continue with his point. Sometimes there were moments of clumsy silence and both of us would go to speak again, and it was just like fingers and thumbs and all things awkward. I had foreseen this possibility – that my mind might go into a blur, that the meeting might be over almost as soon as it started – and was determined none of that would happen. As a fall-back plan I had brought along an information pack on Children in Crossfire. If the silences became too prolonged, I would say, 'I must tell you a bit about the charity.' I could dwell on that for at least forty minutes, which would give us both time to relax.

While we did eventually talk about Children in Crossfire, it wasn't as a fall-back. I don't know if Charles was nervous or not, but I'd definitely settled down after about twenty minutes. I asked him how far he had travelled to our meeting, if he was married and had children. Eventually I broached the subject of the elephant in the room. 'Charles,' I said, 'I think it would be crazy if you and I sat here today and didn't talk about 4 May 1972. But at the same time, I want you to know I'm not here to dwell on it unnecessarily. Nor am I here to make you accountable to me over what happened.' I then told him that I recognised how difficult this meeting must have been for him and that I was delighted he had agreed to it.

Charles reciprocated by saying that he, too, was delighted

we were meeting. He said he totally regretted what had happened that day and that, in hindsight, he wished he had never taken the action he had, as the outcome had been appalling for me. What he said was not dissimilar to what he had written in his letter, but it was quite another thing to hear him say it. Words on a page can be cold and easily misinterpreted, but when you hear them spoken, other senses help you to interpret their deeper meaning. Hearing Charles, on this occasion, express his regret and hearing the words said with sincerity was an immense relief to me. My instincts told me he was genuine.

'Charles, look, I have a couple of hard questions I'd like to ask you, but I want to ask them in a friendly way. I'm anxious that you don't feel I'm in any way being aggressive.'

'No. Go ahead and ask your questions.'

'When I read your letter,' I continued, 'I found it difficult when you wrote that you felt justified in firing the rubber bullet. From my viewpoint, I find it hard to understand how you could feel justified in firing a rubber bullet at a ten-year-old boy, as I was then.'

He explained that at the time he had felt justified in his attempt to get those throwing stones to 'bugger off'. He said that, at the time of firing, he hadn't seen me and that he never meant to cause the consequences I had suffered. He repeated that if he had realised the damage that the rubber bullet was going to do, he would never have fired it and he wished now that he never had.

I listened intently to every word he spoke. 'Do I understand correctly that you are saying, Charles, that you are not justifying blinding me? That when you fired it at the time, you felt you had done it for the right reasons, but you're not justifying the outcome?'

'That is correct,' he answered. He went on to say that he did not use the word 'sorry' because he felt it would be wrong of him to leave me with the impression that he hadn't meant to fire the rubber bullet. 'The truth is,' he continued, 'I did mean to fire it. I just never meant to cause the damage that I did.'

I then asked if he was saying that I was a rioter at the time. 'No, I'm not,' he answered. 'Richard, I didn't even see you.'

I know it would be possible for anyone to pick holes in his answers. I realise that there were all sorts of arguments I could have developed, but I wasn't there to do that. I didn't need to do that. I simply thanked him for his honesty and told him I accepted what he'd said. 'Charles,' I continued, 'for what it's worth, I want you to know that I never had any hatred towards you and I don't now. I forgive you and I have always forgiven you for what happened to me that day.' He thanked me.

I also explained that the letter he had sent seemed a bit cold and insensitive and that when I had shown it to Rita, my wife, she had started to cry. I felt that Charles was saddened to hear this.

By then, both of us were relaxed and he suggested that we go for lunch in the hotel restaurant. What transpired thereafter was both surreal and, in many respects, very moving. Charles took my hand and laid it on his right elbow. He guided me down the steps, through the foyer and into the restaurant. He asked the waitress for a table and I remember thinking, I wish I could explain to this lady the significance of what is happening at this moment in front of her eyes. What she saw was a man guiding a blind man into the restaurant where she worked and helping him into his seat. What she didn't realise was that the man guiding the blind man was the person who had actually blinded him.

After we had ordered our lunch, I produced the photograph of my parents and me, taken in Lourdes a few months after I was shot. He took it and as he looked at it, I said, 'Charles, I just want you to know that my parents suffered badly after I was shot and my mother, I believe, was very close to a mental breakdown.' For the rest of the lunch, the photograph of my mammy and daddy lay on the table. I really felt that both of them were with me.

The next thing I produced was the photograph of Naoimh and Enya. He commented that they were beautiful children and asked me their names. As the afternoon progressed, we chatted on and I asked him about his career in the army and the different places he had been. He asked me about the work of Children in Crossfire, and expressed amazement at what we were doing.

There was a point during our meeting when I needed to go to the bathroom and had no option but to ask Charles if he would bring me. Again, the extraordinariness of the whole experience didn't escape me, and I wondered how he felt to be guiding around a guy he had blinded. But he seemed very comfortable and not at all nervous, as sometimes people are when they must lead a blind person.

After lunch, we went back to our seats in the foyer and eventually I said that I should be getting a taxi to go back to the airport for my flight. He insisted on driving me, and as he led me to the hotel car park and was paying his parking ticket, I still kept thinking how incredible this whole thing was. As he led me to the passenger seat of his vehicle, I thought, I can't believe I am now sitting in the car of the British soldier who blinded me.

We drove to the airport and he accompanied me inside to the ticketing desk. When the attendant suggested that he could leave me over at a seat and she would come and collect me in twenty minutes to assist me to the aircraft, Charles insisted on taking me for a cup of tea to pass the time. I was touched by his commitment and help, and that he didn't want to leave me. By now, we were becoming friends, and he even invited me to visit his home and meet his family. He said, 'I have a bed-and-breakfast and you would be more than welcome to come and stay. But not as a guest, as my friend.'

When it was time to go, he returned me to the check-in desk, where the young woman was waiting for me. Charles and I simply shook hands and parted, expressing the hope that we would meet again soon.

I was on a high because it had gone so well. I liked him. I really did. I had been worried that I might not, that I might find him rude or insensitive, but thankfully I felt that the guy I met had been honest and straight, and hadn't tried to say nice things just to please me.

When I was walking to the plane, my head was in a whirl. I was trying to process the thoughts and also to revisit the conversations we had had. The easyJet lady who accompanied me through Security and brought me to the aircraft was chatting to me, asking me how I was and whether I had been in Scotland for pleasure or business. I told her I'd travelled over from Ireland for a meeting, and she said she hoped it had gone well. I was bursting at the seams to tell someone what I had just experienced, so I began by saying to her, 'You know I'm blind?', then explained that I'd lost my eyesight after being shot in Northern Ireland by a rubber bullet when I was a boy.

I recall her saying, 'That's terrible, just terrible!'

I then said, 'Remember that gentleman who brought me to you?'

'Yes,' she replied.

'Well,' I continued, 'he was the guy who shot me.' I think at that point she must have thought she was guiding a complete lunatic, for she went silent and never asked me another question.

As I boarded the plane for my return flight to Belfast, I realised that the meeting had gone on much longer than I'd anticipated. I also knew that several people back home were anxious to know how I was and, given the long silence, would be worried about me. The last time I'd spoken to anyone was at ten o'clock that morning and now it was almost five o'clock in the evening. The doors of the aircraft were still open so I took out my mobile phone and began to text people frantically until I was instructed to switch it off. I wanted to let everyone know that the meeting had gone well and that I would ring them as soon as I landed on the other side of the Irish Sea.

It was a day I'll never forget: 14 January 2006. Now I place it with almost equal significance alongside 4 May 1972.

The following morning, I woke up in Derry with a really good feeling and for a minute or two I wondered why. Then I realised that something very special had happened the day before. I had sat in the foyer of a hotel and at a restaurant table opposite the guy who had fired the rubber bullet that had changed my life forever. It had been fantastic to tell him that I forgave him, and I was reminded that forgiveness is, first and foremost, a gift to yourself. Furthermore, it is one thing to forgive somebody, but it's an extended blessing to be able to tell them face to face that you forgive them.

I'm not sure if Charles felt he needed my forgiveness, but he got it anyway and, what's more, I felt good about saying it to him. For me, it was a great place to be and it felt good to have been able to do it. I didn't know how he felt about our meeting, but I was certainly a lot happier in myself. What I also discovered was that, after all this time, he was no longer a soldier, but a person. Once you humanise a situation like mine, it's amazing how all the myths evaporate and you begin to see the human being behind the gun who, until now, was like an anonymous machine. I hoped that, for Charles, his encounter with me had helped him to grasp that I and the group of children into which he had fired the rubber bullet were also thinking, feeling and generally good human beings who happened to find themselves, through no fault of their own, in a drama that was the remnant of an unresolved piece of history between Ireland and Britain.

Before Charles and I parted, I had told him I'd like to keep in contact with him, and he had said the same thing. A few weeks later, I was invited to speak in schools in the Newcastle area of northern England. I thought I'd use it as an opportunity to accept Charles's invitation – I was only about an hour away by train from where he lived. When I telephoned him, I was reassured to hear him express warmth and delight at my having called. He said he and his wife would be honoured to have me stay with them and that all I needed to do was tell him the arrival time of my train and he'd be there to collect me at the station.

Having spent the day visiting schools in and around Newcastle, I boarded the train for Scotland. The minute the train door opened at Charles's station, he was there to help me down, and we were picking up where we had left off at Edinburgh Airport. We got into his car and went to collect his wife, Louise, from the supermarket where she was getting a few groceries, then went to their home. The normality of it all was strange. Here we were, meeting for the second time, and he and his wife were just doing the normal things that normal people do. I don't know why it seemed odd. Perhaps, for me, it was the fact that this man, who had once been a member of an army that my community considered a hostile enemy, was a normal human being like the rest of us, not a zombie bereft of all human emotion.

I had often wondered what his life was like, and now I was sitting in his car, relaxing in his home, meeting his family. And it was all so ordinary. I didn't tell Charles I had a fear of dogs. He had two, which slept quietly in the back of the car. When he got out at the supermarket to collect his wife, he left me sitting with them. That was the only time I felt uneasy. I was afraid to move – afraid even to breathe in case they woke up and came near me.

Spending the evening and night in Charles's home was strange for me, as I'm sure it was for him. Louise was a lovely woman, very friendly and welcoming. We didn't chat too much about the shooting, but that was okay. I was there primarily to build trust and to convey this to Charles and his wife.

A career soldier, he had spent most of his army life travelling around the world, serving in places such as Germany and Hong Kong. He had even survived two helicopter crashes. I also discovered he had been previously married and that his first wife had died from cancer. He told me about his children and grandchildren. In many ways, these were the things I wanted to know. It truly is amazing how when we discover each other's humanity, the prejudices disappear, be they racial, religious or political. I didn't see him any more as a soldier, but rather as a grandfather, a father and a man who had had his own difficulties and traumas.

As I needed to go back to Newcastle early the following morning, I went to bed soon after dinner. Charles and Louise helped me around their unfamiliar house and showed me where the bathroom and bedroom were, and all of that was very comforting. Before I went to sleep, I had a private conversation with my daddy and also thought, yet again, of how strange the situation was. I kept reminding myself that I was about to fall asleep in the home of the soldier who had shot me – something that a year and a half before I would never have believed possible. And even more amazing, I liked him! Prayerfully, I murmured to my father, 'Daddy, wherever you are, can you believe I'm here in the soldier's house? I just hope you're happy that this is happening.'

The next morning I heard a knock at my bedroom door at around five o'clock, just before I got up, and there was Charles with my breakfast. It was a friendly touch that made me feel good to be there.

At the station, when the train arrived, Charles helped me to board, with the assistance of a porter, and saw me seated comfortably. As he stepped onto the platform, I heard him thanking the porter for his help. Charles and his wife, in welcoming me to their home, had shown a deep level of caring and compassion, and that was enough for me. I knew it had been another good meeting and I had explained to him about the television documentary and why I hadn't allowed the cameras to be present for our first meeting. Three days later, I received a letter from him in which he said that not having cameras present had been the right thing to do.

Eventually Charles agreed to take part in the documentary and I was delighted for Brendan Byrne and Hotshot Films. He had facilitated my first meeting with Charles, even though he knew he couldn't be present with a camera crew. I had sensed all along, however, that with a little patience we would all be happy, and that was how it was. I was particularly pleased that Charles and I had agreed together that he would appear in the documentary and that the decision had not been foisted on us by the film-makers. It was too important a moment.

# Epilogue

This book is a personal story and therefore covers aspects of my life that I am comfortable to share. It is a life that has been at times challenging, funny and emotional. What have I learned from my life experience to date? First, as an Irish person, I have come to believe that it is our collective responsibility to ensure that our children, and their children, never have to endure the suffering we endured. We must ensure that they don't have to go through thirty years of violence and hatred, so the real challenge is to try to prevent the cycle of hatred, sectarianism and violence from being handed on to the next generation.

I have met with ex-paramilitaries on both sides of the divide. I've met former British soldiers and many victims of their violence. I don't believe that people are born intrinsically evil. I don't believe that people were born into society to be terrorists or to be violent by nature, but we all have the potential to become evil or violent. And I genuinely believe that this is what happened in Northern Ireland.

I am not saying that individuals mustn't take responsibility for their actions. We all have choices in life. Some people choose the peaceful way forward, while others take the violent route. However, I feel that to blame the individual alone, without questioning society and its role, would be wrong. Society in general, and in the case of Northern Ireland this includes British society, must share responsibility for the circumstances that evolved in the Province. Collectively we created an environment that was conducive to violence and it's important that we try to fix it now and ensure it doesn't happen again.

We cannot escape from the fact that all sides of the political divide in Northern Ireland have inflicted awful hurts on each other, and that is wrong. I have always been of the opinion that violence is wrong no matter which side it came from. When one looks at all the positive things we share in Northern Ireland and the many good things we have in common, it almost makes the conflict unforgivable. We have food; we have clean water; we have an educational system as good as anywhere on Earth; we have opportunities; we have homes; we generally like the same music; we have good social lives; we speak the same language and we enjoy all kinds of sport. Catholic or Protestant, the reality is that we share a common Christian faith.

When you weigh up all that we have in common and then look at what we have allowed to divide us, you have to be amazed at how we have allowed what are relatively small differences to dominate so much of our lives and inflict so much hurt. It's as if we're focused on one cloud – that small negative – and have allowed it to spoil a sunny day.

One of the principal factors in helping me to cope with blindness was forgiveness. That I harboured no hatred towards the soldier who shot me or towards the British Army freed me from the burden of bitterness. That I forgave the soldier meant I wasn't carrying that baggage through my life. It left me free to deal with other things and with the practical issues around blindness, such as mobility and developing the necessary skills for the future. Acceptance was also very important in dealing with blindness. I learned very quickly that accepting I would never see again allowed me to focus on what I could do, rather than what I couldn't. I had to accept that I would never be able to drive a car or become a brain surgeon and you certainly wouldn't let me wire your house. All those things that I had to accept were enough without having to deal with anger, hatred and bitterness.

When I thought about bitterness and anger, I could see they were self-destructive emotions that would affect no one but me. Like a cancer, they would have destroyed me from the inside out, and I believe that I would not have been able to function as a full human being if I had been filled with such negative energy. Anything that I have achieved in life I believe I would not have achieved had I allowed anger and bitterness to be the dominant forces.

I have often been asked by others how I was able to accept blindness and cope with it, and why I wasn't scarred for life by the trauma of what had happened. The simplest answer is my parents and their strong faith. It was their total lack of bitterness. Furthermore, while they were more traumatised by my injuries than I was, they began immediately to focus on my future and all that I would need to cope. In truth, they hadn't the time or the luxury to be bitter or to become absorbed in self-pity.

On reflection, I believe that I am at peace with my blindness and what caused it, largely because I forgave the soldier who shot me. Through meeting and listening to His Holiness the Dalai Lama and, of course, my Christian upbringing, I have come to realise that if we are to achieve a full and lasting reconciliation in Northern Ireland, the process needs to begin within each person. Based on my experience, forgiveness is one possible way towards achieving this. Once you resolve such issues within yourself, it makes it easier to resolve them with others.

The process of forgiveness is not going to change the past. By forgiving the soldier, I'm not going to get my eyesight back, but forgiveness can change the future, and that is what happened in my case.

Within a month of having sustained my injuries, I was also given the space to talk about my experience. For at least six months after I was shot, national and international newspapers, magazines, radio and television stations were coming to interview me. Looking back now, I have no doubt that the opportunity to tell my story and explore my feelings had a positive impact on me. I am convinced that as part of any peace process, people on all sides who have lost loved ones or have been injured should be given the chance to be heard with all due sensitivity and respect.

And respect is so important. Throughout this book, I have said that being made to feel important was an enormous help to me. From being just one of hundreds of children in the Creggan, I was suddenly treated as an important person. People like John Hume, Bishop Edward Daly, Dr Raymond McClean, Senator Edward Kennedy, my teachers and the wider Creggan community took an interest in me and helped to transform my blindness into a positive experience.

I am only too aware that there are many disabled people out there whose story has not been heard. I have no doubt that isolation must be very difficult to live with. It gives me pause for thought that maybe all of us should, at some stage in our lives, try to single out somebody and make them feel special and important. I believe it would be a wonderful gift in helping them to cope with their daily lives.

That I went back to a 'normal school' and that my community rallied round to integrate me into it was also very important for me. Back in the 1970s, integration was frowned upon, so it took courage, determination and dedication on the part of my parents, neighbours and teachers to follow this through to such a successful outcome. At this juncture in my life, I look back with a sense of deep and abiding gratitude to all concerned.

It was also important for me to feel like a 'normal' child, that I was able to have a social life the same as my friends. I know that if I had been plucked out of my own community and sent away to a school for blind people, I would have been more traumatised and I doubt I would have coped as well as I have. I'm not saying that those who went to a school for the blind shouldn't have gone or that such schools don't do good work, just that different individuals have different needs. What was right for me may not be right for someone else. In my case, returning to Rosemount Primary School and moving on to St Joseph's Secondary School – having the opportunity to be educated with my friends and to continue living among the community that I had grown up in – were very important for my recovery.

I often ask myself how it was that I, a young boy from an ordinary family in the Creggan estate in Derry, growing up against the backdrop of all the Troubles, was not only able to forgive the soldier who shot me, but also wanted to meet him and, ultimately, become his friend. How was it that that same young boy was able to put his life back together and become involved in the work that I'm doing today?

There's nothing special about me. I'm no different from

anybody else, so how is it that I was able to do it? I used to say it was because I was lucky, but that's not so: luck had nothing to do with it. It was, quite simply, that I was blessed – blessed by the power of my parents' prayers. I genuinely believe it was the devotion of my mammy and my daddy, and their prayers, that ultimately helped me to have such a positive and enjoyable life. Otherwise it's inexplicable.

I have learned that while there are limitations attached to blindness, there are many positive things too. During one of my visits to Malawi, I was standing in a village surrounded by hundreds of people. I was the only white person there, but I was conscious only of being surrounded by fellow human beings. Suddenly the thought struck me that skin colour is superficial. It doesn't matter. I'm like that with everyone I meet. I don't care if a person's hair is pink. I don't care if he or she has an earring through their nose. I don't care if they're dressed in leather or rags. When you're blind, you see the person first. All the other things that sighted people see that sometimes lead them to pre-judge others – even before they speak – are irrelevant when you're blind. I hasten to add that I don't always get it right, but I prefer the non-judgemental approach that blindness offers. If everyone in the world was blind, would racism on the basis of skin colour exist?

Another aspect of blindness is that it is very physical. For example, if I want to board an aeroplane, I need someone to link onto me and direct me across the apron at the airport and show me to my seat. If I get a cup of tea or coffee at home or in a restaurant, I need someone to take my hand and show me where the cup is. Even if I'm to sign a letter, I need someone to direct my hand and lay my fingers on the place where I'm to write my signature. Most people in the Western world, even those who are friendly, don't experience the same degree of physical contact. Yet I often sense that when you have physical contact with a person, your relationship changes. The simple act of guiding a person's hand to sign a letter or a document brings out compassion in the other. In a sense, it is another gift of blindness.

The other thing that helped me to accept my blindness was my ability not to refuse help. I always encourage people to help and I am not afraid to ask for it when I need it. I'm not ashamed of my dependency on others, and why should I be? We all need help in our lives. I just need it sometimes for the simpler things, like dicing my steak at dinner or to be shown to the bathroom in an unfamiliar place. I know that many visually impaired people can do all that for themselves. I can't.

I can't cook. I can't iron. I don't know the front from the back of a washing machine. So I rely on others to help me. It doesn't mean I can't do it, it's simply that I haven't got around to learning yet.

I think, too, that those like me with a disability have an additional challenge. Most people don't have the opportunity to deal with a disabled person and when they come across one they sometimes don't know how to handle the situation. I think there's an obligation on me to take control and understand that people might say the wrong thing without any malicious intent. Often good people fumble awkwardly because they're not sure how to deal with me. I feel it is important that I help to educate them in a sensitive way. Where they might say the wrong thing, for example, by asking, 'Does he take sugar?' instead of speaking to me directly, I find a way of intervening that won't embarrass them but may help them to understand that they can relate to me as they would to anyone else.

In the weeks and months after I was discharged from

hospital, my mother would bring me to the kitchen sink just before bedtime. I wore a vest to which she had pinned every holy medal, scapular and saintly relic she had been given – there must have been thirty or forty pinned across my chest. When I walked, I rattled. She used to stand me by the sink and rub every one of those medals on my eyes, making the sign of the cross. She would get out the Lourdes water and rub that on, then holy water from Doon Well in Donegal and from Knock Shrine in County Mayo. Next came St Anne's oil. Somebody once said to me I was lucky I didn't drown. But while my mother's simple prayer – that I would get my eyesight back – wasn't answered, I received far greater blessings instead.

Writing this book has been an interesting experience. When I started to list all the things I've done, I found myself wondering how I'd had the time to fit everything in. But I did. Even though I am, at the time of writing, in my mid-forties, I still feel very young at heart. But I've also learned, as evidenced in 1996, that people can suffer burnout if they overdo it.

Overall, though, my life to date, in spite of – or perhaps because of – blindness, has been wonderful. Through my blindness I've had fantastic experiences and I can't separate it from all that is good in my life. If I hadn't lost my eyesight, I might not have enjoyed life as much as I have. So where blindness has been challenging at times, with all its limitations, in other ways it has been very positive, which has as much to do with the kindness and compassion of my family, community and friends as it has to do with me.

Having said all of the above, it would be remiss of me not to state that what happened to me was an injustice. My subsequent ability to cope doesn't take away from the fact that what happened to me was wrong. No child, no matter their colour, cultural background or location in the world, should have to endure such trauma and suffering. I'm thinking of friends, Clare Gallagher and Kim Phúc, and the many millic of children throughout the world who have been badly injur through violence. Clare was blinded in the Real IRA bombi of Omagh on 15 August 1998. Kim, 'the girl in the picture became the iconic image of the Vietnam War in 1972 as she ra naked from her burning village with strips of flesh hangin from her body, caused by napalm bombs. It is the responsibility of all of us to try to end such atrocities.

This book is not a recipe book for how to deal with blindness. It is not an A-to-Z manual on coping with disability. It is simply the personal sharing of one person: how I coped with a traumatic incident that left me blind. And it was simple things that made all the difference. I remember that every day of the week, for months after my discharge from hospital, one of my older brothers would come with his car to take me out for a run. If I needed to go to a guitar lesson, there was no shortage of people volunteering to give me a lift. If I needed a ride to school or anywhere else, somebody was always available. That's one of the advantages of having a big family. Even Kevin, who was five years younger than me, assumed a level of responsibility that amazes me to look back upon. He guided me about, making sure I was all right when I was out in the street. From the youngest to the oldest, including both of my parents, everyone worked to minimise the impact of blindness on me, and all this at a time before trauma counsellors. I am filled with deep gratitude and love for all my family, who were, in every respect, victims themselves who needed help. And who was helping them to cope? It was the wonderful neighbours and friends we had in Malin Gardens and the Creggan estate, as well as their partners and families.

I'm sure my brothers and sisters all had their difficult

moments around me: it was hard for them to watch their ten-year-old brother walk into a wall or door or trip over a shoe. My brother Gregory told me he first realised I really was blind when he watched me trying to kick a football and I couldn't find it. They needed to talk about and process these things with somebody, and that somebody was the community we belonged to. Through this book I wish, in some small way, to acknowledge all those people, many of whose names I don't even know, who played such an enormous role in my recovery. They include the friends I grew up with in Malin Gardens and Lower Creggan, and those at school who escorted me from class to class; the friends who recorded class presentations on tape to help me with my homework later; the friends who made me feel normal and included me in their daily lives, who called to the house to take me out to Rosemount Community Centre or to hang out around the shops; the friends who took me for walks around Creggan and sometimes out into the countryside. To them, they might have been just calling for their mate Richard. For me, they were a lifeline. They were an integral part of the process of helping me to rediscover normality in the abnormality of what had happened to me and of helping me to deal with blindness.

So when I talk about accepting blindness and all the positive experiences that have come out of mine, it was my family, friends, teachers and neighbours who made it so easy for me to accept. I have deliberately not named people here for fear that I might leave someone out. All who helped me along the way, in small or significant ways, you were all part of my healing and I wish you to know that my heart is filled with gratitude. I am who I am today because of you.

The generosity of people beyond Derry also, like Dan and Joan Herlihy and their committee in Worcester, Massachusetts, not to mention across the entire island of Ireland, was a blessing. In the aftermath of my shooting, many people wrote letters of solace to my mother. I remember one person in particular: Teresa Matterson, from Castlewellan, County Down, wrote many letters of support to my mother. I just wish that Teresa and all who wrote could know how important their letters were. They made my mother feel important and showed her that there were people out there who cared. Recently I contacted Teresa for the first time to thank her for her friendship to my mother.

A former soldier in England used to send me the latest pop records every month. He wrote to my parents and gave them lots of support as well. It was he who sent me my first Braille watch and also a chessboard. He was losing his eyesight when he heard about me and got in contact with the family. When I was learning how to use the Braille watch, our bread-delivery man, Sean Toye, would come into our kitchen once a week and call to me, 'What time is it now, Richard?' I would check my watch and tell him the time. I was so proud that I could do that. Sean made it fun and I always looked forward to his question. All those 'small' or simple gestures helped me deal with the whole experience.

My teachers had to make special arrangements to have a blind pupil in a class or walking around the school. In Rosemount Primary School and St Joseph's Secondary School, no effort was spared to help me. In St Joseph's, the principal, Ted Armstrong, and his deputy, Niall McCafferty, would regularly invite me to the principal's office to ask how I was getting on, if there was anything more they could do to assist me and to enquire if I was happy at school. My teachers were managing a very difficult situation and they would have moved heaven and earth to make sure I was taken care of. I had many wonderful teachers, such as Marie McCafferty, now Donnelly, of St Mary's College, and Kevin McCallion from St Joseph's, who spent endless extra-curricular hours preparing me for my CSE and A-level exams. And, of course, Michael Doherty, who taught me the guitar. All of them made a special effort to ensure that I was at no disadvantage. Often they adjusted their class lessons to assist me, which was very important not just in my education, but in my future life.

The priests in the Creggan parish were a great source of strength to my parents. I'm sure they saw my mother on many occasions and gave her all sorts of spiritual comfort.

The one thing about the Peace Process that has prevailed in Northern Ireland over the last decade is that it has given peace a chance. It has created the space for us to begin to hear each other. I know that when I listen to the heartrending stories of my aunt Ita, who lost her husband, my uncle Gerard, on Bloody Sunday, or Rita Rosterick, whose son was shot dead in Northern Ireland, or Kathleen Gillespie, whose husband was blown to pieces in an IRA proxy bomb on the Derry/Donegal border, I realise there is no franchise on suffering. I cried when I listened to Rita Rosterick talk about the loss of her boy because I heard in her story echoes of my own mother's suffering and the suffering that all mothers go through.

I have often thought of what it would be like if we were to record on a tape all the personal stories of suffering, then cut it into pieces. If we were to mix up all the bits, then join them together with Sellotape, I don't think we could tell whose story was whose or which side of the political fence each came from.

I've come to realise that it doesn't matter if you're Protestant or Catholic, Unionist or Nationalist, British or Irish, the suffering is the same. And if we're to build a true and lasting peace in Northern Ireland, then one of the challenges will be to deal with the hurts of the past and try to ensure that they are not handed on to the next generation.

While I have enjoyed my blindness and at times have had wonderful fun with it, I hope that I have not in any way made light of blindness. I hope especially that I haven't made anyone feel worse about their own condition. More than anything, I hope I have demonstrated that it is possible to have a full life despite a major disability. No matter how challenging and difficult your situation might be, if you can gain a reasonable perspective on what is possible, life can be a challenge worth undertaking. Thankfully, I'm one of those people who was blessed enough to be able to do just that. I certainly don't take it for granted.

I suppose to sum it up I managed to put blindness into perspective. I focused on what I could do rather than what I couldn't. I focused on my ability, not my disability. While I realised that blindness took many things away from me, I also realised that there was still so much I could do and enjoy. I wasn't going to allow blindness to take those pleasures away from me. In a nutshell, I managed blindness; it didn't manage me. And so far, I believe I'm winning.

I've never forgotten a gem of wisdom my daddy gave me when I was a young teenager: 'Never let one cloud spoil a sunny day.' For me, that cloud represented some aspects of blindness. But I didn't allow it to spoil my sunny days, of which, I am glad to say, there have been plenty.

# Acknowledgements

I would like to thank the following people, as without their help and support it would not have been possible to complete this book:

Bernadette Healy and the McDonagh family for your time and willingness to share wonderful stories with me about your sister Teresa.

Ciara Considine, my editor at Hachette Books Ireland, for all your hard work and enthusiasm. Also Breda Purdue and all the team at Hachette.

Damien Harkin and Paul Kealy, the Principal and Vice-Principal, respectively, of St Joseph's School, for your help and co-operation with the launch of this book.

Des Doherty of Desmond J. Doherty Solicitors for your ongoing support, but in particular for providing the transcription machines for the pool of typists to begin the long process of transferring my story from tape to the written word.

Don Mullan for your hard work and constant encouragement, without which I genuinely don't think I would have even considered writing this book, but most of all for the wonderful friendship we have shared over the years.

Emer Ryan for the sensitive way in which you helped edit this book.

Fran Cotton for your sound advice, professionalism, enthusiasm, friendship and positive encouragement.

His Holiness the 14th Dalai Lama of Tibet for the beautiful things you said. I will always value your message of forgiveness and will never forget all that you have done for me.

Hugh O'Regan for helping to fund this book. I have never had the opportunity to meet you, but I hope you know I am extremely grateful for your support.

Ian Williams, Executive Director of Concern Universal, for your help and solid advice, without which this book would not have been a reality.

Jan Buettner for providing a quiet retreat at his resort in North Germany for Don and I to focus on the book. It was the perfect setting and I appreciate your generosity.

John and Pat Hume for your kind words and the support you have been to me and my family. Your message of peace is an inspiration to us all and I am proud to have you as friends.

Linda Keen for really pushing me to write my story, and for your genuine friendship, support and encouragement.

My cousin Margaret McKinney for providing me with useful and illuminating information regarding the McKinney family tree.

Moya Mullan for letting myself and Don to use your house over a bank holiday weekend to kick start the book.

Mr Tashi from the Office of Tibet in London for your kindness, co-operation and constant willingness to help in any way with anything I needed for the book.

My daughters Naoimh and Enya, and their friends Colleen Ryan, Kathy Kelly, Joanne Morrow and Sarah Gallagher for the endless hours you all spent giving up a bank holiday weekend to transcribe my words from audio tape. This was, after all, the first draft of this book.

My friend and colleague Ursula Moore for the endless time and effort you willingly put in, at almost every stage of this book, not expecting anything in return. You are and have been a true friend.

Naoimh, Colleen and Deborah for allowing their Cyrpus holiday to be interrupted to read the final edit of this book to me.

Paddy Maguinness for your friendship, excellent advice and genuine desire to see this book published.

Rita, my Mother, my sister Deidre and colleague JR for the time spent sourcing the photographs for this book.

Rupert Cadbury and the William Cadbury Trust for your kindness, support, encouragement and also funding towards this book.

**Standing order form for Euro account**
**To support the work of Children in Crossfire**
**XR85661 CHY 14182**

# Standing Order Instruction

Name(s) and address of account holder(s)

Mr/ Ms/ Mrs/ Miss

Email.

Phone No.

Bank/ Building Society Details

Name and full address of your Bank/ Building Society

To:The Manager

Address

Bank/Building Society account number

Branch Sort Code

Instruction to your Bank or Building Society

Please pay Bank of Ireland, accoun no. 45939943, sort code 90-47-55 for the credit of Children In Crossfire.

€ each month* or € each quarter* or € each year*

** please complete your preferred option*

until further notice starting from __ __ • __ __ • __ __ __ __ (date of frist payment)**

** please allow two working weeks from date of signature*

and quoting with each payment the reference number

Signature(s)*

Date

Please do not send this Standing Order Instruction direct to your bank. When completed and signed, please return to:

Children in Crossfire
2 St Joseph's Avenue
Derry / Londonderry, **N. Ireland.**
BT48 6TH
(048) 71269898
Charity No: CHY14182
www.childrenincrossfire.org

**XR85661 CHY 14182**

**Instrcution to your Bank or Building Society to pay by Direct Debit**

**Direct debit mandate for Sterling account**
**To support the work of Children in Crossfire**

**Please fill in the whole form including official use box using a ball point pen and send it to:**

**Children In Crossfire**
**2 St. Joseph's Avenue**
**Derry/Londonderry, Northern Ireland**
**BT48 6TH**

**Service User Number**

| 9 | 6 | 2 | 8 | 2 | 9 |
|---|---|---|---|---|---|

**FOR Children In Crossfire**
**OFFICIAL USE ONLY:**
This is not part of the instruction to your Bank or Building Society.

**Name(s) of Account Holder(s)**

**Bank/ Building Scoiety account number**

**Branch Sort Code**

**Name and full postal address of your Bank or Building Society**

**To:The Manager** **Bank/ Building Society**

**Address**

**Postcode**

**Reference.**

**Instruction to your Bank or Building Society**

Please pay Children In Crossfire Direct Debits from the account detailed in the Instruction subject to the safe guards assured by the Direct Debit guarantee. I understand that this Instruction may remain with Children In Crossfire and, if so, details will be passed electronically to my Bank/ Building Society.

**Signature**

**Date**

**email:** ______________________

**phone number:** ______________________

Banks and Building Societies may not accept Direct Debit Instructions from some types of account

**www.childrenincrossfire.org**